T0329083

# Abdilatif Abdalla: Poet in Politics

Edited by
Rose Marie Beck & Kai Kresse

MKUKI NA NYOTA
DAR – ES – SALAAM

PUBLISHED BY
Mkuki na Nyota Publishers Ltd
P. O. Box 4246
Dar es Salaam, Tanzania
www.mkukinanyota.com

ISBN 9789-9877-53-38-3

Visit www.mkukinanyota.com to read more about and to purchase any of Mkuki na Nyota books. You will also find featured authors, interviews and news about other publisher/author events. Sign up for our e-newsletters for updates on new releases and other announcements.

Distributed world wide outside Africa by African Books Collective.
www.africanbookscollective.com

# Contents

# Kai Kresse & Rose Marie Beck

## Preface and Acknowledgements

This volume of essays presents praise and exploration of the works and the person of Abdilatif Abdalla, poet and activist – and colleague, teacher and friend to many of us.

It was not difficult to select a title for us. *Poet in Politics* is especially appropriate as it encapsulates, in a succinct and concise form, what Abdilatif Abdalla stands for, as a writer and political activist, as verbal artist and a master of riddles – and even prophecy (see Ngũgĩ, this volume). He has been engaged in both poetry and politics from early childhood onward throughout his life, before and after exile from Kenya, which began in 1972 and is still continuing. For Abdilatif Abdalla, political engagement is an inevitable fact of life. As he said in his lecture on the obligations of a poet in his/her society, *Wajibu wa Mshairi Katika Jamii Yake* (given in Dar es Salaam in 1976, first published in 1977, and reprinted here): "Hakuna sehemu yoyote ya mwanaadamu ambayo haikuingiliana na siasa kwa njia mojawapo au nyengine" – there is no human space which is not permeated by politics in one way or the other (in this volume, page 86).

Most of the papers collected here were presented in preliminary sessions at the symposium on 4th and 5th May 2011 on occasion of the retirement of Abdilatif Abdalla from the University of Leipzig, where he had been teaching for fifteen years. A few contributions have been added, to present a more comprehensive perspective on the person we intend to celebrate here. Thus the contributions in this book reflect both the symposium and the dignitary, Abdilatif Abdalla.

The first section, *Poet in Politics,* contains papers that speak about Abdilatif Abdalla (Ngũgĩ, Kresse), the valuation of his poetry and persona (Bakari, Walibora) in contemporary Swahili and East African societies (Rajab) and the problem of translating his works into other languages (Beck, Khamis).

In the second section, we hear Abdilatif Abdalla's own voice speaking directly to us, through important (and now historical) texts that are almost inaccessible today but merit attention. These are his (in)famous (but rarely read) pamphlet *Kenya: Twendapi?*, which criticized Kenyatta's government and in turn brought Abdalla to prison, as well as two essays stating his position on the responsibilities of the writer in post-colonial African societies, written in the intellectually vibrant Dar es Salaam of the 1970s. These are, firstly, the already mentioned *Wajibu wa Mshairi Katika Jamii Yake*, on the social obligations of a poet, and, secondly, a similarly pitched lecture on the problems for a community-oriented 'people's writer' in post-Independence Africa, *Matatizo ya Mwandishi wa Jamii Katika Afrika Huru*, given in Dar es

Salaam in January 1978[1] in protest against Ngugi wa Thiongo's detention by the Kenyan authorities at the time. Finally, we are happy to include a reprint of unique excerpts from Abdilatif Abdalla's prison diaries, translated into English by Abdalla himself and first published under the title *The Right and Might of a Pen* in 1985, in the London-based monthly news-magazine *Africa Events*. The two essays were previously published too (in *Lugha Yetu* 30, 1977; and *Lugha* 3, 1984) and are reproduced here in slight variations, as they were provided to us by the author, whom we thank for the possibility to include all these important texts here, making them more accessible again to a wider audience. They express, in sharp and lucid manner, early criticism of post-colonial rule in East Africa. In these essays – unlike in the pamphlet *Kenya: Twendapi?* – political critique is raised and contextualized within academic debates about language, form, and the obligations of African writers in politics. *Writers in Politics* of course is the title of a well-known essay collection by Ngũgĩ wa Thiongo, one of our contributors here[2], critically commenting upon and contextualizing the activity of creative writing (of fiction or non-fiction; poetry or prose) as first and foremost fundamentally political, within the kinds contexts that post-Independence countries in Africa provided.

The third section contains papers that contextualize Abdilatif Abdalla's work and person with regard to politics (Nassir), literary studies (Rettova) and language (Wolff). Finally this volume also contains congratulatory texts by his colleagues (Miehe, Herms, Othman) and students (Mahazi, students of the University of Leipzig) that were held on occasion of the symposium itself.

Finally, for the phase of finalization of this volume, we thank Joy Adapon for her ready services in copy-editing the texts, Manuela Kirberg for attending to all formal matters, Viola Kup for the design of the cover, and, most importantly, Walter Bgoya and Mkuki na Nyota with whom we are able to publish this volume, and once again, our Elder Brother, Kaka Abdilatif Abdalla, for ready advice and assistance during the process of the preparation of this volume.

Concluding this preface with an '*Asanteni!*' to all who contributed and helped, we now cast an inviting '*Karibuni!*' to all readers. May *Poet in Politics* demand, and reward, your full attention while you read.

---

[1] Kresse (in this volume) provides summary discussions of these essays.
[2] Ngũgĩ wa Thiongo 1981. *Writers in Politics*. Nairobi: Heinemann

# Section 1

---

## Poet in Politics

# Rose Marie Beck

## 'Deep Language' Crossing Borders[3]

### A Symposium

Abdilatif Abdalla approached pension age at the end of April 2011, after 15 years of employment as a lecturer for Swahili at the Institue of African Studies, University of Leipzig. This was half a year after my appointment to the chair of African Languages and Literatures at the institute. Very soon it became clear to me that we should create an occasion to pay homage to this outstanding personality, and I decided to organize a symposium in honour of his lifelong achievements as poet, scholar and political activist.

This would not have been possible without the generous support of all members of the institute – colleagues, collaborators, secretarial staff[4], and students – who substantially contributed all kinds of resources: funds, contacts to funding institutions, knowledge, infrastructure, work time and, importantly, their enthusiasm for the occasion[5]. It speaks volumes about the immense appreciation of Abdilatif Abdalla and his major role in the institute. Thanks to this generous support we were able to invite 15 companions, colleagues and friends of Abdilatif Abdalla from Kenya and Tanzania, Germany, Britain, the US and Turkey to come to Leipzig in May 2011 and speak with and about him.

The symposium reflected the festive occasion in various ways. His students – current and former – bade him farewell in a moving ceremony, reading out a poem that they had composed themselves (see this volume), each of them presenting him with a rose. A reading of his poetry with translation by Irmtraud Herms and Marion Feuerstein-Tubach was followed by a reception at the Mediencampus/Villa Ida. Throughout the symposium the participants visibly enjoyed to be gathered at this occasion to share stories and memories and to discuss politics and literature.

At the conference, the papers mainly reflected two topics: Abdilatif Abdalla as poet and Abdilatif Abdalla in politics. Not all papers that were presented then are collected in this volume (Farouk Topan, Ridder Samsom, Wangui Wa Goro, Walter Bgoya), and some contributions were added later on (Othman Miraj, Alena Rettova). In what follows I try to bring together all the contributions under the title of the conference.

[3] 5 – 6 May 2011, University of Leipzig. Symposium in Honour of Abdilatif Abdalla: "Deep Language" Crossing Borders – Culture as Resource in Political Activism and Resistance.
[4] Prof. Dr. Helmut Asche, Prof. Dr. Ulf Engel, Prof. Dr. Adam Jones, Prof. Dr. Utz Dornberger, Monika Große, Dr. Ari Awagana, Claudia Böhme, Natascha Bing, Hanna Nieber, Susann de Ruijter, and a large bunch of current and former students.
[5] The conference was supported by the DFG (Graduate School Junctures of Globalization), Centre for Area Studies (BMBF), A1 Verlag, Medienstif-tung Sparkasse Leipzig, Heinrich Böll Stiftung, Sulzmann Stiftung, Mainz, Vereinigung von Förderern und Freunden der Universität Leipzig e.V., Institut für Afrikanistik, Universität Leipzig.

## 'Deep Language' Crossing Borders

Born in 1946 in Mombasa, Abdilatif Abdalla[6] grew up in a well-established family and enjoyed a classical education that ideally combines Islamic, poetic and political knowledge. As Farouk Topan, Kai Kresse, Mohamed Bakari, Ken Walibora and others unanimously point out, this complex of culture, religion and politics is constitutive of the cosmopolitan Swahili societies of the East African coast. Abdilatif and his family exemplify this. His elder brothers were influential role models for Abdilatif, Ustadh Ahmad Nassir Juma Bhalo as a renowned poet ('Juma Bhalo', the recently deceased famous *taarab* musician, was his cousin), and Sheikh Abdilahi Nassir as a politican and well-known Islamic scholar. This influence[7] was decisive: soon after Independence, Abdilatif became politically active in the opposition KPU (Kenya People's Union) party which was soon criminalized and suppressed on flimsy legal grounds in the run-up to the elections of 1968. In a series of pamphlets Abdilatif voiced his criticism that culminated in the famous *Kenya: Twendapi?* – 'Kenya, where are we going?'[8], where he raised broader issues such as the shameless exploitation of Kenyan citizens, lawlessness and the establishment of an elite responsible only for their own enrichment.

Abdilatif was arrested, tried for sedition and sentenced to three years of solitary confinement, which he served from 1969 to 1972. In prison he spent some of his time secretly composing poems that were then smuggled outside, collected and compiled, and published in 1973 as *Sauti ya Dhiki* ('Voice of Agony'). Today these prizewinning poems belong to the core of contemporary Swahili poetry for their outstanding beauty, literary quality and topical orientation. The bestowing of two literary awards, both in Kenya (1974, Kenyatta Literary Award) and Tanzania (1977, Saba-Saba Literary Award), document Abdilatif Abdalla's importance as critical poet, arguably in a modern as well as a traditionalist sense, not only for Swahili society, but for East African society on the whole. Until today the volume is widely read and available at Kenyan bookshops – despite the fact that its author was deemed a capital enemy of Kenya by the Kenyatta and Moi governments for many years.

However, since his release in 1972 and his life in exile[9], he has hardly published any more poems, with extremely few exceptions, neither in Swahili nor in English. His exiled voice remained prolific, with essays on the role and responsibilities of the writer in post-colonial Africa (e.g. Abdalla 1976, 1978, reprinted in this volume), in critical journalism and the expression of his opposition to Kenyan and African politics. It was only with the opposition regaining strength in the early 2000s, that we see him return, in parts at least, to literary activity, for instance with a translation of Vaclav Havel's drama *Unveiling*

---

[6] For more extensive biographical characterizations, see Kresse (this volume), Kresse (forthcoming).
[7] See the contribution of Mohamed Bakari (this volume).
[8] The pamphlet is reproduced in this volume, see p. 74-77.
[9] See the contribution of Ngũgĩ wa Thiong'o (this volume) on their joint journey as political activists and friends.

(*Uzinduzi*) into Swahili in 2005, with Alena Rettova. How can we understand the 'silence' of the Swahili poet's voice and the ongoing activist's voice?

It is commonly assumed that through poetry Abdilatif Abdalla was not only able to preserve his sanity and mental health, but also his political identity and personal integrity:

> By writing Sauti ya Dhiki, Abdalla may be said to be trying to claim subjectivity, to create himself from the passivity of an 'object' as the prison system intends for him, to a speaking rational 'subject.' In other words, subject formation or creation is an integral part of the things Abdalla does with poetical words. (Walibora, this volume)

His subjectivity is characterized by many voices (or narrative 'I's, Walibora, this volume) in which insurgency and despair, self-assertion from the isolation of solitary confinement, the hope for a future for himself and his country remain in irreconciliable and incommensurable contrast. In this situation, Abdalla takes recourse to a deeply culturally embedded form of literary expression, that of poetry: the ability to condense thoughts and topics by means of the rigid principles of Swahili poetics, thus achieving a high density of metaphorical language, also known as *lugha ya ndani* – 'deep language'. Such verbal artistic proficiency is a well known poetic ideal (not only) in Swahili poetics (e.g. Shariff 1988: 80) which is further associated with the demarcation and relative closure of Swahili coastal culture (Sheikh 1994: 7).

As Mohamed Bakari and Ken Walibora stress, Abdalla's poetry, in unique and – in their view – even revolutionary ways, bring together the strict norms of classical Swahili poetics with political topics. Herein lies one of its major merits, as Gudrun Miehe said, namely to transpose classical Swahili poetry into a contemporary context and render it attractive for contemporary poets. His poetry is characterized by 'deep language' for its ability to speak the unspeakable:

> Waswahili hupendelea sana kutumia mafumbo, kwa mfano, katika kueleza mambo yenye aibu na yale yenye kuudhi, yasiyofaaa kujulikana na watu ila waliohusika, ili wengine wasielewe msemwa ni nani. (Shariff 1988:81).

> The Swahili love using riddles, for instance when talking about shameful matters or anger which are supposed to be accessible only to those whom it concerns so that others do not understand who the addressee is. (author's translation).

The unspeakable here is the politically unspeakable, that which cannot be uttered without risking one's life, a situation that clearly existed in the repressive Kenya of those times, and that is inextricably linked to the terrible threat of constant control and punishment in prison. As he writes repeatedly, Abdalla used such language in his poems to veil the messages, as he expected that neither his prison warders, let alone the political functionaries of the time, nor even Jomo Kenyatta himself, would be able to unequivocally decipher the meanings of his poetry.

> ... I doubt if they [the prison guards] will be able to make out the meaning of the poems. Even if they will, I have 1001 alternative interpretations for each one of them ('The Right and Might of a Pen', 1985, reprinted in this volume).

Ken Walibora (this volume) shows how in the poem "*Mamba*" (crocodile) Abdilatif imagines the demise of Kenyatta himself as an act of resistance:

> Given the autocrat's imagined and imaginary immortality and invincibility, it takes considerable courage for an imprisoned poet to even think about the autocrat's death; it is tantamount to imagining the unimaginable or thinking the unthinkable. As a matter of fact to have the audacity of imagining or foretelling the President's death was considered as treasonable at the time of its writing as literal killing. In a sense, therefore, Abdalla uses poetical words to 'assassinate' the tyrant and perhaps gets away with such an audacious action.

*Lugha ya ndani* becomes an instrument of intellectual subversion and the extraordinary power of the prisoner, a 'weapon of the weak' (Scott 1985). Perhaps this is one of the reasons for the continued popularity of *Sauti ya Dhiki*, as recounted by Ngũgĩ (this volume, p. 16) in his anecdote on the translation into Gikuyu of one of Abdilatif's poems: the intellectual power of the prisoner is understood in its subversive essence and is especially accessible for intellectually famished people exposed to and stuck in subalternity.

In short, Abdilatif Abdalla used his cultural knowledge to subvert the control of his prison and his suppressors. More than that, he set his cultural and social background of belonging to an old-established family within the cosmopolitan space of Swahili culture and his intellectual superiority against his tormentors. It is a remarkable localization of political activism that draws on cultural meanings of linguistic practice and poetic ideals shared within a small group. This group, his family, seems to have been the prime addressees of Abdilatif's imagination during imprisonment. The poems were smuggled out and found their way to Sheikh Abdilahi Nassir, who recognized their poetic, political and literary quality. It was he who suggested and facilitated the publication of Abdilatif's poems with Oxford University Press East Africa, where he worked at the time.

Therefore, from the point of view of literary production, the situation changes once Abdilatif is out of prison: the relative 'freedom of exile' (as contrasted to the traumatic confinement of prison) enlarges his – imagined and real – audience considerably. Is it possible that the physical end[10] of such an existential threat to life and mental sanity also sets an end to this particular

---

[10] I am aware that effects of traumatic events such as solitary confinement take a long time to end, if they ever end at all.

poetic productivity? Perhaps that which may be perceived as loss of poetic voice can also be seen as deliverance from traumatic experience and its memory.

At the same time it should not be overlooked that Abdilatif Abdalla's poems have so far not been translated into English[11]. Said Ahmed Khamis (Bayreuth) and Ridder Samsom (Hamburg) noticed that this is only partly owed to their complex, encrypted, condensed, metaphorical language. Rather, Abdalla shares the fate of many other East African writers writing in other languages than English who are not translated either and thus are not heard internationally[12]: This is not so much a question of 'Can the subaltern speak?' (Spivak), but rather, critically, of 'Can the subaltern be heard?' and 'Who wants to hear the subaltern?' Therefore I claim that subalternity is not so much produced by an alleged inability to speak – in itself a hegemonic stance – but by the inability of the hegemon to hear and listen (Beck, 2015). Just like other writers, and in contrast to writers whose works are available in English and French, Abdilatif Abdalla therefore does not (yet) enjoy broad international recognition beyond a specialized public, neither as an outstanding poet, nor – and this needs to be stressed here – as victim of post-colonial repression or as an African intellectual.

Of course, his is but one example in the many examples of persecuted intellectuals, writers, or film makers. Ngũgĩ wa Thiong'o was an acclaimed writer *before* he, too, turned to Gikuyu language and community theatre as a means to reach those who were excluded from political participation. He thus played on the difference between English and the local languages as means of control and subversion. This raised the fear of the then ruling elites that those excluded might rise beyond their control. Ngũgĩ, as is well known, was incarcerated for his activities and exiled later on. But while Ngũgĩ could draw on his already existing reputation as a political writer in English to muster international solidarity, Abdilatif has remained less visible. Nuruddin Farah, another example, wrote one of the first novels in Somali in the alphabet which was invented and standardized under the regime of Siad Barre, only to have it banned. In order to be heard, he changed his literary activities to English, which promised a much larger readership and political influence – albeit rather beyond Somalia than within it (Farah 1988). Again another example is Phaswane Mpe, a Sepedi writer from South Africa, who could not publish his novel in Sepedi, because, as his editor pointed out, he would not find a readership for his criticism in this community, since Sepedi was used as a medium rather for harmless 'traditional' stories than political topics. He, too, settled for a publication in English under the title *Welcome to our Hillbrow* (2001). In the novel he lets Refentse, one of his characters, talk about the

---

[11] Some of his poems were translated into German by various translators (for example, Irmtraud Herms) and read on many occasions, but not published. There was also a reading and translation of his poetry on May 5, 2011, at the Mediencampus Leipzig, as part of the symposium. There are currently ongoing activities towards the publication of an English translation of 'Sauti ya Dhiki', though.

[12] But see the translation of selected poems by Euphrase Kezilahabi, 'Stray Truths', to be published 2015 by Michigan State University Press, translated by Annmarie Drury. I am grateful to Kai Kresse for having drawn my attention to this.

entanglements of politics and language. In South Africa, contrary to the other examples, the assumed danger inherent in literature in African languages is diffused by a banalization of their importance.

As these few examples show, the reactions of political-poetical activists to the specific political conditions in their countries with regard to the choice of language and medium thus varies greatly, geared to the intentions of the writer with regard to his/her audience, but also as a cultural capital to draw upon in order to be able to resist and subvert the attempts at control by those in power. In this light Abdilatif Abdalla's biography highlights how intensively culture that finds expression in highly specialized linguistic practices (poetry and stylistic mode of *lugha ya ndani*) can be a significant resource for resistance against the oppression by ruling elites in Africa, but at the same time is not necessarily productive for the achievement of broader political goals.[13]

The characteristic amalgamation of the poetic and the political through metaphorical language in *Sauti ya Dhiki* remains unique, not only for Swahili literary expression, but also with regard to Abdilatif's later writing. His text, *Kenya: Twendapi?*, does not make use of 'inside language' either. In two of his articles on the role of the author in society (reprinted in this volume) he does not make much reference to a particular linguistic style, but rather highlights the burden of the engaged writer to guard and guide the struggle for freedom of his country, even at high personal cost. Swahili political language seems not to be vested with particular stylistic properties in a strong sense as is the case for a notion such as 'inside' or metaphorical language[14].

While *Sauti ya Dhiki* is in many senses foundational for his further reputation as a Swahili scholar, intellectual and political activist, Abdalla has not exploited its programmatic poetic potential in his further work. However, his linguistic proficiency was highly esteemed at the University of Dar es Salaam where he was part of the team that worked on the Standard Swahili Dictionary at TUKI (Taasisi ya Uchunguzi wa Kiswahili) until 1984, and again later when he was in Germany at the University of Leipzig and involved in Gudrun Miehe's philological work on various aspects of Swahili classical poetry (see Miehe, this volume). Overall, during his years at Leipzig, Abdalla was politically not very outspoken and kept a low profile. He nevertheless has always spoken his mind, he was an important mentor to many of his students at the Institute of African Studies. It may well be, too, that the Leipzig period and his academic engagement with Swahili literature were also a time of rest and recuperation after very stressful years, starting in 1968 with his political activism in Mombasa and imprisonment, and the following years of exile in Tanzania and England.

As the contributions to the conference showed, and as is also visible in the contributions to this volume, the political side of Abdalla's life was discussed

---

[13] This is, more generally, true for Swahili writers on the whole.
[14] Shariff (1988) remains silent on this issue.

in a different vein, i.e. making reference to the broader East African and post-colonial context.

All contributions on Abdalla's political work shared a similar fundamental dissatisfaction about contemporary Africa in general and Kenya in particular. There were accounts of the hardships of underground work and the difficulties to produce presence and visibility among those whose support was needed by the group (Wangui wa Goro). The atmosphere in the 1980s must have been terribly oppressive, even in exile. The combination of secret underground work and bread-winning employment led to individual exhaustion, but also to deep friendship and reliability amongst the activists. Attempts of Kenyan secret service to intimidate not only the political opposition working abroad, let alone the exiled, but also the 'normal' Kenyan expatriates, gave evidence of the existential and social difficulties of the activists even in their closest environment.

It is no surprise that in spring 2011 at our conference meeting the veteran activists present at the symposium expressed high hopes with regard to the Arab Spring for the revolution to spill over to Kenya. And there were slight undertones of envy, too: the oppression in the Kenya of the 1980s was so overwhelming, and so powerful, that a similar movement would not have been possible then. The reminiscent mood of the symposium was strongest at that moment: encouraging developments of the past 20 years in Kenya were brushed aside, showing how very difficult it was for the long time exiled activists to rid themselves of the harrowing atmosphere of those times. The round table discussion on the last day of the symposium (facilitated by Helmut Asche) thus rather reified and summoned the repressive Kenya once again: the critical voices of Kenyan and German students on the panel as well as sophisticated statements from the audience were not able to counter the romanticizing images of revolution and the 'voices of the discontented'[15].

While Abdilatif Abdalla's poetry was praised as revolutionary, inspiring and identification-creating, participants were somber, disillusioned, angry or hopeless about the state and future of Kenya[16]. This was the case even for Sheikh Abdilahi Nassir's presentation, whose experience of old age drafted a vision of breakdown and restitution.

## Conclusion

Taking into consideration both the symposium and the papers assembled here, I am confident in saying that this volume presents unprecedented takes on, and original discussions of, Abdilatif Abdalla as a Swahili poet and Abdilatif Abdalla as political activist in exile. Abdalla the poet has been treated, broadly, within a framework of Swahili Studies (Kresse, Khamis, Bakari, Walibora, Miehe, Rettova). It seems Swahili Studies provide an already established context

---

[15] Kresse, this volume.
[16] Wangui wa Goro, Ahmed Rajab, Khamis Ramadhan with his photo exhibition about political protest in Kenya, Walter Bgoya with reference to (East) Africa in general.

against which it is possible to speak about Abdilatif's work as poetry-cum-politics. However, when talking about Abdilatif's exiled political existence, there is no reference to this academic context, and no one else is called upon instead. Abdilatif is either the subject of fond memories (Rajab, Othman) or he disappears behind politics (Nassir). Once again it was Ngũgĩ in his keynote who stepped outside the box and drew our attention to the writer's relationship to time:

> I believe that writers come from a prophetic tradition. A prophet looks at the existing conditions and is able to deduce the future that would inevitably come to be if current trends continue. He voices a warning. He points out, poses questions, challenges, and then calls for a change in the moral direction of a community. When society fails to heed the warnings and then the consequences follow, they turn around and ask: how did you know that this and that would happen? How could you have predicted this? I am sure that Abdilatif has fielded those kinds of questions many times. But rarely in the history of prophecy has a prophet asked a question that lives on, continually posing new challenges to new generations. Abdilatif managed to do this in his question, Kenya: Twendapi? (Ngũgĩ, this volume).

Certainly, Swahili is at the core of Abdilatif's life. And although it seems his 'deep language' has not crossed borders, nevertheless his poetry has inspired the East African diaspora as well as academics around the world. While it is true that the hegemon is structurally 'dumb', it is possible to listen to the strong words of this poet in politics and his most beautiful poetry.

## References

Beck, Rose Marie. Schweigen als Praxis und Praktiken des Schweigens in Michael Dobstadt, Christian Fandrych, Renate Riedel (eds.), *Linguistik und Kulturwissenschaft . Zu ihrem Verhältnis aus der Perspektive des Faches Deutsch als Fremd- und Zweitsprache und anderer Disziplinen*. Frankfurt: Peter Lang. Pp. 251-271.

Farah, Nuruddin (1988). Why I Write. *Third World Quarterly* 10, 4: 1591-1599.

Kresse, Kai (forthcoming). 'Kenya: Twendapi?' – Kenya: where are we going? Re-reading Abdilatif Abdalla's political pamphlet fifty years after Independence, *Africa: Journal of the Internatinal African Institute*.

Mpe, Phaswane (2001). *Welcome to Our Hillbrow*. Pietermaritzburg: University of Natal Press. [2011. Ohio: Ohio University Press].

Scott, James (1985). *Weapons of the Weak: Everyday Forms of Peasant Resistance*. New Haven, CN: Yale University Press.

Shariff, Ibrahim Noor 1988. *Tungo Zetu*. New York: Red Sea Press.

# Ngũgĩ wa Thiong'o

## Abdilatif Abdalla and the Voice of Prophecy

Though Abdilatif and I come from two different regions of Kenya, he from the Coast and I the Highlands, and we are of different ages, he born in 1946 and I, in 1938, our two lives are interwoven with the post-colonial history of Kenya and have crossed at key moments of that history. I published my first novel, "Weep Not Child", in 1964 at the age of 26; he published his first epic, "*Utenzi wa Maisha ya Adamu na Hawaa*", in 1971 at the age of 25. In "*Kenya: Twendapi?*", the leaflet that Abdilatif published clandestinely in 1968, he had questioned the direction our country was taking, decrying the denial of the democratic space, and warning against an encroaching dictatorship, the beginnings of it at least. Though very strong on the question of democracy, the pamphlet had the shortcoming of seeing the emerging dictatorship in ethnic terms, denouncing "*wajumbe ambao wamewekwa ili kulifanyia kazi kabila fulani ili lizidi kudhulumu makabila mengine.*" (1968: 3). In the preface to my third novel, *A Grain of Wheat*, published in 1967, I had warned against similar anti-people trends but in class terms; I lamented the fact that the reality of the post-colonial situation was painful, and added, sometimes too painful for the peasants and workers who fought against the British and who now saw all that they had fought for being put on the one side. Despite this difference on the interests the new dispensation was serving, essentially both of us were warning against the consequences of the directions taken by the independent state and this, only a few years into our independence.

Abdilatif had written his warning, following the disqualification, on technicalities, of all KPU candidates in municipal and mini-general elections of 1968. Thereafter, the banning of Kenya People's Union (KPU) of which he was a member, and the subsequent virtual silencing of its leadership including Jaramogi Oginga Odinga and Bildad Kaggia, took place. The grounds for disqualification were the whimsiest: that all the KPU candidates had not filled their papers properly and all KANU candidates had filled the same papers properly. It was a crude play on the minds of Kenyan people, actually an act of contempt, a case of openly laughing at the populace. They used a fabricated legal technicality to subvert actual legality; enonomy of truth to subvert truth; lip-service to the democratic process to subvert democracy. For pointing out this truth, that the state had subverted the form and spirit of the law, Abdilatif himself was accused and convicted of sedition, and placed in a maximum security prison in Kamiti in March 1969.

It was about the same month, the same year that I resigned from the University of Nairobi as a lecturer in English in protest against the banning of a prospective talk by Oginga Odinga at the invitation of the students. I was not a member of KPU but I felt equally strongly about the shrinking of the democratic space, a shrinking which had been extended to an institution founded on the

values of academic freedom, the right to read and hear clashing ideas. This led
to my first exile, voluntary though it was. I first went to Makerere, Uganda, in
1969, on a writing fellowship, and the University of Northwestern, on a visiting
professorship, returning to Kenya to head the department of literature in 1972,
the year that Abdilatif returned home from prison. He had been three years in
prison: I, three years in my first exile.

On his return he published *Sauti ya Dhiki* in 1973; and on my return, I
published the novel, *Petals of Blood* in 1975. Both documents took a consistent
class position in the analysis of Kenya society. This approach was best captured
in Abdilatif's dramatic poem, *Mnazi: Vuta N'kuvute*, in the depiction of the
struggle between Badi and Alii for the fruit of the collective inheritance,
"*Mnazi ni wa shirika*", as Alii argues. In conceiving it, Abdilatif may have had
Kenyatta and Odinga in mind, but here, in the poem, Badi and Alii become
representatives of class social forces and not of biological ethnic entities. Badi
and Alii are like Kīgūnda and Kīoi in the play, *Ngaahika Ndenda*[17], performed
at Kamīrīthū in 1977, and which continued the class themes of *Petals of Blood*.
The publications of *Petals of Blood* and *Sauti ya Dhiki* had two opposite though
ironic results: *Sauti ya Dhiki* won the Kenyatta literary prize; my novel and the
play won me Kenyatta's wrath and a place at the Kamītī Maximum Prison. I
was thus the second writer to be so imprisoned in post-colonial Kenya.

As if to make the point clear, I was placed in a block not too far from the one
where Abdilatif had been held for three years: some of the prisoners would point
to the cell from where he wrote *Sauti ya Dhiki*. I wrote down my prison notes,
literally drawing from the same prison air and environment he had breathed,
and later, in interviews following the publication of my memoir, *Detained: A
Writers' Prison Diary* in 1981, I was able to acknowledge Abdilatif's pioneering
role in post-colonial prison literature. It is ironic that with all these parallels
and close encounters, including sharing friends like Grant Kamenju, Walter
Bgoya, Ben Mkapa, and my visits to Dar es Salaam where, in exile, Abdilatif
worked in the Institute of Kiswahili Research, before he moved to London to
work for the BBC and later edit *Africa Events*, we had not met face to face.

Little did I then know that in the following year I would join him in London
in forced exile from a Kenya that had moved from a *de facto* to a *de jure* one
party dictatorship, soon changing from a party into a personal dictatorship. It
was during the post-1982 period that I came to know Abdilatif Abdalla and
forged a political, literary and personal friendship that continues to this day.
If I may say so, the personal was sealed forever following my insistence that
Abdilatif be invited to a literary conference in Hamburg: it was then that he
and Betgen Hage met, their heart beat each to the other, and years later the
encounter of Betgen and Abdilatif gave birth to my friend, Muyaka, whose
name makes us go down memory lane to the great poet of classical Kiswahili
literature, Muyaka bin Haji (1776-1840).

---

[17] Translated in English as "I Will Marry When I Want", the play was written by Ngũgĩ wa Thiong'o and Ngũgĩ
wa Mĩriĩ, its performance banned by the Kenya government on 16th November 1977.

Now, together in London, as writers in exile, Abdilatif and I joined the other members of the London Committee for the Release of Political Prisoners in Kenya, who included Wanjiru and Wanyiri Kihoro, Nish Muthoni, Yusuf Hassan, Shiraz Durrani, Naila Durrani, Wangui wa Goro and our Caribbean and international friends led by the late John la Rose. We would meet at least once a week, for the next seven years, to agitate for democracy and the release of all the political prisoners in Kenya. We rejected the legal fiction which the Kenyan state had used to condemn those convicted in a law court as criminals, reserving the term political detention to those supposedly held without a formal trial and conviction. Under that fiction Maina wa Kinyatti, many university students, and hundreds of others accused of connections with the coup attempt, would have been regarded as convicts and those like Kamoji Wachira, Edward Oyugi, Alamin Mazrui, Willy Mutunga, were held under similar conditions, as properly political detainees. To us, they were all political prisoners because they had been taken in and punished for their opposition to the shrinking democratic space. Prison became a metaphor for the Kenya of the Moi dictatorship, echoing the lines quoted by Abdilatif Abdalla in *Sauti ya Dhiki*, from Muyaka bin Haji: *Ngome intuumiza, naswi tu mumo ngomeni*.

It was also during those struggles that I looked back to the pamphlet, *Kenya: Twendapi?*, and realized its prophetic character and import. In our different ways, and with different details, we, in the Committee, were really asking the same question over and over again, trying, in the process, to offer a vision that we thought provided the correct response. The Committee, formed in July 1982 under the chairmanship of John la Rose, faced two enormous challenges: breaking the culture of silence and fear within Kenya; and the international culture of benevolent indifference to what was happening in Moi's Kenya.

It is difficult, in the light of the democratic gains in the country today, for people to quite imagine the fear that had gripped Kenya society, especially after the failed attempted air-force coup of 1982. Mass terror followed the failed coup; the right to organize, in any way, shape or form, was criminalized. Any individuals deemed to be challenging or even simply defending the right to organize were hauled into prisons, forced into exile, or killed. Since universities had always been seen as centers of dissent, they became the object of the state's wrath. Not surprisingly, students and university professors were among those targeted by the regime. Kamoji Wachira, Alamin Mazrui, Edward Oyugi, Maina wa Kinyatti, Willy Mutunga, to mention only a few, were among the victims. Again, this pouncing on leaders of thought, or those whose very *raison d'etre* was to work in ideas, had the effect of intensifying the culture of silence and fear. The terror and its inducement of fear had affected even those abroad: every member of the London Committee could tell tons of stories of incidents of some Kenyans fleeing to avoid meeting the so-called dissidents in the streets or corridors of universities abroad. Although inside Kenya people were organizing underground, it was also very important for them to know that Kenyans abroad were organizing aboveground and thus legitimizing the right to organize. We kept the idea of the right to organize in all the documents that we smuggled inside the country and that we published abroad. When later we formed UKENYA (United Movement for Democracy in Kenya) as an aboveground organization, we provided a model for the others that later emerged in Kenya, including the terminology: names like "Forum for Democracy in Kenya" clearly echoed our naming.

At the same time, Kenya was deemed, in the West at least, to be an island of democracy and stability. Initially the Committee had difficulties in puncturing that outlook, especially the more difficult formulation of "Kenya is not as bad as, say, Uganda or Tanzania". I can remember the skepticism with which the Security Committee of the British House of Lords received our documented claims about the 1984 Wagalla massacre in Kenya. Without the benefits of the internet – it did not exist in those days – we had to scour newspapers line by line to provide the data that provided proof. Abdilatif, in his strategic employment in the BBC, had access to many newspapers and reports from news agencies. We also helped organize sister committees all over the world – USA, Sweden, Denmark, Norway and Nigeria – that spearheaded campaigns of information and enlightenment in their own territories. We worked closely with other human rights committees for Chile and the Philippines, as well as with Amnesty International. By linking with forces inside, we were also able to obtain details of torture in the underground chambers of the Nyayo House. It was one of us, Wanyiri Kihoro, who after returning to Kenya, - against, I must say, our general warning - got arrested and tortured in Nyayo House. Through Wanjiru Kihoro, he managed to smuggle the then unknown details of torture, which we passed on to Amnesty International, who then produced the special issue on torture and human rights violations in Kenya in 1987, and which finally turned the world around to our view.

The regime reacted to our activities by having us denounced as dissidents, and traitors; in 1984, it had even sent its Foreign Minister, Elijah Mwangale, to Britain to plead with the British government to have us expelled from London. Within the country the regime organized the public burning of our effigies and then throwing them into the sea. There were even attempted assassinations, mine in particular thwarted by the Zimbabwe intelligence in Harare. To all their threats, we reacted in the words of Abdilatif Abdalla in his famous pamphlet: "*Kitisho sicho kimfanyacho mtu kuacha lile aaminilo kuwa ni sawa ... sisi twaamini kitisho huzidi kumpa mtu ushujaa wa kuendelea na lile alifanyalo.*" (*Kenya: Twendapi?*, 1968) This was a position that the writer had also immortalized in the poems, "N'shishiyelo ni Lilo", "Siwati" and "N'sharudi", in *Sauti ya Dhiki*.

The poems serve to remind us of the obvious: that Abdilatif Abdalla is primarily a poet and not a politician; and that his real voice, the enduring voice, the voice that will survive him, is the one infused with the spirit of the words, rhythms and imagery of his poetry, reminding us of the Keatsian words that truth is beauty and beauty is truth. At its best and most powerful, the aesthetic is also ethical. The verses also serve to remind us of another obvious fact: that Abdilatif writes in Kiswahili, the national language, an African language.

Lest we forget, Abdilatif is one of the greatest poets of the Kiswahili language – part of a long line of others that go back to Fumo Liyongo, Muyaka bin Haji and Shaaban Robert. He is also a central figure in the modern Kiswahili renaissance that has seen an explosion of novelists like Mohamed Said Abdulla of the detective tradition; Ben R. Mtobwa of the tough crime busters and thriller tradition; Said Ahmed Mohamed of the serious political novel tradition; and the rise of a completely new Kiswahili critical and theory tradition with such figures as Kimani Njogu and Rocha Chimerah; the massive translations into Kiswahili, which means that virtually all the Europhone African writing is now available in Kiswahili; and the general spread of Kiswahili as a language having the vocabulary and language to cope with all aspects of modern science and technology.

These two obvious facts of his being a poet, and in an African language, are also links that further bind Abdilatif and me. We may have travelled along different linguistic paths but it is surprising, almost uncanny, how we have arrived at similar practices. I started writing and publishing in English, a non-African but official language. Today I write primarily in Gikuyu but criss-cross among the three languages – English, Gikuyu and Kiswahili – through directly writing in them or through translations. Abdilatif started writing primarily in Kiswahili but now he also works in English, in fact he edited *Africa Events*, an English language magazine, but he has had his poems translated in Gikuyu, thus also criss-crossing the three languages. This once led us to a moment I would like to share with you.

It was in 1994 that Abdilatif and I, along with other Kenyans - among them being Karimi Nduthu, Tirop Kitur, Maina wa Kinyatti, Ngũgĩ wa Mirii and Khamis Ramadhan, attended the 7th Pan African Congress held in Kampala, Uganda. Outside the formal proceedings, the conference had attracted small traders from as far away as Kenya. These ordinary men and women had set up a temporary open air market, hoping to sell their ware to the participants that came from all over the world. Abdilatif and I had not been in Kenya for many years and the ache of being in touch with the folk from home drove us to the new market place. The women, mostly Gikuyu speakers, were really excited to see the faces of these two dissidents: they knew me as a writer but not so much Abdilatif, the writer. After I introduced him I offered to read them one of his poems written in prison:

## Siwati

*Siwati nshishiyelo, siwati; kwani niwate?*
*Siwati ni lilo hilo, 'talishika kwa vyovyote*
*Siwati ni mimi nalo, hapano au popote*
*Hadi kaburini sote, mimi nalo tufukiwe*

*Siwati ngaadhibiwa, adhabu kila mifano*
*Siwati ningaambiwa, 'tapawa kila kinono*
*Siwati lililo sawa, silibanduwi mkono*
*Hata ningaumwa meno, mkono siubanduwi*

*Siwati si ushindani, mukasema nashindana*
*Siwati ifahamuni, sababuye waungwana*
*Siwati ndangu imani, niithaminiyo sana*
*Na kuiwata naona, itakuwa ni muhali*

*Siwati nimeradhiwa, kufikwa na kila mawi*
*Siwati ningaambiwa, niaminiyo hayawi*
*Siwati kisha nikawa, kama nzi; hivyo siwi*
*Thamma nakariri siwi, na Mngu nisaidiya*

**(Abdalla 1973:9)**

In Gikuyu translation, it reads:

### Ndigaatiga Witikio Wakwa[18]

*Ndigitiga witikio wakwa, ndigiutiga; nguutiga ni ki?*
*Ndikaautiga uguutura uguo, ndiuruumirire hindi ciothe*
*Ndikaautiga ni nii na guo, guuku kana o ku na ku*
*Nginya tugaathii kabuurini, nii na guo tuthikanirio*

*Ndikaautiga o na ndaaherithio atia, mahera mithemba iriku*
*Ndikaautiga o na ingiirwo, ni nguheeo iria noru*
*Ndigaatiga wa kihooto, ndingiurekia kaimana*
*O na ingirumwo atia kana atia, guoko ndingikuregeria*

*Ndikaautiga na ti ngarari, njiirwo ni cio ndaacookia riiko*
*Ndikaautiga ikaraai muui, gitumi gia kuuga uguo*
*Ndigaatiga witikio wakwa, witikio wakwa wa goro*
*Kuurekia ni ndiroona, ni undu itangihota nii ri na ri*

*Ndikaautiga o na gutuika, magerio ni maingi muno*
*Ndikaautiga o na ingiirwo, witikio wakwa ti wa ma*
*Ndingiutiga njooke nduike ta ngi; uguo gutingihoteka*
*Ni nguuga o ringi nii ndingihota, Ngai wakwa ari mbere*

The women were in tears; the poem spoke to them directly in Gikuyu about the situation in Kenya. Some, obviously forgetting that I had introduced him as a Kiswahili writer from the coast, said loudly: So he knows Gikuyu? I had to explain to them once again that he wrote in Kiswahili, that this was a Gikuyu translation. They now knew him not only as a political dissident but also as a writer who

---

[18] Translated from Kiswahili by Kimani wa Njogu, and published in the journal *Mutiiri: Njaranda ya Miikarire*, No. 1, Newark, New Jersey: Mutiiri Abirika, 1994, p. 73.

voiced their concerns and anxieties. Their reaction left a big impression in my mind about the importance of writing in African languages to connect with the *mwananchi* and, equally important, translations as a way of making our languages dialogue with each other to the same end of reaching *wananchi*.

I believe that writers come from a prophetic tradition. A prophet looks at the existing conditions and is able to deduce the future that would inevitably come to be if current trends continue. He voices a warning. He points out, poses questions, challenges, and then calls for a change in the moral direction of a community. When society fails to heed the warnings and then the consequences follow, they turn around and ask: how did you know that this and that would happen? How could you have predicted this? I am sure that Abdilatif has fielded those kinds of questions many times. But rarely in the history of prophecy has a prophet asked a question that lives on, continually posing new challenges to new generations. Abdilatif managed to do this in his question, *Kenya: Twendapi?*

In a recent internet interview[19], Kimani wa Wanjiru, asked Abdilatif if the pamphlet was still relevant to Kenya and whether the issues raised therein had been adequately addressed, more than 40 years later; to which Abdilatif responded:

'My very brief answer is that I would like to believe that the question is still very relevant, because I think as a nation, we have not yet sat down to seriously and thoroughly discuss what kind of country we would like Kenya to be, and also have the courage to take practical steps to bring about the structural changes needed.'

So we continue to ask *Kenya: Twendapi?* in our poetry, fiction and essays. It is only in terms of new economy, politics, culture, mental make-up and hence spiritual strivings for a new Kenya, that we can meaningfully address that question. It calls now, as it did then, for the economic, political, cultural, psychological and spiritual empowerment of the ordinary man and woman of Kenya, Africa and the World, irrespective of their gender, ethnicity and religious affiliations. It is indeed a question that speaks to the whole world today.

It is only right and proper that, as we gather here in Leipzig, the city of Karl Marx and Sebastian Bach, to celebrate a life of a beloved poet, political activist, humanist, teacher, editor, maker of dictionaries, broadcaster, we invoke the question: *Abdilatif wendapi?* But we already know the answer: he may be retiring from marking essays and attending departmental meetings, but he will continue asking questions that have always driven him and his voice of prophecy for the benefit of Kenya, Africa and the world.

Thank you, Abdilatif Abdalla.

---

[19] See *Pambazuka News*, issue 500, 14 October, 2010, http://www.pambazuka.org/en/category/African_Writers/67813.

# References

Abdalla, Abdilatif. 1968. *Kenya: Twendapi?* (Kenya: Where Are We Heading?). Unpublished manuscript.

Abdalla, Abdilatif. 1973. *Sauti ya Dhiki*, Nairobi: Oxford University Press.

# Kai Kresse

## Abdilatif Abdalla: Poet and Activist
### Voice of the Discontented, Voice of Humanity[20]

*Kweli itashinda kesho, kama leo haitoshi*
*Truth will win tomorrow, if today is not enough*
(Shaaban Robert, 'Kweli', in *Masomo Yenye Adili*)

Shaaban Robert's statement, that truth will ultimately prevail, if not today then tomorrow, can be read as a commitment to hope, and confidence, that forces of the good will in the end succeed, even against the odds and the adverse powers that may dominate 'today' (*leo*). This statement is quoted by Abdilatif Abdalla at the very end of his lecture on the obligations of the writer in society, given at the University of Dar es Salaam in 1976. There, it encapsulates a bottom line about the writer's moral and social obligations (*wajibu*), as the need to do what must be done and say what needs to be said. From a writer's perspective, it is to give voice to such demands and concerns – especially when facing regimes that disregard justice and trample upon the principles of a humanity shared by all people. This is an attitude that Abdalla himself had just elaborated upon in the lecture, with reference also to Bertold Brecht.

Looking at Abdilatif Abdalla as a writer in social context in this brief essay, I will engage with some key terms and conceptual phrases from a selection of his texts (written between 1968 and 2009) and attempt to carve out a conceptual framework that underpins Abdalla's writings. I argue that Abdalla should be understood according to his own terms, both as writer *and* political activist. These are two dimensions that he himself has treated as indivisible and mutually inclusive. On the one hand, the gifted verbal artist needs to take care to give voice (*sauti*) to the currently relevant demands and concerns in society. On the other, the political agent needs to find appropriate public expression for such demands and concerns in order to pursue them successfully. Being a socialized human being (*mtu*), a member of society, embedded in a wider unity of people living in shared space, and being sensitive to its established moral principles and normative guidelines, fundamentally connects both roles. In each case, people have an obligation to act with reference to such principles and guidelines, in Swahili summarized by the term *utu* (humanity; goodness), and with the wishes and demands of their social peers in mind[21]. In Islam, this principle of 'commanding right and forbidding wrong,' as an active obligation of Muslims to their peers, has been worked out as a central ethical principle for all believers (Cook 2000; 2003). A wide scope of variations of this principle can

---

[20] I am grateful to Abdilatif Abdalla for many conversations and discussions over the last five years or so, and particularly also for his comments on an earlier draft of this chapter.

[21] For better orientation and contextualization of my discussion here, see my previous reflections, on *utu* as a key concept covering morality, goodness and humanism in the Swahili context, see Kresse 2007 (Chapter 5). On the moral obligation for the knowledgeable, to inform and educate their social peers, see Kresse 2009.

be found in Islamic pamphlet literature throughout the Muslim world and in the Swahili context specifically – such as, for instance, in a representative issue of the Islamic newspaper *Sauti ya Haki* (Mombasa, November 1974), where the importance of forbidding evil (*umuhimu wa kukanyana maovu*) is flagged up and contextualized in a lead article.

Referring once more to our initial quote, we can say that the confidence with which Shaaban Robert's statement expects truth to prevail, tomorrow if not today, relates to the conception of (a potential for) social unity within which all social actors are embedded. If they can show themselves able to unite, even and especially against adverse powers, the public expression of their unity, and thus the unified public expression of their concerns (of resistance, of liberation, or other) as a performative force constitutes the conditions for the kind of 'truth' (*kweli*) that Shaaban Robert's quote talks about, prevailing ultimately against all other forces. This success then builds on (the possibility of) social unity, and on the side of individual actors this is linked to the idea of a sincere belief (*imani*) in a just and common cause. If this is held and expressed by all social actors concerned in unity (especially the underprivileged and neglected), Abdalla can be seen to argue below, a forceful dynamic is acquired that is ultimately more powerful than all repression[22].

What I would like to get across in my essay here, by drawing from textual samples and quotes from Abdilatif Abdalla at different stages and points in his life – and, partly, by relating these briefly to Kenya's political history – is a sense of how being poet, writer, political activist and a concerned and sensitive person can overlap and coincide. More than that, I would like to show, while working on some illustrative quotations, how his literary and political work can be characterized as performances of a 'voice of the discontented', *sauti ya wasiotosheka*, and, at the same time, as an avowedly moral voice, *sauti ya utu*, 'voice of humanity/being human'. These are two complementary aspects of a morally driven political agenda which is about voicing critique and speaking truth to power, while picking up on social demands and upholding moral standards and normative guidelines. While the writer is embedded and somewhat bound by social conceptions, demands and expectations around him, he does not cease to be free. However, Abdalla argues, for the writer as well as other members of society, becoming a 'slave to freedom', someone who blindly follows ideas and promises of freedom without being grounded in a moral framework, makes for a potentially dangerous perspective. The exercise of freedom should be balanced and guided by principles of *utu* and the like.

In focusing on the phrase *sauti ya...* (voice of...) for my characterizations here, I am of course also following the title of Abdalla's most famous collection of poems, *Sauti ya Dhiki* (Voice of Agony), written secretly in prison between 1969 and 1972, and published in 1973. Understanding this phrase more widely,

---

[22] One could of course question this position and discuss the necessity of an assumption of a divine guarantor for it, but this goes beyond the scope of this paper.

voicing personal suffering and political discontent, anger and disillusion, by means of a creative and original language that resonates with and speaks to a wider public is what Abdalla has been engaged with as a writer, both of literary and political texts. Such voicing has made the aggrieved sentiments audible as part of a common experience of many ordinary Kenyans, impossible to be ignored by the powerful and politically responsible who are taken to task. This social engagement as a poet earned him the honorific title *Sauti ya Utetezi* (Voice of protest, or opposition) in a work of critical appraisal in literary criticism (Nyaigoti-Chacha 1992). Based on this sketch, I now turn to discuss Abdalla's texts in chronological order, without being able to go into the details of contents and contexts of each text as much as they would deserve.

### Kenya: Twendapi? (1968)

Using the Swahili expression *sauti ya wasiotosheka* (voice of the discontented) for a characterization of Abditalif Abdalla, I pick up on his own idiomatic label of the *WASIOTOSHEKA* (those who are discontent, the discontented) as he employed it himself. He used it (in capital letters) to sign off on the series of political pamphlets that he wrote as a young oppositional KPU supporter, criticizing Kenyatta's increasingly authoritarian post-Independence KANU government. These pamphlets were written in 1968, and they culminated and ended with *Kenya: Twendapi?* (Kenya: where are we going?) as the seventh pamphlet, which was circulated in November 1968. The pamphlets spoke up on behalf of Kenyans who were dissatisfied with the more and more dictatorial tendencies of the government that they were experiencing, either as oppositional activists or as ordinary citizens. *Kenya: Twendapi?* can thus be characterized as conveying the 'voice of the discontented', *sauti ya wasiotosheka*, to a wider public of social peers, on a local and national level, to people who share a sense of violated justice and the need to fix it. The pamphlet transmits a stern message of discontent from the ordinary Kenyans to the ruling party KANU, accusing them of having become dictatorial and oppressive. The 'discontented', used by Abdalla as an anonymous alias to sign his KPU pamphlets, stands for a larger body of aggrieved citizens who are deeply disappointed and upset with their government. As a kind of symbolic leitmotif, the term may well be applied more widely to discontented and alienated Kenyans through different periods of the post-colonial experience.

In the pamphlet, a collapsed state of affairs of political order and democracy in independent Kenya in 1968 is described, just a few years after Independence. Things have become so bad that the opinion is voiced that 'the times of the colonizer were better' (*ni afadhali wakati wa Mkoloni;* 1968: 3) – an almost unthinkable statement in the light of previous anti-colonial struggle – and a loss of faith in 'democracy' in Kenya is expressed. Describing the one-party regime of KANU and its suppression of dissenting political voices, the young and bold Abdilatif Abdalla goes as far as to compare Kenyan 'democracy' under Kenyatta and KANU with that of the Apartheid regime in South Africa:

'This is indeed the KANU government's boer-like democracy', he says. (*Hii ndiyo demokrasi ya sirikali ya KANU ya kikaburu*; 1968: 3). His sharp critique specifically refers to the systematic obstruction of KPU's activities by the government. As the pamphlet also expressed the wish, and a call, to get rid of the KANU government, Abdalla, who was later identified as the author by Kenyan authorities, was in consequence put on trial and imprisoned for three years in solitary confinement in Kenya's maximum security prison.

The label '*wasiotosheka*' is used twice in the *Kenya: Twendapi?* pamphlet, both times with the claim to an active collective authorship of the text. Initially, the label is printed in capital letters that stand out, marking its importance: '*sisi (WASIOTOSHEKA)*' – we (THE DISCONTENTED). Here, the disgruntled oppositionals describe themselves as those who know that the government is after them 'in every way' to silence them, 'so that we will not continue *to open people's eyes* any further'. This last expression indicates a self-understanding of a group with a liberating and consciousness-building agenda, and the *wasiotosheka* can be said to be on a two-fold mission: to voice common (openly visible and clearly justified) discontents, and to make this process audible among the (similarly discontented but silent) masses, so that discontent may grow and take up a larger and potentially critical force which would then make the realization of political change possible. In this self-understanding, the name 'WASIOTOSHEKA' is then used again, a second and final time, at the end of the document to sign off, in terms of authorship. The choice of the term is rhetorically clever because of its inherent invocation of the silent masses (of Kenyan peers, as real or potential readers of the pamphlet and supporters of the cause) who are invited as well as implied to be part of this radical challenge to the authoritarian government.

As a group, the potentially numerous and powerful political force that is invoked by the pamphlet, the WASIOTOSHEKA are not to be intimidated by threats and force. As the pamphlet says,

> Threats and terror (kitisho) are not what makes a person turn away from what he believes is right. Far from it, we believe that threats and terror increase giving that person courage (ushujaa) to go on with what he is doing.

> Kitisho sicho kimfanyacho mtu kuacha kufanya lile aaminilo kuwa ni sawa. Bali sisi twaamini kitisho huzidi kumpa mtu ushujaa wa kuendelea na lile alifanyalo. (1968: 1).

Thus we can see, by using this rather under-determined but clearly oppositional label, the spectre of masses of dissident citizens is evoked, posing a challenge and threat for the government perspective. At the same time, this collective label joining opinions and forces against political oppression by an authoritarian government, also seems to instil a lot of confidence and strength to the defenders of this cause – leading to a belief of its possible success. This happens through a belief (*imani*) in the unity and subsequent power of the discontented masses.

*Imani*, the word for belief, faith, or inner conviction here in the pamphlet is spelled in capital letters too, a clear pointer to its relevance. Abdalla uses it to refer to the righteous and moral belief that what one does is just, right and good – and that such belief indeed lends an immense power to its carriers, to implement political change (for example, the success of the Mau Mau fighters against the British colonialists). As the pamphlet says, in the name of the discontented,

> It is such a BELIEF that will indeed give us the strength and the courage to expel those who rule like dictators in the KANU government; rulers whose skin and whose faces have African features, but their hearts and their actions are those of boers. We did not expel the white boers in order to place black boers in their stead. This is not any more the time of a 'leadership of names'. Now we want a 'leadership of deeds'.

> Na ni IMANI kama hiyo ndiyo itakayotupa nguvu sisi, na ushujaa, wa kuwaondoshea hawa watawala wa kidikteta wa sirikali ya KANU. Watawala ambao ngozi zao na nyuso zao ni za Kiafrika, lakini nyoyo zao na vitendo vyao ni vya Kikaburu. Hatukuwaondoa Makaburu weupe ili tuweke Makaburu weusi. Wakati wa 'viongozi majina' sio tena huu. Sasa twataka 'viongozi vitendo'. (1968: 4).

As we have just seen in the interplay between belief (*imani*) and courage (*ushujaa*), a firm confidence seems to be established that the strength of one's own position will surge due to, firstly, the just cause at its basis, and secondly, the (potential) number of supporters involved. The clue here is about unity: once the discontented unite and stand up together, all is possible and can be realized: 'if the hearts of human beings unite in order to realize what they are determined to do, there is nothing that can beat them' – not even death (3).

## Sauti ya Dhiki (1973)

I will not get involved substantially here with Abdilatif Abdalla's most famous collection of poems, the volume *Sauti ya Dhiki* (Voice of Agony). This well-known book was written secretly in the three years of Abdalla's solitary prison confinement that followed prosecution for having written the pamphlet 'Kenya: Twendapi?' – but it has to be integrated into the perspective of discussion. *Sauti ya Dhiki* was published in Kenya in 1973, after Abdilatif's release from prison and his emigration to Tanzania, by no one less than Abdalla's older half-brother and mentor, Sheikh Abdilahi Nassir, then in a leading position with Oxford University Press East Africa. The volume ironically won a literature prize named after Kenyatta, the same autocratic president whose suppression of dissenting voices had not only sparked off Abdalla's pamphlet and activism in the first place, but also brought him into jail.

Let me quote one statement of appreciation of this volume that was expressed by Shihabuddin Chiragdin in his foreword to *Sauti ya Dhiki*, and that goes along with the general gist of my argument here. Chiragdin, one of the foremost authorities on Swahili literature at the time, congratulates the admirable young poet 'for teaching us that we should not run away from agony' (*kutufunza kuwa tusiikimbie dhiki*; 1973: xii), as a lot may be learned from the process of living it through and expressing it powerfully. Indeed, the author's voice of agony shaping this volume might be seen as an accentuated example of voicing discontent and pain about wrongful and regrettable ways in which the social world is seen to run.

Perhaps the poem *Siwati* (1973: 9) most clearly and radically illustrates Abdalla's attitude of moral insistence and perseverance. The message of this poem seems to be that not only should we not run away from agony if we see it coming, but we should stick to our beliefs and convictions and never let go of them, no matter how adverse the circumstances will be. '*Siwati*' means 'I don't give up' (or 'I will not let go'), and Abdalla's dense four-stanza poem of this title presents a series of urgent repetitions of the need not to give up, under any conditions, what one believes is right. Thus the statement '*Siwati lililo sawa*' (line 7), 'I won't give up what is right' is at the core here. The inner convictions about the truth and justice that one's actions are aiming at, and dedicated to, are, so to say, the most existential and defining features of one's being. Not only do they (*lililo sawa*) provide moral guidelines for one's actions, they also stand for a social goal to be realized. If we were to give up on this inner driving force of moral conviction – that which has motivated us and kept us going in our actions in the first place, despite adverse conditions – then we ultimately give up ourselves, what we know we should be and what we aspire to be. Without this, we are nothing, 'like flies', in fact (*kama nzi*; line 15) – yet as long as we don't give up, Abdalla's poem implores us, we cannot be broken and even the strongest oppositional powers and the biggest oppressors do not have real power over us, and have not gained victory over us – yet.

Thus the need *not* to give up, not to yield, not to let go, if one believes and knows one is right in what one is doing, is central not only for the cause of truth and justice in a general and abstract sense. Yes indeed, for the possibility of realizing them at some point in the future, the standards of 'what is right' (*lililo sawa*) must not be abandoned. But also, as Abdalla's poem puts it to us, on an individual level, too, giving up what is right (what one sincerely believes is right), under whichever kind of circumstances, would amount to self-negation, the giving up of one's self – the defining features that matter – and ultimately one's freedom. This is why Abdalla, here speaking from the immediate experience of imprisonment and in anticipation of possible death, keeps alive and puts across so pleadingly – to himself, as much as to anyone else – the need not to give up, as giving up would mean the end of meaningful existence, also with a view to a potential of realizing what is right (*lililo sawa*) in the future. *Siwati...*'– in the words of Abdalla's narrating subject, what 'I' will not give up is, in the end, what is ultimately worth living or even dying for; and what defines me as a free human being with a conscience and will that is (yet) unbroken – '...*lililo sawa*'.

## The Writer and Poet in Society (1976 & 1978)

In two short lectures given at the University of Dar es Salaam in the 1970s, Abdalla provides conceptual sketches of the ways he sees the poet and writer embedded in society, particularly the politically sensitive scenarios of the young post-colonial African states. He comments on the kinds of challenges and demands they face and need to address, as part of their obligation to society. His reflections here are insightful and inspiring. They seem, on the one hand, to be building on the experiences that Abdalla himself had previously undergone in Kenya (as imprisoned pamphlet writer, as poet). On the other hand, they reflect critically on the political contexts of Tanzania's *ujamaa* politics under Julius Nyerere at the time. Over the course of both lectures, Abdalla carves out a vision of 'a writer/ poet *of society*' (*mwandishi/mshairi wa jamii*) and discusses pressures and expectations that these verbal artists 'of the people' face and need to address.

The first lecture, on the obligations of a poet in his society (*Wajibu wa Mshairi Katika Jamii Yake*,' 1976), emphasizes the need for the poet to be in touch and knowledgeable about his society, to know what is going on, and to compose based on his own experience of having lived among people and participated in their everyday lives. If he takes this on as a serious and dedicated obligation, then he will be able to produce meaningful art that engages with central issues and problems of society, illustrating and discussing them in beneficial ways (1976: 3). This would then qualify a true 'poet of society', a '*mshairi wa jamii*' (4). Such a poet identifies with, and speaks out for, the many who are being ruled; he takes their side and speaks up against any abuse they are suffering from, even and especially when such abuse is performed by the new African elites (ibid.). Here Abdalla explicitly refers to the (real and/or potential) abuse of power, also by the new post-colonial African rulers who have taken over from the colonials (4). Poets *must* maintain a critical distance to rulers, he says, they *must not* simply follow directives from above, and praise and 'sing "*ujamaa* and self-reliance"' or other slogans (4). They should, however, act independently as 'critics and guardians of the interests of society', based on their experience of living among the people (4).

Thereby, it is the task of society (and those in charge) to provide the writer with possibilities for sufficient experience and (self-) education so that he can take on such a role. Thus Abdalla insists on the critical freedom of verbal artists that must not be interfered or messed with by governments with their particular ideological interests. The writer should remain free and independent, but his freedom is constrained and qualified by the guidelines within which he has to pursue and fulfil his social obligations. Thus in his freedom as 'a writer of society' (*mwandishi wa jamii*), he should not become 'a slave of freedom' *(mtumwa wa uhuru)* in the sense described above, as someone who has lost any sense of guidance and measure. Rather, he should use his freedom responsibly to put into words and express what his critical conscience tells him to, on behalf of the people among whom he lives (5). The writer's aesthetic and creative freedom is not a resource that can be employed at one's liberty; it has to follow the obligation (*wajibu*) to society that the writer has internalized. Fulfilling this role mindfully and conscientiously, the writer then can be seen to serve freedom *and* society.

In a second lecture from 1978 (published 1984), given on the occasion of an academic meeting dedicated to Ngũgĩ wa Thiong'o who had just been imprisoned in Kenya by the Kenyatta regime, Abdalla consolidates the image of such a 'people's writer' (*mwandishi wa jamii*), and discusses the problems he is facing in post-independent 'free Africa' (*Matatizo ya Mwandishi wa Jamii Katika Afrika Huru*). However, the political situation in post-colonial African countries has proven to be a major disappointment, as Abdalla describes. The people's writer, when looking around at his peers, sees no difference in their quality of life when compared to colonial times (1978:4). What has changed, he remarks, seems simply to be the colours of the flag that is hoisted (4), or the colours of the skin of the rulers (ibid.). Circumstances and actions initiated by the colonials driving many Africans into hardship, hunger and suffering, continue to haunt people; only they are now administered by those who had agreed to act as 'servants' (*viboi;* from 'boys') to those in charge of the international economic networks (4).

'The people's writer' (in English, I prefer this term to the more literal translation, 'writer of society') constitutes one of four identifiable groups of writers in society, according to Abdalla. He is the one who does not run away from problems, but stands with his brothers and sisters, in order to inquire and convey the truth about their continued oppression and instrumentalization under the mantle of nationalism (5). The other three groups of writers are: those who continue to work for the powerful few who control the economy; those who disagree with such ongoing exploitation but have no will-power to speak up, criticize or interfere; and those who avoid telling the truth to people and instead write about irrelevant things that do not concern the necessary fundamental critique to be raised nor contribute to improving people's lives (5).

Thus the point about the people's writer, the only truly 'meaningful writer' (*mwandishi wa maana;* 6), is about taking on freedom and the possibility of (fundamental) critique and improvement of the social life-world around him – and this has to be done through free and active engagement. Those artists who submit to directives of political rulers and make no attempts to build and voice their own opinion (which, in any case is forbidden by the post-colonial rulers), or who only express sanctioned or prescribed statements by the post-colonial regime, are in a state of 'mental slavery' (*utumwa wa mawazo;* 6) – which Abdalla calls 'a kind of death-like state' (*aina nyengine ya mauti*), as those writers/artists who agree to follow demands from above and stay quiet (when it would have mattered) have basically agreed to kill themselves (*amekubali kujiua mwenyewe*).

Fortunately, says Abdalla, there are some true and meaningful writers in post-colonial Africa, who address fundamental problems in their societies and are seeking to guide and guard their peers. However, for them to be successful, writing should not remain the only form of mediating critical discussion and fruitful suggestions. A wealth of diverse forms of performing art and narrative in Africa deserve to be taken up and employed by people's artists in – and for – a truly free Africa (6-8). Abdalla points to a remarkable popularity of literary works when their message is mediated not in print, but in a vivid format that can be more easily accessed, processed and understood. The narrative qualities of performances employing visual, oral and mimetic elements are flagged up, as we encounter them in film, theatre-play, and oral literature. These, he says, are recommendable ways for African writers to engage with and take on, so that their messages may reach a wider audience more naturally and easily. Here, Abdalla directs us at (now famous) examples of Sembene Ousmane, who developed his own way of Wolof story-telling through film; and of Ngũgĩ wa Thiong'o, who collaborated in play-writing with Kikuyu workers and re-learned and re-developed his own language anew, as a narrative means for the critical story-telling he pursued. Both writers draw from traditional forms of oral literature and story-telling that African societies have in abundance, in order to communicate their critical messages across more effectively. Such a re-engagement of traditional forms as vivid and effective narrative means is recommended by Abdalla. It illustrates an internal and integral working of literature or (verbal) art within society, and for it – along the lines of the writer's obligation sketched out by Abdalla in the first place.

### The Right and Might of a Pen (1985)

In September 1985, when based in London and working for the BBC Swahili service, Abdalla published a few excerpts of his prison diaries from the period of his three-year incarceration period in Kamiti Maximum Security Prison in Nairobi. These five brief entries, corresponding to five days between May 1969, shortly after he was moved in, and May 1970, are the only remaining entries from his secretly written prison diaries that he could recover and reconstruct (decoding the secret code he had made up when writing them). The heading used here, 'The right and might of a pen', represents a kind of re-iteration of his credo in the ability and power of writing in society, as a means for its improvement and a weapon against its abuse.

These accounts of five somewhat randomly selected days of Abdalla's prison experience give us a hint of an insight into what he was actually going through. From being arbitrarily subjected to insults, attempts of humiliation, violent attacks and solitary confinement, to the effects of loneliness and bad food, a wide range of factors creating an adverse reality that Abdalla had to confront and tackle in prison, are described. What comes across also and especially, is a calm sense of moral conviction about having done the right thing, to have stood up conscientiously for truth and justice when it mattered.

What we see, looking at these few exemplary days of Abdalla's prison experience, is how faith in, and resilience about, doing the right thing, by speaking out for the discontented and raising his voice in their name, provides orientation, inner strength and self-support during the difficult experience of undergoing prison and solitary confinement. We also gain a sense of the importance of the (forbidden) practice of writing under such conditions, and its meaningfulness, both as a channel of ongoing resistance against the unjust authorities as well as a resource of strength and personality building. In this latter respect, the performance of writing represents a proof, to oneself and the world, that the writer's will, spirit and determination have not been broken. We may see here that writing can create a separate personal space – even where there is no space. From inside prison, writing can leave palpable expressions of protest, and, to put it another way around, of freedom.

## Peace, Love and Unity: for Whom? (1989; poem)

Another text by Abdilatif Abdalla that illustrates resilience, freedom and the determination to raise one's voice, however strong and powerful the adversaries, is the poem 'Peace, Love and Unity: for Whom?' written in 1989 in English, remarkably, as only few of his poems are, this poem takes on the systematic rhetorical delusion that was fabricated by President Moi's so-called *nyayo* ideology shaped during his rule after he took over the presidency following Kenyatta's death in 1978. Characterizing the one-party state that presented itself as following the example and demands of first President Jomo Kenyatta – not least through its key term *nyayo* (indicating 'footsteps' to follow, in Swahili) – this ideology not only demanded blind following. It also clad itself with a deluding cover, of statements that emphasized 'peace, love and unity' as the key terms of an over-arching pseudo-humanism in the name of the Kenyan nation. De facto, however, as also Ngũgĩ and others have noted, what was demanded was a blind and silent following of presidential wishes and demands.

Engaging from exile in London, now with the no less autocratic regime of President Moi, Abdalla emphasizes his resistance, which he performs as an insistent verbal refusal to accept the deceiving words used in Moi's *nyayo* ideology where 'peace, love and unity' are used in an effort to quash any critical or protesting voices. After all, who would dare to be seen to act against peace, love, or unity?

Abdalla begins each stanza with an emphatic, 'I refuse!', a refusal to even consider engaging in communication that would accept the platform set by these deluding terms. This indicates, again, the forcefulness of discontent and the need to speak up in the face of injustice, as already seen when looking at *Kenya: Twendapi?* and the poem 'Siwati'. Also, the deep belief and conviction (*imani*) in the truth and rightfulness of one's case come up again here, in the name of those many who were mistreated and thus mocked by the wordplay and false semantics of *nyayo* politics. The author's moral impetus and social solidarity are expressed as well, and a sense of the extraordinary resulting potential of power arises as the poem spells out refusal to engage in any kind of dialogue with the perpetrator-government, in the name of the many people killed or treated unjustly:

> *...How can there be 'peace' between us?*
> *When I'll never accept to bury the people's anger in the tomb of my*
> *verse?*
> *How can I forget decades and decades of my people's suffering and pain?*
> *Of tears and blood pouring from their struggling limbs like rain?*
> *How can I ask them to sing your songs in high volume*
> *To stifle the tormented sounds of those you torture and maim?*
> *How can I draw veils over their eyes*
> *To conceal and eclipse the scenes of numerous massacres?*

Texts such as this illustrate the importance of being discontent, of being driven by discontent, and of the possibility of using it as a driving-force (or, as here, a counter-force) for building a vocal moral agenda of social improvement. This is observable in the way that Abdalla emphasizes his refusal to give into, or even negotiate with, the unacceptable, as this would happen on unacceptable grounds. This insistence on a fundamental public disapproval of the kind of unjust and inhumane state that Kenya has become during the politics of *nyayo*, which is also an insistence on the public recognition of what is wrong, marks the strength and forceful energy of this poem. If this is true, then the poem also exemplifies the force of the voiceless discontented masses for whom the poet has chosen to speak up – though whether this force is forceful enough to change things is another matter. Following the logic and reasoning of discontent as expressed through Abdalla's texts, speaking up and lending a voice was something he had to do, as the fulfilment of a commitment to a moral obligation that the poet (or writer, or composer more generally) has to his community.

Abdalla also pointed out this commitment very clearly in conversation with me; the poet should represent his society with a view to those who have no voice of their own, vis-à-vis their more powerful counterparts inside and outside the community. He should speak out in public on their behalf, as already expressed above by the image of *mwandishi wa jamii*, 'a writer of society' or 'of the people'. This illustrates a continuity of Abdalla's thought in conceptualizing the vision for a just society, or at least the necessary struggle towards it, based on the obligation towards one's peers.

## A Political Address (1994)

In 1994 Abdalla was still politically active against the Moi-regime and its *nyayo* politics. As a representative of the *United Movement for Democracy in Kenya*, he gave a brief address at 7th Pan-African Congress in Kampala that shows features that may consolidate our observations made so far. While positioning the political movement he represents in stark opposition to Kenya's current government, with an emphasis on the need for a 'second liberation struggle against neo-colonialism and imperialism' (p.4), he outlines two main objectives of the United Movement.

The first is 'to expose to the world the repressive and dictatorial nature of the MOI-KANU regime, which the Western world used to present as the most stable, the most developed, and the most democratic country, particularly in the East African region' (p.2). Such unveiling of a delusion that has been able to persist because of lack of sufficient initiative to make clear to a wider (global) public what is actually happening can again be characterized as an act of voicing discontent.

The second main objective of the United Movement, which he describes is 'to organize, sensitize, and involve Kenyans living abroad in the struggle for democratic and meaningful changes for all our people in Kenya' (p.2). This correspondingly can be seen as an act of responding to, or acting upon, discontent. This is envisaged to be done in a systematic way with a view to all the people concerned, by way of social connections and common engagement, for a democratic Kenya enabling all its citizens to participate meaningfully in politics. Here, too, we may say that voicing discontent and acting upon the ways that discontent has been experienced constitute two major axes of Abdalla's political engagement.

### Risala kwa Washiriki Katika Tamasha la Kitamaduni la Lamu (2009)

As a final text, let us look at another brief address, on the occasion of the dramatized performance of Abdalla's dialogical poem *Mnazi: Vuta N'kuvute* at the Lamu Cultural Festival in 2009. This dialogical poem itself constitutes a kind of parable-like commentary on the political state of Kenya after Independence, originally during the early years in the 1960s (it was written in prison and included in the *Sauti ya Dhiki* collection). Its look at two competing leading figures opposing each other (then, Jomo Kenyatta and Odinga Oginga) as well as its expression of a general disappointment about the state of affairs could be usefully transferred to 2009, when Mwai Kibaki and Raila Odinga were the main opponents. Abdalla's address was read out as a letter to the audience as the poet was not able to attend in person.

It is possible to make some comparisons with the early political pamphlet *Kenya: Twendapi?* with a view to the disillusioned vision for Kenya, and about the prospect of improving things. With an explicit view to the 46th anniversary of Independence, celebrated that year, Abdalla remarks with regret how disappointing it was for him to see that in 2009 there was no visible improvement of ordinary people's standard of living in Kenya when compared to the period before Independence. Rather, he says,

> *The state Kenyans are in today is worse than it was then. And nobody will be able to change this state of affairs other than the Kenyans themselves (hali ya Wakenya hao hivi sasa ni mbaya zaidi kuliko ilivyokuwa nyakati hizo. Hakuna atakayeweza kuibadilisha hali hiyo isipokuwa Wakenya wenyewe).*

So, just like in the early pamphlet, we encounter a frustrating assessment of the political situation in contemporary post-colonial Kenya: things are worse, and Kenyan citizens worse off, than during the colonial rule of the British, he says. Notably, Abdalla allocates the agency for change, and the responsibility to bring about change, to lie with all Kenyans – it is up to the citizens to stand up and bring their country in order. In the end, this is also where Abdalla's hope lies. He wishes for the younger generation to be able to learn from history (and specifically the historical political situation his poem covered):

> *My hope, especially for the young, is that we study our history so that we understand it well, and also that we learn from that history so that the mistakes that were made back then will not be repeated, and so be able to achieve true change in our country (mabadiliko ya kweli) – change that will benefit every Kenyan irrespective of their tribe (kabila), colour or religion. We are all placed together inside one large dhow (dau), and therefore our prayer (dua) need to be unified as well!*

> *Matumaini yangu, khaswa kwa vijana, ni kwamba tutaisoma historia yetu tuielewe vizuri, na pia kwamba tutajifunza kutokana na historia hiyo ili makosa yaliyotendeka hapo zamani yasiwe yakirudiwarudiwa, ili kupatikane mabadiliko ya kweli katika nchi yetu – mabadiliko ambayo yatamfaidi kila Mkenya bila ya kujali kabila lake, au rangi yake, au dini yake. Sote tumo katika dau moja, na kwa hivyo dua yetu lazima iwe ni moja!*

'True' or 'real' change is what would matter and put Kenya and its people on a good track again. In this respect the appeal goes on to all people concerned: it is up to them (at least *also* up to them), through combined and sustained efforts, to bring about the kind of social and political change that can in the end said to be lasting. For this, the invocation of social solidarity and a needed unity among people is highlighted. Also, the common shared basis of membership to the Kenyan community, here marked by passengers in a dhow, is flagged up. Not however, with any kind of exclusive reference to ethnicity (*ukabila*) or religion (*dini*), as is common in popular discourse, but rather as having been (historically, yet coincidentally) assembled in the same vessel that needs to be kept afloat and manoeuvrable in order for all passengers to be content, or at least able to see perspectives for their respective journeys. This picture of a shared passage on a boat may be quite befitting and realistic: precarious as it may be, a successful journey is reliant on the fact that all stick to certain basic rules (of mutual recognition, among others) so that the boat may stay afloat and reach its (next) designated harbour. People need to submit themselves to the community of the ship, so that the shared goal of moving forward can be seen to be accomplished. Otherwise, it is implied, the ship of the Kenyan nation is doomed to sink.

**In Conclusion:** *Sauti ya Utu* and *Sauti ya Wasiotosheka*

Let me conclude by discussing once more the overarching conceptual bracket, between the 'voice of the discontented' (*sauti ya wasiotosheka*) and the 'humane voice' (*sauti ya utu*) that I worked upon here. In Abdilatif Abdalla's writings, I suggest, we can see 'discontent as a resource' coming into play in a valuable and creative manner. It seems to infuse the writer with constructive yet critical energy to identify and challenge injustice, while ultimately seeking to re-establish morality or humane standards of social interaction (*utu*). Generalizing from here, we may conclude that for the writer, a certain level of discontent is needed to trigger his critical creativity into addressing matters of social injustice publicly. The writer's obligation to speak up for those without a voice – as Abdalla once put it to me – for those with little influence, power, and means of proper articulation of their concerns, is a continuous one.

In his work, the writer's invocation of humanity, the work of his '*sauti ya utu*' so to say, marks a common standard of moral principles valid for all. Complementary to the potential of 'discontent as resource' we can speak of the work of '*utu* as a base' against which social action is measured and judged. When *utu* is violated, people as a rule become discontent and the poet, as moral voice of the community, has to speak up in order to address these matters. Thus we seem to have a kind of dynamic cycle in place, within which moral knowledge and sensitivity, belief (*imani*) and action (*kitendo*), including verbal expression or performance are interrelated and somewhat interdependent aspects of how the social dynamics of the role of the writer play out, following the specific examples given in Abdilatif Abdalla's texts discussed above. For a wider comparative perspective, across Africa and beyond, this kind of model framework could usefully be extended further, to include other African contemporary political writers and activists in discussion (like Ngũgĩ, Achebe, Ousmane, Okot p'Bitek and others), or historical examples of Swahili poets (like Liyongo, Muyaka, or Shaaban Robert) – and ultimately indeed, writers and activists around the world, as Abdalla himself did, invoking Brecht. But this is where I have to stop for today.

## References

Abdalla, Abdilatif. 1968. *Kenya: Twendapi?* (Kenya: Where Are We Going?). Unpublished manuscript.

Abdalla, Abdilatif. 1973. *Sauti ya Dhiki*. Nairobi: Oxford University Press.

Abdalla, Abdilatif. 1977. Wajibu wa Mshairi Katika Jamii Yake (The Obligations of a Poet within his/her Society). *Lugha Yetu* 30, Journal of National Kiswahili Council of Tanzania.

Abdalla, Abdilatif. 1984. Matatizo ya Mwandishi wa Jamii Katika Afrika Huru . Lugha 3, Journal of Department of Afro-Asian Languages, Uppsala University, Sweden.

Abdalla, Abdilatif. 1985. The Right and Might of a Pen. *Africa Events*, September 1985: 25-26.

Abdalla, Abdilatif. n.d. Peace, Love and Unity: for Whom?. Manuscript, 30-34.

Abdalla, Abdilatif. 1994. A Statement Given by Abdilatif Abdalla, Chief Coordinator of the United Movement for Democracy in Kenya, to the 7th Pan-African Congress, Kampala, Uganda, on 3-8 April, 1994. Manuscript.

Abdalla, Abdilatif. 2009. *Risala kwa Washiriki Katika Tamasha la Kitamaduni la Lamu* (Address to the Participants of the Lamu Cultural Festival). Unpublished manuscript.

Chiraghdin, Shihabuddin 1973. '*Utangulizi*', in A. Abdalla, *Sauti ya Dhiki*. Nairobi: Oxford University Press, ix-xii.

Cook, Michael. 2000. *Commanding Right and Forbidding Wrong in Islamic Thought*. Cambridge: University Press.

Cook, Michael. 2003. *Forbidding Wrong in Islam: An Introduction*. Cambridge: University Press.

Kresse, Kai. 2007. *Philosophising in Mombasa: Knowledge, Islam and Intellectual Practice on the Swahili Coast*. Edinburgh: Edinburgh University Press.

Kresse, Kai. 2009. Knowledge and Intellectual Practice in a Swahili Context: 'Wisdom' and the Social Dimensions of Knowledge. *Africa: Journal of the International African Institute*, Special Issue (Knowledge in Practice), vol.79, no.1: 148-167.

Nyaigotti-Chacha, Chacha. 1992. *Ushairi wa Abdilatif Abdalla: Sauti ya Utetezi*. Dar es Salaam: Dar es Salaam University Press.

Robert, Shaaban. 1971 (1959). *Masomo Yenye Adili*. Dar es Salaam: Nelson.

# Said Ahmed Khamis

## Whither Swahili Literature? Translation and the World Recognition of Abdilatif Abdalla's Sauti ya Dhiki

> *I am an invisible man ... I am a man of substance, of flesh and bone, fiber and liquids – and I might even be said to possess a mind. I am invisible, understand, simply because people refuse to see me ... That invisibility to which I refer occurs because of a particular disposition of the eyes of those with whom I come in contact. A matter of the construction of their inner eyes, those eyes with which they look through their physical eyes upon reality.*

Ralph Ellison, *Invisible Man*

### Wither Swahili Literature?

In a general implicit sense, the above title informs what Casanova (2004:175-204) calls: *small literatures*. By small literatures we mean literatures which are hardly recognised in a global scene, or literature(s) whose heritages are betrayed, their differences denied and their values always alleged to be derived from the great literary traditions as if the so-called great literatures are completely devoid of influences from other literatures and cultures of the world.

However, the idea of 'purity' attributed to great traditions and dominant literatures is but a façade which presents respectively the opposing dualities *conspicuous-high* and *invisible-low* looked at in comparison as 'dominant literatures' or 'cultures' and 'small literatures' or 'cultures'.

Casanova challenges the idea of dominance, self-absorption and exclusiveness engulfed in the so-called great traditions and dominant literatures. Casanova (175-176) puts this challenge in the following statement:

> *Every literary space, including that of France, has been subject to domination at one moment or another of its history. And the international literary universe as a whole has taken shape through the attempts made by figures on the periphery to gain entry to it. From the point of view of the history and the genesis of worldwide space, then, literature is a type of creation that is irreducibly singular and yet at the same time inherently collective, the work of those who have created, reinvented, (re) appropriated the various means at their disposal for changing the order of the literary world and its existing power relations. Thus new genres and forms have come into being, foreign works have been translated, and popular languages have acquired literary existence.*

Goethe introduced the term *Weltliteratur* (world literature) to emphasize the universality of literature. However, Goethe's *Weltliteratur* is not conceptualised in the duality of *conspicuous-high* and *invisible-low*, instead it connotes 'relational terms' such as 'globalism', 'diversification' and 'comparability' within the alleged sense of 'universality'. Goethe advisory statement goes:

*I therefore like to look about me in foreign nations, and advise everyone to
do the same. National literature is now a rather unmeaning term; the epoch
of world literature is at hand, and everyone must hasten its approach. (cited
in Damrosch 2003:1).*

Though Goethe's formulation of Weltliteratur is regarded as a turning point
in comparative literary studies, Damrosch (2003:1) challenges the term in
the following questions: *What does it really mean to speak of world literature?
Which literature, whose world? What relation to the national literatures whose
production continued unabated even after Goethe announced their obsolescence?
What new relations between Western Europe and the rest of the globe, between
antiquity and modernity, between the nascent mass culture and élite productions?"*
In this barrage of Damrosch's questions I would place, the question *Whither
Swahili literature?*, a relevant question that hints at the impasses surrounding
the notion of universalism vis á vis worldwide recognition of Swahili literature
in general and Abdilatif Abdalla's *Sauti ya Dhiki* (1973) / "Voice of Agony" in
particular, and this despite the fact that we know that Swahili literature exists,
and it exists robustly.

To this effect, Damrosch reminds us of Franz Kafka, Katib Yacine, Henrik
Ibsen and James Joyce – all found themselves faced with the same alternatives
and curiously discovered the same way out from the same dilemma of smallness.
In some cases they managed to bring about successful revolutions and to pass
through the mirror and achieve recognition by changing the rules of the game
in the centres of the literary world (176). In this case less dominant literatures
must sustain evidence, resistance, resilience and efforts to achieve a successful
breakthrough towards world recognition and acceptance of Swahili literature
and other small literature in general.

## Sauti ya Dhiki and the Idea of Breakthrough

*Sauti ya Dhiki* (1973) "The Voice of Agony", is born out of political ferment
and of fighting spirit of a young activist cum-poet Abdilatif Abdalla who was,
in 1968, detained by the government of Kenya for writing and circulating a
seditious document called *Kenya: Twendapi?*/"Whither Kenya?". The document
accuses the government of silencing the opposition by using intimidation and
coercive means. In *Sauti ya Dhiki* therefore, we learn of the poet's political
conviction and his quest for the right to speak out and to participate in political
activities and contribute constructively towards the progress and development
of his country. Here is the first stanza of Abdalla's poem *Siwati* (9)/"Never Will
I Let Go", which shows Abdalla's unwavering stance:

Siwati
*Siwati n'shishiyelo, siwati; kwani niwate?*
*Siwati ni lilo hilo, 'talishika kwa vyovyote*
*Siwati ni mimi nalo, hapano au popote*
*Hadi kaburini sote, mimi nalo tufukiwe*

## Never Will I Let Go

Never will I let go what I hold dearly, I'll not abandon it - why should I?
Never will I let go, for what it is, I'll firmly hold it, come what may
Never will I let go, it's me and what I believe in Be it here where I am, or somewhere else
Till both of us are thrown into a grave together[23]

The insistence of 'never will I let go' is profound, deliberate and hyperbolically poignant in a self-assertive way. The alliteration in Swahili language is not only pleasant to the ear, but it is also emphatic in Abdalla's appeal. This by itself determines Abdalla's resolute stance and conviction, not to mention his dexterity which contributes to his poetic excellence.

### Appreciation of *Sauti ya Dhiki*

In the early years of 1970s when his anthology *Sauti ya Dhiki* emerged, most of us interested in Swahili literature read it with a pleasant surprise. First, it was the first Swahili poetic anthology written by a detainee and smuggled out of prison to be published and read by both common readers and academics. Although *Sauti ya Dhiki* was well received by East African audience, it created ambiguities regarding the place and manner in which the poet dared to compose his poems not only in a marvellously new style, but also in a critical and incisive treatment.

When I read *Sauti ya Dhiki* for the first time, I found that the collected poems were not only written in different thematic lines, but they were all stressing anger, courage, uprightness, protest, resistance, resilience, lament, love and hatred. Immediately I realised that Abdalla was influenced by Muyaka bin Haji Al Ghassany, a 19th century poet of high reputation. In addition to that I was drawn by his revolutionary views based on such questions like: *how can a poet who is detained dares to write the subversive poems in confinement? Why and how could he develop and balance romance and innocence amidst the major themes of agony, protest, etc – and this with unbelievable boldness if not recklessness.* Thus, after reading *Sauti ya Dhiki* in conjunction with alleged seditious document *Kenya: Twendapi?*, Abdalla's dare-devil became more believable to me, and hence my full admiration to the poet and his work were reinforced. Therefore *Sauti ya Dhiki* greatly influenced me as a poet, and I guess also a number of Swahili poets, students, readers, critics and academics as well.

I read *Sauti ya Dhiki* for the first time in a poetry class at the University of Dar es Salaam in 1976. Abdalla's revolutionary spirit made an impact on me. I quickly absorbed and digested what I considered the poet's naked truth, his advocacy and appeal to Kenyan citizens to fight for their rights, which was by implication the appeal to all African people and all oppressed people in the world. I therefore started to draw parallels between Kenyan and Tanzanian

---

[23] All poems translated by the author.

political situations and their ramifications. At that time Kenya and Tanzania were two different countries separated politically and ideologically at least on the surface, though at the underlying level, they were two countries whose citizens were disillusioned with how their governments were running the countries as (neo)colonies. It was as if some of us were blinded and tongue-tied, and *Sauti ya Dhiki* immediately opened our eyes and made us not to be afraid to speak out our plights and predicaments.

Adorably, I myself was more inspired by Abdalla's poetic skills and noble ideas: the ideas of courage, determination, dedication and commitment to fight for real freedom and dignity. These were ideas that most of us cherished not long time ago as our people were fighting for independence from colonial powers. We were in fact also aware of French revolution, of USA civil war and war of independence, of the Russian revolution, of courage and steadfastness of those engaged in the First and Second World Wars, and of the Chinese and Korean wars against Japan imperialism. I was therefore convinced that I should write something to support Abdalla's cause, which was also my cause. I started composing one poem after another, till I obtained a fill in an anthology called 'Sikate Tamaa (1980)/ "Never Despair". I dedicated the anthology to Abdalla with the following words appearing on the first page: *Salamu: Abdilatif Abdalla na Sauti ya Dhiki ... nimesoma mengi* – "Greetings to Abdilatif Abdalla and *The Voice of Agony* ... I have learnt a lot."

Abdalla kindly wrote an introduction to my anthology. It was an act of honour to me. My first poem has a clear ring of Abdalla's of *Sauti ya Dhiki*. In fact it was written to encourage my mentor, and in so doing, the poems encouraged me and the rest of the audience at the time if not today. Here is the first stanza of my poem *Sikate Tamaa*:

Sikate Tamaa
*Umeanguka, inuka, simama kama mnazi*
*Umechunika, inuka, tia dawa kwa ujuzi*
*Sasa inuka, inuka, kijana ianze kazi*
*'Sikate tamaa!*

Never Despair
You have fallen down, rise up, stand up like a palm tree
You've been stripped off your skin, rise up,
You need look for an alternative way
Rise up now, rise up, start again the fight
Never despair!

My admiration however, was (and still is) not only based on *Sauti ya Dhiki's* revolutionary spirit, but also on Abdalla's renovation of Swahili traditional poetic forms. *Sauti ya Dhiki* constitutes of verses of varying number of measured lines; of changing visual shapes, of metric patterns and balance based on different syllabic counts, of line segments appearing in different lengths, of variable rhyme schemes at mid- and end points of rhythmic waves, of diction which provides words which are brightened up for aesthetic and semantic effects – old words which are now made to appear in new senses and new contexts, such as *mwenzangu* (a partner, a companion) *swahibu* (a lover, an intimate friend), *jipu* (remorse), *mamba* (a leader who rules with an iron fist), *mnazi* (nation wealth) *kunena* (to speak out) *telezi* (carelessness leading to falling in a trap) etc. These words are in one way or another connected with key concepts as love of one's spouse, one's comrade or a reference to agony, courage and revolutionary spirit. In Abdalla's anthology words of everyday usage are beaten into new shapes, images, and symbols for a number of meanings and nuances.

However, the most visible aesthetic quality of Abdalla's *Sauti ya Dhiki* is the rendering of cadence in his poetry. This is done by repeating the same words with the same sounds in close proximity in sequence of sounds in their horizontal relation. Kwame Dawes (2007:11-19) emphasizes the essence of cadence in poetry as a culmination of "political convulsions and craft in art". This is how he contends:

> But not everyone succeeds in dealing with the conundrum of content and craft. Not all artists find the aesthetic that allows them to treat the political convulsions of these last hundred years in ways that do not make us question the very validity or relevance of art. But a handful have managed to make us believers – believers in the power of craft … One good thing about music, when it hits, you feel no pain. It is not so much what it teaches, but what it fills, and how it manages to touch us in ways that are only explained by the beauty of the crafting of the words. To teach this to students is sometimes difficult for they want answers, they are not always interested in finding a salve for souls through the music of words placed side each other or the tenor of the sounds that emanate from the sound system in the lecture hall…

The poem *Nakukumbuka* (11) "I Remember You", is a good example of power of music in Abdalla's poetry crafted by a repetition of the line segment *Mi nawe mbali tungawa* and variation of rhyme schemes at the mid- and end points of rhythmic waves:

Nakukumbuka
*Mi nawe mbali tungawa, nakukumbuka*
*Lau ngekuwa na mbawa, ningaliruka*
*Ni muhali hili kuwa, nasikitika*

*Mi nawe mbali tungawa, muhibu wangu*
*Kamwe hayatapunguwa, mapenzi yangu*
*Hili kaa ukijuwa, wewe u wangu*

I Do Remember You

Though you and I are far apart, I do remember you
If I were to grow wings, I would (surely) fly to you
But that is not possible, I am afraid to say
Though you my darling and I are far apart
Never will my love to you diminish
Rest assured that you'll always be mine

In *Kuno Kunena* (23) the poet uses the agglutinative nature of Swahili word-formation to create different kinds of musical patterning:

Kuno Kunena

*Kuno kunena kwa nini, kukanikomea kuno?*
*Kwani kunena kunani, kukashikwa kani vino?*
*Kani iso na kiini, na kuninuniya mno*
*Kanama nako kunena, kwaonekana ni kuwi*

That Act of Speaking Out

Why the act of speaking, ended up in me being imprisoned?
What is there in my speaking, that made it so much irritable?
Is it all those baseless allegations that made me hated so much?
Alas! speaking out is seen as something evil?

## Impasses

If we accept the fact that *Sauti ya Dhiki* is one of the 'flowers' of Swahili literature, why are we not resolved to remove the invisibility that threatens it and other works of Swahili literature? Why is everybody shunning the idea of translating *Sauti ya Dhiki* into major languages? Is it because *Sauti ya Dhiki* has been written in Kimvita, a Swahili dialect that is linguistically not accessible to most people? But how do we determine and remove the obscurity and inaccessibility of a text? Is it because *Sauti ya Dhiki* is written in Swahili language ranked as one of the smallest language? Is it because some of us feel that *Sauti ya Dhiki* is too political, which is not absolutely so? And if it were, is it not a fact that most works of successful writers are overtly or covertly political?

The answers to these questions happen to be reflected in Casanova's statement which asserts that, "The creative liberty of writers from peripheral countries is not given to them straight away: they earn it as the result of struggle" (177). Therefore, one way of securing creative liberty is to earnestly start translating Swahili literature in major languages with a target to provide the global audience with texts which have been translated with a fidelity that is stressed by Cornel West's idea of *Paideia*, an old Greek word meaning 'education'. In its modern sense, according to West, the word *Paideia* means an education that connects you to profound issues in serious ways. It instructs us to turn to our attention from the superficial to the substantial, from the frivolous to the serious. Paideia according to West is a cultivation of self, the way you engage your own history, your own memories, your own morality, your own sense of what it means to be alive, as a critical, loving, aware human being (2009:22) – in other words, it is the idea of 'liberating the mind'.

## Translation

According to Casanova (175)

> (a) literary space, is not immutable structure, fixed once and for all in its hierarchies and power relations. But even if the unequal distribution of literary resources assures that such forms of domination will endure, it is also a source of incessant struggle, of challenges to authority and legitimacy of rebellions, insubordination, and, ultimately, revolutions that alter the balance of literary power and rearrange existing hierarchies. In this sense, the only genuine history of literature is one that describes the revolts, assaults upon authority, manifestos, inventions of new forms and languages – all the subversions of the traditional order that, little by little, work to create literature and the literary world.

Translation is one the strategies of creating communication through literatures of different languages and cultures. However, the kind of translation project that we need is a geopolitical one which must be used to alter the balance of literary power and rearrange existing hierarchies. Such a translation project must first and foremost deal with the issues of 'power relations', 'purpose of translation', 'choice of source texts', 'choice of target language', 'choice of translators in terms of whether they have sufficient 'competence' and 'ideological commitment''.

So far the criteria for the implementation of a geopolitical translation have never been thought out in Swahili literature. As a result we will mention in passing two main streams of translation: namely 'translation of Swahili literature in major world languages', and 'translation of world literatures in Swahili'. The translation of Arabic/Islamic literature in Swahili already started in the 16th century. These translations[24] especially from Arabic to Swahili were undertaken by leading Muslim clerics with the aim of restoring the Islamic values and sensibility threatened to disappear after over 200 years of Portuguese rule in East Africa (Gérard, 1976:7).

Then there followed the translation of English texts in Swahili, a project that was undertaken during the colonial period in East Africa. Some of the translations, to name a few, are *The Bible, Pilgrim's Progress, Aesop's Tales, Treasure Island, Mowgli's Stories, Gulliver's Travels, Alan Quarterman, King Solomon's Mines* and *The Honourable Blackman*. Most of the texts translated in this phase were meant to change African psychology through certain ideologies designed to create mental enslavement in African minds.

Swahili translations from African literatures in English which appeared in the 1960s and 1970s were produced for the purpose of creating cultural

---

[24] Some Swahili scholars reject any reference of the term translation when referring to Swahili Arab/Islamic poetry of this period except for *rewriting, paraphrasing, reinvention, (meta)literary compositions* etc.

referents that would inspire Africans with a sense of nationhood. It was a collaborative project that involved nationalist leaders, writers, literary scholars and local publishers. Some of the translated titles are those of Chinua Achebe, Aye Kwei Armah, Peter Abrahams, Ngũgĩ wa Thiongo, Mungo Beti, Sembene Ousmane, Wole Soyinka, Camara Laye, Okot p'Bitek, Agostinho Neto, Peter Palangyo and Cyprian Ekwensi, to name a few. Other titles within this group are those of Shakespeare, Gogol, Gorky, Brecht, and Orwell.

Swahili translation of contemporary Swahili literature which includes a few works of Shaaban Robert in Russian, Shafi Adam Shafi in German and French, Said A. Mohamed in Japanese, Italian and English, and Euphrase Kezilahabi in French, is the last group we know so far. However, the translation of Swahili literary text at this period does not appear to be doing very well since publishers in East Africa are more interested in producing original Swahili literary works. As a result of this, translating Swahili literary texts in English is considered by East African publishers as not viable economically. The enthusiasm that prevailed in the 1960s and 1970s to promote local literature(s) and culture(s) has considerably dwindled. Publishing firms of the like of East African Publishing House, East African Literature Bureau and Tanzania Publishing House, have completely collapsed. Private firms, local and multinational, have now taken over. These private firms are not interested in promoting East African literature(s) and cultures(s) but in making money. It is not surprising therefore to find that only a few Swahili literary works have been selected for translation in this phase, and these have been translated and produced by foreign publishers for foreign tastes.

In this case it is necessary for ministries of education to plunge into the project of designing literature syllabi to include Swahili texts translated in English to promote both African language literatures and African European language literatures. After all, if European language literatures and translated Swahili literary texts exist mutually, they should be feeding into each other. This must happen, if we are to envisage the translation of *Sauti ya Dhiki* and other Swahili literary texts into major languages of the world. Such translated Swahili texts will be an evidence of the status quo of Swahili literature in whether or not it deserves global recognition or not.

## Concluding Remarks

In concluding we will posit the following salient features regarding our topic:

In comparative terms, modern literatures exist in an unequal distribution(s). Some occupy a dominated peripheral position. Others occupy dominating position as they exercise powers on dominated literatures. Yet, the small dominated literature never ceases to take into account the variety of solutions for overcoming literary dependence. In this case writers and scholars who are engaged in Swahili literature and the so-called small literatures should maintain steadfastness towards global standards of such literatures like *Sauti ya Dhiki*. Also we must maintain the use of translation as a way of disseminating

Swahili literature and other small literatures to the world beyond East Africa for scrutiny and evaluation. It looks inevitable therefore to consider English as the target language for translation of Swahili literary texts such as *Sauti ya Dhiki*. Such a translation should be undertaken with a target to pave the way for global reception and recognition and in consideration for *Paideia* – a deep education and the liberation of the mind.

## Works Cited

Abani, Chris. 2007. *Kalakuta Republic*. London/San Francisco/Beirut: Saqi.

Abdalla, Abdilatif. 1973. *Sauti ya Dhiki*. Dar-es-Salaam/Lusaka/Addis Ababa: Oxford University Press.

Casanova, Pascale. 1991. *The World Republic of Letters*. Cambridge/Massachusetts/London: Harvard University Press.

Damrosch, David. 2003. *What is World Literature*? Princeton/Oxford: Princeton University Press.

Gérard, Albert S. 1976. Structure and Values in Three Swahili Epics. *Research in African Literatures* 7, 1: 7-22.

Khamis, Said A.M. 2015. 'Nguvu' versus 'Power': Resilience of Swahili Language as Shown in Literature and Translation in Lutz Diegner and Frank Schulze -Engler (eds), *Habari ya English? - What about Kiswahili? East Africa as a Literary and Linguistic Contact Zone.* (Matatu vol. 46) Leiden/Bosten: Brill/Rodopi, 49-65.

Mazrui, Alamin. 2007. *Swahili: Beyond the Boundaries – Literature, Language and Identity.* (African Series, No. 85). Ohio/Athens: Ohio University Research in International Studies.

Ngaboh-Smart, Francis. 1997-98. Science and Representation of African Identity in Major Gentl and the Achimota Wars. *Connotations: A Journal for Critical Debate* 7, 1: 58-79.

West, Cornel & Ritz, David. 2009. *Living and Loving.* Carlsbad: Smiley Books.

# Mohamed Bakari

## The Poetics of Abdilatif Abdalla's Agony

Abdilatif Abdalla was charged with sedition in 1968 after publishing and distributing an article in Swahili entitled *Kenya: Twendapi?* (Where is Kenya Headed?). The trial and the subsequent three-year sentence made Abdilatif the first political prisoner in post-independence Kenya. Bwana Mataka, the nineteenth century local ruler of the town of Siyu in the Lamu archipelago, is arguably the first Kenyan political prisoner. He was the husband of the famed female Swahili poet Mwanakupona Binti Mshamu who composed the famous *Utendi wa Mwana Kupona* in 1856(Allen 1971). He had been cunningly lured to Zanzibar after defying the then ruling Sultan and promised reconciliation, only to be held prisoner and repatriated to Mombasa to be jailed at the Fort Jesus prison, where he was to die in detention. His courage and defiance has been eulogised in a famous poem in the Ki-Siyu dialect. In Abdilatif's case, this was a mere five years since the country had gained political independence from Britain in 1963.

Jomo Kenyatta, the charismatic politician and a 'prison graduate' who had himself served seven years in political detention, was then the president of the newly founded Republic. He had been imprisoned by the British colonial authorities for allegedly belonging to a proscribed political movement, the Mau Mau Movement. This was an insurgency movement centred around the Kikuyu ethnic group that had taken up arms when all recourse to an amicable solution was exhausted. The Central Highlands, which were inhabited largely by the Kikuyu, were alienated and parcelled out to various European settlers virtually as a reward for fighting in the World Wars I and II. Kenyatta, having returned to Kenya from a seventeen-year sojourn in England and Europe, imbued with the Pan-Africanist spirit of liberating all colonial territories under European colonialism, from the Maghrib to the Cape of Good Hope, immersed himself in the anti-colonial struggle in Kenya, as part of the grand game plan mooted by the emergent African intellectual elite in collaboration with other Black activists.

The grand strategy, the collective ideas of African-American and African intellectuals of the early part of the twentieth century, seems to have worked with precision since the key figures, an aggregation of romantics, idealists and hard headed pragmatists, ended up in the driving seats of the newly independent African countries. Julius Nyerere of Tanzania, Kwame Nkrumah of Ghana, and Kenya's Jomo Kenyatta were representative of these various strands in African political struggle. In Kenya, Kenyatta was annointed the 'Father of the Nation'. Through public adoration he was gradually transformed into a mythical figure, beyond reproach. He succeeded, through his proxies, to entrench himself as the sole Big Man of Kenya, drive the opposition into oblivion and create a *de facto* one-party state. Through the available repressive colonial laws like the notorious Preventive Detention Act, Kenyatta was able to silence his opponents and intimidate any potential nemeses. The cult of personality that grew around Kenyatta meant that one could not offer honest criticism of the regime. Cheerleading was the order of the day for those with political ambitions. The most apt description of the man that Kenyatta became was given by the most famous critic of the regime, Ngũgĩ wa Thiong'o (1981), in his prison diary, *Detained*, when he described him as a 'failed Moses'. Kenyans, intoxicated by the euphoria of independence, were oblivious of the kind of regime Kenyatta's government was willing itself into: dictatorial, tribal and above all, kleptocratic. A clear disconnect was emerging between the Kenyan impoverished masses and the government on one hand and the intellectual elite and the government on the other.

Within a short span of time, Kenya was becoming a class-ridden society in the classical Marxist sense. The intellectual elite, especially in the University College, Nairobi, was veering increasingly to the extreme left, within the context of the Cold War. At this time, barely out of his teens, Abdilatif Abdalla had a more heightened political consciousness than was common among his age-mates. That this was the case was not surprising because he came from a politically engaged family. His elder brother was already a controversial politician who was advocating secessionism for the Coast because of the fear of political dominance by the two largest tribes of the country, the Gikuyu and the Luo. This elder brother, Sheikh Abdilahi Nassir, was to become one of the most important of coastal politicians. He was charismatic, uncommonly articulate, and a largely self-educated public intellectual in the way of Swahili Muslim sages. A protégé of Maalim Ghazali, who was himself a student of Sheikh Al-Amin Mazrui, Sheikh Abdilahi, as he is affectionaly referred to by his admirers, was a man steeped in the Islamic intellectual tradition and aware of what was happening around him. Looking around, he was persuaded that he could be a better representative of coastal aspirations than many of those who thought that they could defend those interests. He threw himself into the fray and this inevitably alienated some of those who followed his public lectures earnestly because they felt that a person perceived as a Muslim scholar had no business throwing his lot into the murky business of politics. He did not last long in politics. It was clearly his decision that Kenyan politics as they were then shaping, could not fit his temperament as a Muslim scholar. But this short experience in politics must have had an impact on his younger brother. After school Abdilatif joined the Mombasa Municipal Council as a clerk but, coming from a political family, could not conceptually separate his role as a municipal worker and a socially committed private citizen. At that time there was also the perception that municipal workers were not quite like civil servants working with the central government. Municipal workers had to deal with elected councillors to such an extent that they were perhaps the most politicised workers in the country. Besides, some of these councillors were so poorly prepared to do their jobs because of a low literacy level, lack of an understanding of what their work entailed apart from collecting a monthly stipend, that they had very low esteem among their council workers and those they alleged to represent. In this context it is easy to see how municipal workers had no option but to fill this vacuum by taking an interest in political issues that affected them.

In a recent interview with the mass circulation Kenyan daily, *The Daily Nation*, Abdalla provided the context for his prosecution. The paper noted that 'The Municipal and mini-general elections of 1968 came as a shocker for him when all the KPU candidates were disqualified from running on 'technicalities''. Abdilatif was adamant:

> *I was so enraged by the kind of injustice that our party suffered. That all the 1,800 KPU candidates had not filled in their papers properly while all the KANU candidates had filled in the same papers properly would not make sense even to an insane person. (Sunday Nation, July 8, 2012, 'Lifestyle', p.4)*

This was the beginning of his travails. Abdilatif had another career as a poet. He had shown precociousness already when he composed a 670 stanza creation epic based on an Islamic view of the story of Adam and Eve and their banishment from Paradise, *Utenzi wa Maisha ya Adamu na Hawaa* (Abdalla 1971). It is important to note that it is here that Abdilatif acknowledges the main influence in his budding interest in poetry. He pays due homage to his elder brother Ahmad Nassir Juma Bhalo as his master from whom he learned the craft of poetry:

630
*Fundi wangu mashuhuri*
*Wa kutunga mashairi*
*Ni Ahmadi Nasiri*
*Juma Bhalo nawambiya*

631
*Naye ndiye ndugu yangu*
*Aliye mkubwa wangu*
*Mamake yeye na wangu*
*Ni huyo huyo mmoya*
*(Abdalla 1971)*

Actually he had apprenticed himself to the finest Mvita poet, and arguably the finest poet of his generation, and he was to take over his brother's mantle as the finest poet of his generation composing in Swahili. In his preface to an earlier anthology of Ahmad Nassir's gnomic poetry, the late Professor Lyndon Harries observed of him:

> *When I read some of Ahmad's poems to Sheikh Faraji Bwana Mkuu*
> *of Lamu, an authority on Swahili poetry, he expressed surprise that so*
> *young a person should have written poems of such traditional character*
> *and with so rich a vocabulary. Words classified by Sacleux in his great*
> *Swahili-French dictionary as inusité appear here and there in these verses.*
> *Obviously the poet did not think them up, and it is certain that he was*
> *unable to consult Sacleux's dictionary. The very existence of such words in*
> *his work indicates that the poet is the recipient of an oral tradition. Many*
> *of the fixed gnomes are generally known and used by Mombasan families*
> *in daily speech. (Harries 1966: xviii)*

Several decades later Kai Kresse still found Ahmad Nassir had lost none of his poetic sparkle and his wit was as sharp as ever. Kresse describes him as 'a highly respected and knowledgeable healer and poet, well known in Mombasa and far beyond for his exceptional wit and virtuosity in the use of language.' (Kresse 2007: 2). His brother is perhaps the greatest single influence in the cultivation of Abdilatif's influence. But then, Ahmad Nassir himself is directly influenced by the 18th/19th century Mvita poet, Muyaka bin Haji. Just like in the elder brother's poetry, one feels instant echoes of that classical Swahili poet in the poetry of Abdilatif. Muyaka's influence is ubiquitous in the poetry of both Ahmad Nassir and Abdilatif Abdalla. Muyaka was a people's poet, and his poetry was poetry of the ordinary and the quotidian, expressing the concerns of the collective community whose moral compass was provided by Islamic ethical and moral values. Harries famously described Muyaka as a poet who removed poetry from the mosque to the market place, essentially meaning that his themes took an increasingly secular trajectory. Yet it is the language use that set Muyaka apart from both his contemporaries and the earlier poets because of the demotic character of his language. So was it to be with Ahmad Nassir and as was later to be emulated by Abdilatif. The Islamic backdrop is also constantly present in the poetry of both poets, but it is the proletarian concerns that sets off Abdilatif from his brother, whose main interest is the preservation of Swahili culture and its worldview. Abdilatif, having grown up in a different social and cultural environment, embraces the new Kenyan reality of cultural, ethnic, sectarian and ideological diversity; Ahmad Nassir remained a quintessentially Swahili poet, completely immersed in local traditions and concerns, and this difference is nowhere more evident than in their use of language. Ahmad Nassir is steeped in the local while Abdilatif embraces the new cosmopolitanism. The local in the poetry of Ahmad Nassir is epitomised in his handling of the language of everyday life. Again, Harries notes this linguistic inventiveness that elevates the language of everyday life to one of a vehicle of poetic imagination:

> *The linguistic environment from which the language of Ahmad's poems*
> *derives is Mji wa Kale, Mombasa. The dialect is Kimvita. Those acccustomed*
> *to Standard Swahili or to the southern dialects will find the language of*
> *these poems very difficult indeed, but it cannot be overemphasized that*
> *this is not some literary form of the language. The basis of these poems is*

> the everyday speech of the Swahili people of Mombasa. It is undoubtedly
> of richer lexical content than everyday speech because, as in most literary
> work, it preserves in smaller compass a fuller range of words than might
> normally be used in dealing with the same or similar subjects in everyday
> speech (Harries 1966: xix).

Ahmad Nassir was, and evidently continues to be, preoccupied with moral and ethical issues. On the other hand, although Abdilatif is also interested in the moral dimensions, he is more concerned and engaged with the pressing issues of his time. It is not far-fetched to describe Abdilatif Abdalla as a Swahili existentialist poet, without despairing or experiencing personal alienation or anomie. His existentialist poetry is wrapped up in the conventions of classical Swahili prosody. He could not tear himself off from those prosodic conventions because if he did he was going to lose part of his Swahiliness. Ahmad Nassir's poetry is playful, reflective, humorous, that of Abdilatif, rather earnest. Abdilatif's poetic sensibility brings home man's inhumanity to man when he graphically portrays the post-colonial dungeons where political prisoners are thrown and forgotten, where political dissent is criminalized and local dictators have a field day emptying national coffers with impunity, where the cult of personality stifles and ultimately replaces functioning national institutions, where slogans are elevated to national philosophies. Abdilatif brings home the reality of the inhumane conditions under which prisoners are held. I do not know of any poetic description that captures so vividly the plight of prison inmates as Abdilatif's poetry does. Here are some of those lines, from the opening poem of *Sauti ya Dhiki*, that shame us out of our complaisance, unwittingly abetting and aiding the torture and abasement of prisoners of conscience:

9

*Kweli menifunga ndani, ya chumba nde sitoki*
*Kutwa kucha ni chumbani, jua kuota ni dhiki*
*Na mlinzi mlangoni, yu papo kattu ha'ndoki*
*Nilindwavyo bilhaki, ni kama simba marara*

10

*Kweli yanilaza tini, ilo na baridi kali*
*Ningawa burangetini, natetema kweli kweli*
*Na maumivu mwilini, daima ni yangu hali*
*Shauri ya idhilali, ya kulazwa simitini*

11

*Kweli japo ni ngomeni, kwenye kuta ndefu nene*
*Kabisa sitangamani, na mahabusu wengine*
*Na lengo kubwa nadhani, ni: nilonalo 'sinene*
*Hazuwa mambo mengine, kwa kuambukiza watu*

(from *"N'shishiyelo ni Lilo"*, Abdalla 1973: 2)

But Abdilatif, given his social and political context, had no choice but to become an engagé poet. African politics of the early years of independence was largely left-leaning and Abdilatif, although now much mellowed, could have been vaguely described as a Muslim socialist, a species that was a melding of Islamic sense of justice, Maoist peasant politics, populism, utopian idealism and third worldism. No wonder that Abdilatif Abdalla has a closer affinity to Oginga Odinga (or as his coastal supporters used to call him, "Odinga Odinga") brand of populist politics than Kenyatta's pragmatic capitalism. This political and literary context was to fatefully determine his future career as a political activist and a literary avantgarde. These two trajectories were to lead to literary and political agony. Abdilatif's embrace of the larger humanity is reflected in his early poetry and his activism was to lead to political imprisonment and exile from a culture that totally claimed his Weltanschaung. It is the view of this writer that the experience of exile removed him from the wellsprings of his creative imagination and Abdilatif never quite recovered his fertile poetic imagination. Dante's temporary exile did affect his creativity. It may also be noted in passing that the theme that Abdilatif tackled in *Utenzi wa Maisha ya Adamu na Hawaa* was almost identical with what the great English poet John Milton tackled in 'Paradise Lost, Paradise Regained'. Milton railed against corruption as Abdilatif was to do in his own time. Both were incarcerated for their political views. It is certain that at seventeen, Abdilatif had never read or heard of Milton, but his epic rises to the same sublimity as Milton's. Yet because Abdilatif's poetry has never been translated into other world languages, his work is familiar only to a circumscribed circle of readers in East Africa. Milton's poetry is full of intertextuality, drawing heavily from classical learning, from Egyptian and Greek and Roman mythologies, Christian sources that construct Satan, the Devil, Mephistopheles and his army of celestial rebels. Abdilatif creatively re-imagines the sparse Qur'anic outline of the story and builds a suspenseful drama out of the creation story.

Although he composed less and less poetry, his linguistic sensibilities found another outlet in Swahili prose. He can be described as a master prose stylist in Swahili. His essays on literary issues that he engaged in in the late 1970s shine with clarity and aptness of phrase so rare in other writers of this time. Because Swahili had become an instrument of Nyerere's African Socialism, Ujamaa, it was becoming more clichéd, rhetorical and almost Orwellian in its doublespeak; my favourite was this statement on Radio Tanzania: '*Mapinduzi si lelemama, ni kujitolea mhanga katika mstari wa mbele wa mapambano!*' (A revolution is not like a ladies' dance, it requires total commitment at the forefront of the struggle). Abdilatif did a lot to bring down the language to reality.

Abdilatif Abdalla's poetry, just as that of Ahmad Nassir, is full of feminine influence. Idioms, expressions and lexicon associated with feminine sensibility are replete in his poetry. Both the brothers appear to have come under the spell of female relatives, those matriarchal pillars of Swahili society: articulate, forthright and deadpan. In a sense his poetry can be described as both streetwise and full of domesticity. This affinity for the feminine idiom is what makes Eve in his *Utenzi wa Maisha ya Adam na Hawaa* so realistic and full of suspense, because Hawaa is enabled to speak in her own voice by Abdilatif.

## The Exile as a Lexicographer: Abdilatif as an African Dr. Johnson:

The 1970s were a decade of great expectations in much of East Africa. Nyerere's socialist experiment attracted a lot of idealists to Dar es Salaam, Tanzania's capital city. Among those socialist leaning activists was Abdilatif Abdalla. One of the only true successes of Ujamaa was the genuine attempt to forge Swahili as a language of national cohesion. And this could only be achieved by the modernization of the language. The subsequent modernization of Swahili is the living legacy of Nyerere, himself a master of the Swahili language. Abdilatif found a natural home at the Taasisi ya Uchunguzi wa Kiswahili, Tanzania's Institute of Kiswahili Research.

The Institute remains one of the finest centres of lexicography in Africa. Scores of young Tanzanian scholars were sent out to acquire degrees in the scientific study of language, in major departments of Linguistics in American universities, principally at the University of California, Los Angeles, and the University of Wisconsin, Madison; the University of Indiana at Bloomington, and the University of Texas, Austin. These were four of the most important centres for the study of African languages and literatures. Those who came back formed the nucleus of scholars who made important contributions to the modernization of Kiswahili. Lexicography was at the heart of this project. Abdilatif thrived in this Institute dedicated to the catapulting of an African language to the modern era. The collegiate atmosphere appeared to have won him over, and ensured that he worked in an area that suited his talents. This was far from the Kafka-esque bureaucracy that he worked in before suffering incarceration in Mombasa. The poet was now wedded to lexicography and turned himself into a harmless drudge, a situation that evokes that of the eighteenth century English lexicographer, Dr. Samuel Johnson. Abdilatif became instrumental in moderating the excessive enthusiasm of the Tanzanian lexicographers' partiality for only the putative standard forms in the new Swahili lexicon. He has a matchless familiarity of a large spectrum of Swahili dialects and thus helped to make the Kenyan voice heard at this historic project. Paradoxically, although he is associated with the Kimvita dialect of Mombasa, he spent only five years of his entire life in Mombasa. The rest was spent in other dialect areas along the Kenyan Coast, and later, in Tanzania. He picked the Mombasa version from his adoptive mother and other near relatives among whom he lived. This is certainly the main source for a rather compelling feminine voice in some of his poetry, including more intensive use of this particular voice in *Utenzi wa Maisha ya Adamu na Hawaa*. He ensured that all necessary words from these dialects were included in the final version. His presence in the committee was important because the majority voices were partial to the standard forms only, associated with Zanzibar, but which in reality was increasingly drawn from the Dar es Salaam based forms. Dar es Salaam had replaced Zanzibar as the political and cultural capital of the Swahili language. It was because of this that the important Zanzibar rural dialects were overlooked while compiling the dictionary. The result has been that many of the words found in the fiction of important writers like Said Ahmed Mohamed, who uses many words from Pemba, for example, are not included in the final product. The new dictionary had more partiality towards the new coinages from politics, law, bureaucracy and such related social areas. Dialectal forms were considered as forms of archaisms and were sometimes included and other times relegated to the realm of the oral to await their destiny. Like the legendary Dr. Samuel Johnson, Abdilatif could be relied upon to locate the sources from which words of archaic and near obsolete usage could be found to illustrate their earlier use within the spectrum of Swahili literary history. These sources could be in any of the Swahili dialects, whether from written sources or transmitted oral tradition.

It is appropriate at this juncture to challenge the view that the northern Lamu dialect was the basis of literary Swahili. This was a myth that started with scholars like William Hichens who wrote on Swahili literature in the early part of the twentieth century, and taken up and institutionalised by Lyndon Harries and scholars who came later like W.H. Whiteley. The fact was that northern poets whose work had been preserved were often *ulama* whose language would be adorned with many words of Arabic origin for purposes of balancing the right metrical pattern or merely out of force of habit. Indeed, what was sometimes deemed a literary version of the language was no more than the usage of literary tropes as part of what Erich Auerbach (2003) had described in his *Mimesis* as the tendency of Western literature to be self-referential, meaning that creators of literary works will draw from the common earlier sources like Greek and Roman mythologies as we alluded to earlier, and the Bible and other classics that form the Western canon. Pre-twentieth century Swahili literature is full of references to the founding texts of the Islamic tradition. These are part of this literary and intellectual tradition and no writer can escape from dipping into its resources whether that writer or composer is viewed as religiously inclined or secular. Whether one is looking at the poetry of Muhammad Kijumwa, Muyaka or poets who came after them or earlier before them, from any of the dialect areas, the tendency is the same.

With his wide-ranging linguistic and editorial skills, Abdalla could easily be imagined to have also played a role in revising into shape Sheikh Abdallah Saleh Farsy's prose, in the commentaries and footnotes of his important Swahili translation of the Qur'an, when Maalim Yahya Omar teamed up with others in London to make it more coherent and fluent than it initially was. This text was the first complete translation of the Qur'an by a Swahili mother-tongue speaker (Farsy 1969). Although very learned in the Islamic disciplines, Farsy lacked the proper writing skills to hone his conversational style in his work to a fluent written prose. His original commentaries sometimes sounded like the stream of consciousness writing found in modern English fictional work. Farsy's translation now remains one of the most important reference works not only in Qur'anic translation studies in Swahili but also as a literary model for compact prose. It is a good source for technical terminology of religious provenance, but also for other areas such as law, commerce and ethics, since some of these terms have found their way into the specialist lexicon in secular aspects of life.

Translation is another of those areas in which Abdalla was active. Although he may not be identified as a full-time translator, he accomplished an important translation of a major author. In the seventies he translated one of the most important fictions of the late 60s and early 70s, Ayi Kwei Armah's *The Beautyful Ones Are Not Yet Born*' (Armah 1976). As is to be expected from a poet and writer of Abdilatif's stature, the translation was creative, elegant and flawless. He has also worked on translation of drama. This further confirms Abdilatif as a versatile intellectual who has put his linguistic skill to use wherever his linguistic talent was constructively needed.

Earlier on we noted that Abdilatif fashioned himself as a Swahili linguistic nationalist and constructed and guarded his identity around the notion of Swahiliness. But Swahili identity has been changing over the centuries and least of all it has not been an exclusionist label or notion. It was perhaps the most inclusive of local identities because it was not based on any notion of putative common origin or blood ties. Swahili citizenship, or amity, was predicated on the notion of urbanity, cultural sophistication and civility. To labour on this point is to go into the sterile debates of the early part of the twentieth century and their re-enactment within the ethnic politics of the decades after independence, when cultural authenticity was worn on the sleeves. Everyone had to fit in within the anthropological category of the tribe. As Ngũgĩ wa Thiong'o cogently and recently argued, there was nothing inherently wrong with the category of tribe, since this was a way of expressing one's being. It only becomes suspect when it begins to be put to exclusionist ends by politicians that the term acquires its notoriety. But as a term to denote an imagined community, as Benedict Anderson put it, is a great framework to articulate a group's sense of shared values. I think Abdilatif has this sense of belonging, rather than a desire to claim an exclusionist identity.

To obsess on this kind of singularity of identity, rather than accepting that our constructed subjectivity, in the poststructuralist sense of the constituted subject, is a complex of historical and social forces beyond our control, enables one to accept that we are a bundle of identities and that we should, and do, negotiate these identities within the contexts in which we find ourselves.

Abdilatif's self-perception as a Swahili poet first and foremost prevented him from appreciating and drawing inspiration from other cultures, both local and international. He would have been an even greater poet if he had borrowed a leaf from other creative geniuses who dipped into other cultures to draw what the genius of those cultures had bestowed to humanity and refashioned those resources to create a new cultural synthesis. I cannot even imagine what his poetry would have turned out had he immersed himself in the mainstreams of his adopted cultures in both Britain and Germany. He might even have experimented his poetic talent on these languages. Even if he had stopped creating in Swahili and acquired and fine-tuned these languages for his creative purposes he would have contributed to world literature. Ngũgĩ wa Thiong'o, my own Professor at the University of Nairobi who is with us in this symposium, may accuse me of trying to roll back our literary gains as Africans, but contrary to received wisdom, we have been part of the stream of universal civilization through our encounter with great civilization across the Indian Ocean.

I should perhaps end with an anecdote related to James Joyce. He was often taunted for being an Irishman who spoke another language less authentic to him. He retorted that while the English gave the Irish the English language, the Irish gave the English their literature. For what passes for English literature is substantially the outstanding contribution of Irish literary intellectuals, from W.B Yeats, James Joyce, Bernard Shaw to George Orwell.

## References

Abdalla, Abdilatif. 1971. *Utenzi wa Maisha ya Adamu na Hawaa*. Nairobi: Oxford University Press.

Abdalla, Abdilatif. 1973. *Sauti ya Dhiki*. Nairobi: Oxford University Press.

Armah, Ayi Kwei. 1976 (orig. 1968). *Wema Hawajazaliwa* (translated by Abdilatif Abdalla). Nairobi: East African Educational Books.

Auerbach, Erich. 2003. *Mimesis: The Representation of Reality in Western Literature*. Princeton: Princeton University Press.

Farsy, Abdallah Saleh. 1969. *Qur'ani Takatifu*. Nairobi: Islamic Foundation.

Harries, Lyndon. 1966. *Poems from Kenya: Gnomic Verses in Swahili by Ahmad Nassir bin Juma Bhalo*. Madison: University of Wisconsin Press.

Kresse, Kai. 2007. *Philosophising in Mombasa: Knowledge, Islam and Intellectual Practice on the Swahili Coast*. Edinburgh: Edinburgh University Press.

'Utendi wa Mwana Kupona', in J.W.T. Allen (ed.), 1971. *Tendi: Six Examples of a Swahili Classical Verse Form with Translations & Notes*. Nairobi: Heinemann.

Ngugi wa Thiong'o 1981. *Detained: A Writer's Prison Diary*. Nairobi: Heinemann.

Waliaula, Ken Walibora. 2013. *Narrating Prison Experience: Human Rights, Self, Society, and Political Incarceration in Africa*. Illinois: Common Ground Publishing.

*Sunday Nation*, July 8, 2012:

http://www.nation.co.ke/Features/lifestyle/Why+Kenyatta+sent+me+ja il/-/1214/1447590/-/item/2/-/7hbds1/-/index.html

# Ken Walibora Waliaula

## Doing Things with Words in Prison Poetry[25]

**[B]ut can words alone bring down a tyrant?**
**Kunle Ajibade,** *Jailed for Life*

In March 1969 Kenyan Swahili poet and political activist Abdilatif Abdalla appeared before a Mombasa court on sedition charges. The magistrate found him guilty and sentenced him to eighteen months in prison for the offence. But the attorney general Charles Njonjo successfully appealed against the sentence, claiming the magistrate had been too lenient. Abdalla's sentence was accordingly doubled to three years. The sedition case thrust Abdalla, then aged 22, from relative obscurity to the national limelight in post-independence Kenya. Writing subsequently in the preface to his anthology of prison poems, *Sauti ya Dhiki/* "Voice of Agony" (1973), Abdalla would state with unequivocal candour, that he was imprisoned because of being found guilty of writing and distributing in a number of towns on the Kenyan coast, a pamphlet entitled *Kenya: Twendapi?* "Kenya: Where are we Headed?" (1968). Abdalla's anti-government activities had not gone unnoticed, and he was, therefore, compelled to feel the full force of the Jomo Kenyatta regime for rubbing it the wrong way.

*Sauti ya Dhiki* encapsulates the many and varied moods and affective states that engulfed the poet as he figuratively journeyed in the psychic landscape that the prison ambience fostered. The poet evinced and expressed a wide range of emotions including bitterness, defiance, confidence, regret, and self-doubt as he "travelled" under the conditions of deprivation and dehumanization that this figurative prison journey occasioned. As Soyinka stated regarding his own prison poetry, "the poems are a map of the course trodden by the human mind during the years of incarceration" (quoted in Afejuku 2001: 21). Soyinka's conception of prison poetry as a map suggests that in such poetry readers are able to trace the inmate's mental, psychic or philosophical journeys. As a map would consist of any number of details and destinations, prison poetry contains a whole range of mental or psychic courses or journeys. The prisoner as poet is also impelled to speak in many tongues, to paraphrase Sidonie Smith & Julia Watson (2001: 134), whose conception of self as well as Bakhtin's idea of speech variability in "Discourse in the Novel" (2006) inform this analysis.

## The Multiple "I"-s and Speaking in Tongues

Following J.L. Austin's concept of "doing things with words," (Urmson & Sbisà 1975) I examine the various voices and guises that the poet adapts and adopts to do things that help remake his world unmade by the prison experience. I argue that the poet's "I" appears in many guises and is heard in multiple voices so as to problematize the notion of a stable, unitary self.

---

[25] This paper was first presented at Africa at Noon Lecture at African Studies Program, University of Wisconsin-Madison, September 22, 2010.

As Sidonie Smith & Julia Watson have remarked, the very notion of a stable unitary self has increasingly come under attack in recent autobiographical criticism. Smith and Watson see as misreading initial interpretations of the "I" which hinged on the assumption that the concept of individuality was sufficient as a determining force in life writing (2001: 129). They call for a more nuanced reading of the "I" in life narratives, a reading that goes above and beyond the facile fascination with an "I" exclusively bound to an autonomous and concrete individuality.

The idea of a fragmented self or subject has lately become commonplace, and so is the complicated and often conflicted interplay between subject and object. One could perhaps claim that as early as the early 19th century W.E.B. Dubois (1994: 2-3) was well aware of the instability of the "I" when he conceived of the "double-consciousness" of the African American experience. Smith & Watson posit the existence of at least four types of the "I": the historical, the narrating, the narrated, and the ideological. Thus in their purview, the traditional approach to studying the "I"- then - and the "I"- now - is also inadequate in making sense of the manifold manifestations of the pronoun (2001: 129).

As Smith & Watson further state, the historical or real "I" is a person located in a particular time and place, whose story the autobiographical act enacts or narrates but whose life is far more complex and transcendent than the story can possibly fully contain or fully embrace. One could think of the autobiographical mode as offering only a slice of that life while other slices exist elsewhere (e.g. in the archives of the police, hospital, schools, churches, family album, or in the malleable memory of others). Nevertheless, this "I" that lives in the real world, they posit, is unknown and unknowable. In other words the "I" representing the real historical Abdalla is much more complex than the one presenting the carceral imagination and experience of the late 1960s and early 1970s. The real Abdalla is scattered in the public and private archives of his native Kenya and the countries of his exile (e.g. the schools, airline manifests, payrolls, mosque registers, family albums, prison and court records, conference panels) and cannot be fully represented by the "I"-s or personas of his poetry. One could argue that even the media's characterization of Abdalla as a "revolutionary young man" in 1969 is but a symptom and a consequence of a shifting interpretive impulse, which does not adequately capture the quintessence of Abdalla's authentic historicity. Are we, then, left with no viable option but to cling to the "agnostic" belief that despite or because of his poetry Abdalla's real "I" is both unknown and unknowable?

It would seem that what readers encounter is the narrating "I," the one telling the story whose range of vision is limited and remains within the confines of the story and lacks the broader experiential history of the historical "I". Yet this narrating "I," though knowable and known, is equally complex. Smith & Watson assert that the narrating "I" is neither a unified nor stable subject; it is "split, fragmented, provisional, multiple" (2001: 60).

The narrating "I" in Abdalla's *Sauti ya Dhiki* speaks in many voices, "speaking in tongues" as it were, and in doing so does many things. The narrating "I" of the preface written in the Tanzanian commercial capital Dar es Salaam on February 22, 1973, where the poet was newly exiled upon release, differs markedly from the various narrating "I"-s or voices of the poems written in prison. Presenting the poet as a political exile in a neighbouring country, the "I" of the preface consists of a candid, if tacit, recovering of the memory and deciphering of the meaning of a just ended carceral experience. It is characterized by a detached prose at once commenting on and summing up the substance of the prison poetry that preceded its writing. It is "writing about writing" that is self-reflexive and explanatory. It is the narrating "I" that comes in the form of a historian of self, writing the history after the fact, and a critic of one's own earlier literary productions, produced under different circumstances. On the other hand it would seem the poet crafts each poem such that it has its one or more of its own grammatical narrating "I"-s, speaking in multifarious voices and exhibiting any number of colours and coming in different guises (e.g. defender of truth, political activist, prisoner, potential martyr, sage and agent of change, self-doubter and neophyte, unborn foetus, disinherited kin, patriot, Panafricanist, brother, friend, philosopher, consensus builder, etc).

It bears noting that Smith & Watson distinguish between the narrating "I" and the narrated "I" by viewing the former as the subject of history and the latter as the agent of discourse (2001: 60). In other words the narrating "I" is the speaking subject while the narrated "I" is the object, the protagonist of the narrative. The narrated "I" is a version of the self that the narrating "I" projects to the readers. Yet like the narrating "I" the narrated "I" is also multiple, fragmented, and heterogeneous. The similarity between the tags of the narrating and narrated "I"-s does not imply that they are one and the same thing. The similarity of the tags mainly lies in the fragmentation the "I"-s embody. Yet there are still differences because the narrating "I" comes across as, for example, the philosophical storyteller, while the narrated "I" is the philosopher character whose story is told.

Lastly, the ideological "I" is to be seen, Smith & Watson argue, as the definition of self that is contingent on prevailing ideological, cultural, and historical notions of personhood during one's own time (2001: 61). In other words, the cultural and historical situatedness of the autobiographical narrator is determined by the particular moment in history in which he or she lived or lives. The overarching ideological concept of self enjoys primacy here, the idea of one's relations to society or estimation of what is evil or good. All these factors are, therefore, present in the auto-biographer's time and space and influence his definition of personhood. In this post-structural perspective, it is possible to read Abdalla's ideological self, particularly his Marxist temperament, as a product of the cultural context that shaped and moulded him. Abdalla had been exposed to and enthused by Marxist literature and ideology that became a crucial catalyst in his political activism. In essence, Abdalla "seeks to be heard in different terms, to be accountable, to count" (2001: 131-132) as Smith & Watson would put it.

## Why Write

The account Abdalla seeks to give of himself, one could argue, is a self-study that attempts to extrapolate upon the carceral experience and imagination with the tools of poetic prosody, and Kimvita, a dialect of Kiswahili that the British hegemony in East Africa minoritized and marginalized. One could argue that Abdalla's use of Kimvita is not only an indicator of cultural nationalistic tendencies, but represents, in its intent and intensity, a resolute counter-hegemonic endeavour. Yet, the post-colonial context of Abdalla's writing and incarceration means that the thrust of his counter-hegemony is, in the main, levelled against not a colonial autocrat but a post-colonial autocract, in Achille Mbembe's terms (2001: 111). The context is, therefore, both different and the same: the transition from the West or colonial autocrat to the post-colonial autocrat did not change the reality of autocratic rule. In both situations the incarcerated individual feels inhibited, dehumanized, demonized, and deprived, and is probably driven by the emancipatory impulse to narrate herself or himself into being, to tell her or his own story, to count. By writing *Sauti ya Dhiki*, Abdalla may be said to be trying to claim subjectivity, to create himself from the passivity of an "object" as the prison system intends for him, to a speaking rational "subject." In other words, subject formation or creation is an integral part of the things Abdalla does with poetical words.

I am prompted by the "dialogic reverberations" in Abdalla's poems in *Sauti ya Dhiki* to extend the frame of reference for the idea of heteroglossia and dialogism beyond the novel genre, contrary to Bakhtin's earlier configuration of the concept (Bakhtin 2006: 499). I am also attentive to the way in which Abdalla participates in a social dialogue in his poetry, both taking and giving at the same time so that in Bakthin's terms, his word "in language is half someone else's" (2006: 505). I argue that there are in *Sauti ya Dhiki* fragmented, multiple, and heterogenous "I"-s that imbue it with a sense of unmistakable multivocality. In other words, in his collection of poems, Abdalla speaks in tongues, in different languages and accents to articulate the feelings and imaginings of multiple "I"-s. Pinpointing the multiplicity of languages at play in the social heteroglossia, Bakhtin wrote:

Thus an illiterate peasant, miles away from any urban center, naively immersed in an unmoving and for him unshakable everyday world, nevertheless lived in several language systems: he prayed to God in one language (Church Slavic), sang songs in another, spoke to his family in a third and, when he began to dictate petitions to the local authorities through the scribe, he tried speaking yet a fourth language (official –literate language, "paper" language). All these are *different languages*, even from the point of view of abstract socio-dialectological markers (2006: 506).

In a sense, I claim for Abdalla's poetry, the "illiterate peasant's" capacity and tendency to speak "different languages" by different "I"-s that the poet parades to us in an attempt to narrate himself, to orchestrate different themes, to serve his various "semantic and expressive intentions" (Bakhtin 2006: 498). The difference in utterances and voices accounts for the varying subjective positions and subjectivities that are embodied in the "I" of Abdalla's poetry.

In sum, I use Bakhtin's notion of the dialogic and heteroglossia to demonstrate the various voices that emerge in Abdalla's prison poetry as evident from his style and thematic concerns, and how prison as a writing site impinges on the writing. I bring to the fore the multivocality of his poetry and to demonstrate how it speaks to Bakhtin's concept of dialogism. In this regard, I want to propose that the title "*Sauti ya Dhiki*" loosely translated into English as 'Voice of Agony,' is not one singular voice, but is perhaps better interpreted as multifarious voices of agony or anguish expressed by the one prison poet (Ohly 1974: 82). The multiplicity of voices is evident not only from the diversity of themes that preoccupy Abdalla, but the various stylistic and linguistic strategies he employs in his anthology. Moreover, Abdalla purports to speak for others - the underprivileged and deprived - in expressing disillusion with the illusion of prosperity in post-independence Africa in general and Kenya in particular. His *sauti* or voice is hence a synthesis of many voices, not a cacophony, but a polyphony through which we vicariously hear the unspoken agonies of the silent fellow sufferers or unspeaking others.

## Swahili Prosody and Poetry as Autobiography

*Sauti ya Dhiki* is a collection of 40-stanzaed poems that Abdalla wrote in the period of his incarceration between March 1969 and March 1972, with only one poem, *N'sharudi* (I am back), being written after the completion of his prison term. All the poems adhere strictly to the rules of Swahili prosody. Since all the poems are dated chronologically, I concur with Ohly who describes this anthology as a kind of "poetical diary" that registers Abdalla's varying moods, his feelings and thoughts, while he languished behind prison walls, so much so that we can follow them "month by month" (1974: 87). I hasten to add that the presentation of these various moods, feelings and thoughts could indeed be seen as instances of self-creation and self-narration whose outcome is the re-enactment of the poet's various selves. The poems trace in almost chronological fashion the wide range of thematic concerns that preoccupied the poet, therefore accentuating the polyphony of his prison poetry. The polyphony enables the poet to do multiple things with words including "carving a public monument out of his private lives" as William Howarth would put it (1980: 92). Yet, what is revealed foremost in the content and context of *Sauti ya Dhiki* is the spirit of defiance and resilience as an examination of the wide range of themes in the volume. In other words, Abdalla's poetry comes across as a form of resistance to what he perceives as tyranny and bad governance in post-independence Kenya.

## Masking the Message

Yet, there are also instances in which Abdalla uses his poetic ability to do things with words that intentionally mask his message. Abdalla's poem "*Mamba*" (Crocodile) is a classic example of the use of metaphor as a stratagem for deconstructing a regime he found wanting, immoral, and rotten. Clearly, the recourse to metaphor as a weapon of critique is hardly new across Africa. For instance, under the totalitarian rule of President Kamuzu Banda in Malawi, the country's poets Felix Mnthali, Frank Chipasula, Jack Mapanje, and Lupenga Mphande and others used metaphor as a weapon to undertake the hazardous task of criticizing the regime. As one report shows, overt mention of the president and his cronies would have proved suicidal because it was common knowledge that Banda detained, assassinated, or fed to the crocodiles of Shire River any and all real and imagined critics of his rule.

In harmony with the practice of using metaphor as a subtle tool for deconstructing and disrupting the status quo, Abdalla wrote:

*Nami nambe, niwe kama waambao*
*Niupambe, upendeze wasomao*
*Niufumbe, wafumbuwe wawezao*

*Kuna mamba, mtoni metakabari*
*Ajigamba, na kujiona hodari*
*Yuwaamba, kwamba 'taishi dahari*

*Memughuri, ghururi za kipumbavu*
*Afikiri, hataishiwa na nguvu*
*Takaburi, hakika ni maangavu*

*Akumbuke, siku yake itafika*
*Roho yake, ajuwe itamtoka*
*Nguvu zake, kikomoche zitafika*

*Afahamu, mtu hajui la kesho*
*Hatadumu, angatumia vitisho*
*Maadamu, lenye mwanzo lina mwisho.*

Let me also speak, so I can be like those who speak
Let me adorn the poem, and make it appealing to the readers
Let me compose a riddle, that those who can may untangle [it]

In the river there is a crocodile, highly conceited
He brags, and regards himself as invincible
He claims he will live forever

> He is a braggart, thumping his chest foolishly
> He imagines his might will not dissipate
> For indeed pride is before a fall
>
> He should remember, when his day comes
> He should know, his spirit will leave him
> His might will reach its end
>
> Let him know, no one knows about tomorrow
> He will not last forever, even if he uses threats
> As what has a beginning must also have an end. (1973: 10)

In this poem written in the *tathlitha* genre, (three lines in each stanza), Abdalla presents the riddle of a rapacious and supercilious reptile deluding itself with the possession of an illusory and elusive immortality. He openly challenges the readers to unravel the riddle. The oral performance involving an artist presenting riddles to audiences and challenging them to unravel them is not uncommon in the African oral tradition. It is instructive that in declaring his intention in the beginning of this poem, Abdalla uses the contraction of *niambe* namely *nambe* literally meaning 'I speak' rather than to *niandike* / 'I write,' reflecting consciously or unconsciously the orality within which riddles are usually encoded and decoded. The relative brevity of the poem harmonizes with the nature of the genre of *mafumbo* in the Swahili oral tradition; just long enough to provide clues for the audience to respond to the conundrum. The power and beauty of metaphor is a distinguishing feature of riddles.

On the surface the riddle in Abdalla's poem gives the impression of the simply ludic, even childish pastime. Yet unraveling the tenor represented by the vehicle *mamba* or crocodile in this poem would hardly have been "pleasing" to the ruling regime in Kenya. Therefore, the poet's use of metaphor is a stratagem in which he assails Kenyatta's arrogant leadership and false sense of security and fake immortality. Kenyatta is the *mamba* or crocodile of Abdalla's cryptic poem. The point of the poem is that no matter how powerful Kenyatta may be and no matter how long he holds the reins of power, there is bound to be an end to his rule and his life. Abdalla reminds Kenyatta that as a mortal man his time to expire must surely come, sooner or later.

The overall brevity of the poem, apart from situating it within the tradition of performance of riddles, also accentuates the brevity of human life and the inevitability of death. In other words, Abdalla attempts to imagine the demise of Kenyatta, and the end of tyranny in Kenya. Thus the crocodile of Abdalla's poem is synonymous with what Achille Mbembe calls the "post-colonial potentate" or "post-colonial autocrat" who is blinded by a rather warped attitude toward mortality and his own subjectivity. As Mbembe argues, the autocrat's ostensibly absolute subjectivity is hallucinatory, fake and empty. Its facticity lies in caricature only: "The absolute does not exist in reality" (2001: 165). Given the autocrat's imagined and imaginary immortality and invincibility, it takes considerable courage for an imprisoned poet to even think about the autocrat's death; it is tantamount to imagining the unimaginable or thinking the unthinkable. As a matter of fact to have the audacity of imagining or foretelling the President's death was considered as treasonable at the time of its writing as literal killing. In a sense, therefore, Abdalla uses poetical words to "assassinate" the tyrant and perhaps gets away with such an audacious action. It goes without saying that artistic taunting and imaginary killing of Kenyatta, the post-colonial potentate, is made possible by what words at the disposal of a consummate wordsmith can do in spite of ,or because of, the actuality of incarceration.

This bold poem at once aptly represents Abdalla's angst and anger and anticipates Kenyatta's death, an eventuality that came to pass on 22 August 1978, eight years after the poem was written. It signifies the "killing" of Kenyatta before his actual death. The poet therefore demonstrates that he did not have the fear and inhibition that plagued even the bravest of critics then.

## A Range of Miscellaneous Voices

Nonetheless, the fact that the voices of dissidence suffuse Abdalla's collection of poems does not preclude the presence of other voices with which the poet speaks or imagines and represents his various real and imagined selves. Doubt and didacticism, for example, seem to be strange bedfellows, but in Abdalla's poetry they go hand in hand. This synthesis of points of view that seem antithetical to each other recalls Bakhtin's proposition that an individual does not have one single point of view, but he or she inhabits multiple 'worldviews' through the various social discourses he or she speaks (2006: 450). As mentioned earlier, Abdalla's marriage of art and activism lends itself to arousing the readers to action. It is therefore in harmony with this rabble-rousing stance that we encounter poems calling upon the masses to awake from their slumber and to act against tyranny.

Abdilatif Abdalla captures his affective responses to the ontological and existential reality of the deplorable prison conditions while remaining keenly aware of the fact that writing itself is an act of defiance; a bold reaction to the post-colonial autocrat. And in reading his prison poetry we embark on an exploration or mapping of his psychic journey as we "listen" to his articulation of a wide spectrum of voices. The multiple voices he uses do things with poetic words, that not only help remake the prisoner's unmade world, but also undo the world of the imprisoning state apparatuses. Emerging from prison as a site for writing, *Sauti ya Dhiki* is, therefore, a supreme example of how prison literature can and does do counter-hegemonic things with words.

# References

Abdalla, Abdilatif. 1968. *Kenya: Twendapi?* (Kenya: Where Are We Heading?). Unpublished manuscript.

Abdalla, Abdilatif. 1973. *Sauti ya Dhiki*. Nairobi: Oxford University Press.

Afejuku, Tony E. 2001. "African Prison Poetry." *Encyclopedia of Life Writing.* Ed. Margaretta Jolly. London: Fitzroy Dearborn. Pp. 21-22.

Du Bois, W. E. B. 1994. *The Souls of Black Folk*. New York, Avenel, NJ: Gramercy Books.

Bakthin M.M. 2006. "Discourse in the Novel." *The Novel: An Anthology of Criticism and Theory 1900-2000*. Ed. Dorothy J. Hale. Malden, MA, Blackwell. Pp. 481-510.

Howarth, William L. 1980. "Some Principles of Autobiography" in *Autobiography: Essays Theoretical and Critical*. Ed. James Olney New Jersey: Princeton University Press.

Mbembe, Achille, 2001. *On the Postcolony*. Berkeley, University of California Press.

Smith, Sidonie & Julia Watson. 2001. *Reading Autobiography: A Guide for Interpreting Life Narratives*. Minneapolis: University of Minnesota Press.

# Ahmed Rajab

## The Urgency of Memory in an Age of Greed

A word of warning: those expecting an exposition of some aspect of the work of Michel Foucault would be disappointed although one can without difficulty find a linkage between some of Abdilatif Abdalla's poetry and Foucault's 'archeology of knowledge' or, arguably, his concept of *épistèmes*. But I will not embark on such an exercise because we are here to celebrate, and celebrations are meant to be light affairs. So let me first of all say how honoured I am to have been invited here to celebrate the life and times of Abdilatif Abdalla who I first met in 1974 at Dar es Salaam University.

I had gone to Dar es Salaam from London to interview him for a BBC Swahili Service cultural programme which I was presenting and which was called simply *Utamaduni* (Culture). As fate would have it, Abdilatif would later present the very same programme after joining the BBC. Needless to say, his presentation was more nuanced, more informed and hence more sophisticated. Much like Foucault, he analyzed cultural forms as a series of events and his analysis paid special attention to the 'negative structures' of society.

I can never forget the moment when I first met this tall, rangy and thundering poet who insists he is not a poet. I bet that no one can ever forget their first encounter with the man called Abdilatif or Atif to his closest friends. His warmth, humility, crashing laughter, effusive manner and *joie de vivre* are infectious. Nor can one leave him without being impressed by his moral posture and resolve to fight for justice.

We bonded the moment we met. We became more than friends, more than blood brothers. We became comrades, fighting together on many levels, sometimes in the same trenches, other times in different trenches.

I have found him on my side fighting corruption and oppression of all kinds. He found me on his side striving for the purity of our beloved Swahili language and culture. The fact that he hails from the Kenyan coast, and I from Zanzibar, has added to our feeling of familial belonging.

Later, for many years, we sat on opposite sides of the microphone as we broadcast from the studios of the BBC in Bush House, London.

I can't remember which of his books first endeared him to me, whether it was *Sauti ya Dhiki*'(The Voice of Agony) or '*Utenzi wa Maisha ya Adamu na Hawaa*' (The Epic Poem of the Life of Adam and Eve). It certainly was not the political tract, which questioned the rule of Kenya's first President Jomo Kenyatta, *Kenya: Twendapi?* (Kenya: Where Are We Heading To?), because by the time I first met him I had not laid my hands on it.

*Kenya: Twendapi?* was the seventh in a monthly series of anti-government publications written by Abdilatif in close collaboration with some of his comrades, mostly members or supporters of Jaramogi Odinga Oginga's opposition Kenya People's Union (KPU.) Each series had a print run of about 5,000 copies. They were all cyclostyled on a Gestetner duplicating machine and were distributed by Abdilatif and his comrades by deploying guerrilla-style tactics. For example, they surreptitiously pasted copies on walls at night. They also left bundles of copies at bus stops or at the Likoni Ferry Crossing or at the Nyali Bridge so that passersby could help themselves with the material.

Abdilatif had been warned before by some government officials to stop his 'subversive' activities but he remained defiant. One can imagine the young revolutionary leader darting from street to street in Kuze, in the heart of Mombasa's Old Town, where he grew up, conspiring with his comrades in agitation against the Kenyatta government which they viewed as corrupt and anti-people. They had endless clandestine discussions on what should be done and what should appear in the monthly pamphlets.

When *Kenya: Twendapi?* started to have an impact with the people the authorities decided on a clampdown. Someone who was privy to Abdilatif's subterranean political activities snitched on him. He was arrested during the holy month of Ramadhan at the offices of the Mombasa Municipal Council where he was working as an accounts clerk. He was charged with sedition.

Abdilatif, then 22-year-old and already married, was described during his trial as 'a young man full of revolutionary ideas.' He was convicted on three charges of sedition and sentenced to 18 months' imprisonment by a Mombasa court. (*East African Standard*, 20 March,1969). Following his conviction he was incarcerated in Shimo la Tewa Prison, near Mombasa. However, the State lodged an appeal demanding a sterner sentence. This was given by Kenya's High Court when it doubled the 18-month prison term given to Abdilatif, whereupon he was transferred from Shimo la Tewa to Kamiti Maximum Security Prison. A few months before his release he was returned to Shimo la Tewa where he completed his prison term in March 1972.

Abdilatif was the first intellectual to be detained in post-independent Kenya for his dissenting views. Others were to follow during the reign of President Daniel arap Moi (1978-2002). They included Ngũgĩ wa Thiong'o, Alamin Mazrui, Katama Mkangi, Maina wa Kinyatti, Chelagat Mutai, Wahome Mutahi and Willy Mutunga.

In a way it was *Kenya: Twendapi?* which brought him to the wider world. I say this because were it not for that pamphlet, *Mzee* Jomo would probably not have imprisoned him and he would probably not have ended up in Tanzania and later beyond East Africa.

In one of his poems which he recited at a reading during our conference in Leipzig, there is a line which says: '*ni muhimu kukumbuka*' (It is important to remember). He also evokes the significance of remembering in his poem *Jana na Leo na Kesho* (Yesterday, Today and Tomorrow).

In Kenya, in this age of greed, it is important to remember how *Mzee* Kenyatta and his henchmen hijacked the country's liberation struggle for personal gain. It is important to remember what Kenya's Mau Mau war of liberation was all about, how it was hijacked and how the people were betrayed. It is important to remember all this so that the people are enlightened on why they remain poor. More importantly, future generations must also remember all this to prevent them from making similar bad choices.

A friend of some of us here, Pheroze Nowrojee, the eminent Kenyan lawyer, human rights crusader and a bitter critic of the Kenyatta, Moi and Kibaki regimes, blames Jomo Kenyatta for bad choices. He wrote the following in the Kenyan daily newspaper *Star* of November 4, 2009:

> He [Kenyatta] chose to let his Government move resources from the poor to the rich. His followers moved from legitimate sources to illegitimate sources. They took public land, trust land, Government money, donor money and parastatal money, always actively disregarding the fact that the land and money were the land and money of the poor.

As it partly documents this thievery and gives courage to those who are out to catch the thieves, *Sauti ya Dhiki*, the collection of poems which Abdilatif wrote while incarcerated in Kamiti Maximum Security Prison, is more than reminiscences of his prison ordeal. The volume distinguishes him not only as a poet, despite his denial that he is one, but also as a revolutionary. *Sauti ya Dhiki* succeeds in making the revolutionary and the poet one and the same.

In fact, much of Abdilatif's published poetry is a poetics of *mapambano* — in the service of struggle. And this struggle is in its own way a 'tribal' struggle in as much as we claim it to be a class struggle because it is *mapambano* between what Ngũgĩ wa Thiong'o, a close collaborator of Abdilatif's, has called Africa's only tribes: the largest tribe of the 'have nots' against the miniscule tribe of those who have.

The tribe of those who have is the one which has betrayed not only Kenya's hard-won independence but also that of much of Africa. This is the tribe of the *wabenzi* (those who move about in the air conditioned comfort of Mercedes Benz cars) and of the *mafuta mingi* (the fat cats). Members of this tribe are either outright thieves or have acquired their wealth through means which can only be described as chicanery.

I recently went to a bookshop in Nairobi looking for a newly-published memoir by Joe Khamisi, a former broadcaster and former MP from Bahari in the coast. The title of the book, which is all the rage in Kenya, is: *The Politics of Betrayal — Diary of a Kenyan Legislator* (2011). When I asked the Asian bookseller whether they stocked it, he was delighted. 'Yes,' he said.' And it is selling like hot cakes, it is,' he added. 'For this reason, I keep copies already wrapped. It is important that these things are documented and the people, especially future generations, read about them. Here is your copy,' he said after I handed him 1,500 Shillings.

The bookseller was, in effect, talking about the importance of remembering and for 'these things' he meant the shenanigans of Kenyan politicians. When he handed me the book it was carefully wrapped in brown paper, which reminded me of the 'brown envelope' as the epitome, the quintessence of much of the politics of Kenya.

Khamisi's book of memoirs may not be a work of art in its own right but it is a good read and contains many acute albeit comical observations and accounts of Kenyan politics. Much of what is in the book is already in the public domain but some *risqué* details are not.

Writing about the MPs' newly acquired offices in Continental House, which is next to Parliament Buildings, Khamisi makes the following observations:

> *Some lawmakers turned their cubicles into some sort of lodging facilities and private business centres, where import and export enterprises thrived. The business of selling one brand of vitamin supplements was particularly rampant along the corridors of Continental House. Young, beautiful girls, some brought in from far-flung villages, ostensibly to work as personal assistants, did more than just typing and filing. (2011: 262)*

> *Khamisi also notes on the same page that:*

> *The most embarrassing event during the Ninth Parliament was when an MP was accused of raping a woman in his office. The matter was widely publicized and became a subject of unkind jokes by radio disc jockeys... The reputation of members was further tarnished when it emerged that the sewage system at Continental House had clogged due to careless disposal of used condoms. The blockage, which was reported more than once, forced the administration to post notices on the corridors and in washrooms asking occupants not to dump used condoms in toilets.*

Politics in Kenya, as Khamisi aptly observes, opens opportunities for business, and for exploiting the poor for personal gain. In a chapter entitled 'Do you want to be an MP in Kenya?' Khamisi gives 16 tips for aspiring MPs, including how to 'steal votes' and how to bribe electoral officials. Khamisi's book, however, is not in the genre of Abdilatif's committed poetry. It only recounts but does not encourage its readers to take a militant stand against the rulers.

It is a measure of Abdilatif's influence on Kenyans, for example, that his *Sauti ya Dhiki* is still in print over 35 years since it was first published. Although Khamisi's book lacks *Sauti ya Dhiki*'s literary stamp, if not critical stance, it is nevertheless a welcome addition to the impressive list of works by Kenyan authors which 'remember' the struggle and which document what went wrong after the attainment of independence. These include JM Kariuki's *Mau Mau Detainee* and Gakaara wa Wanjau's *Mau Mau Author in Detention: An Author's Detention Diary*. Both recount the authors' experiences as detainees of the British colonial authorities. Other interesting works of the same period are Waruhiu Itote's autobiographical *Mau Mau General* and *Mau Mau In Action*. Itote, whose *nom de guerre* was General China, was a key Mau Mau leader alongside Dedan Kimathi, Stanley Mathenge and Musa Mwariama.

We should not dismiss the importance of works by establishment figures, for example *Walking in Kenyatta Struggles* by Duncan Ndegwa, the first African governor of the Central Bank of Kenya, or *Beyond Expectations: from Charcoal to Gold*, a rags to riches autobiographical treatment of the life of Njenga Karume, a Kenyatta acolyte. They too are important in making us remember.

In addition to *Sauti ya Dhiki*, other prison memoirs produced during the post-independence period include Maina wa Kinyatti's *Kenya: a Prison Notebook* and *Mother Kenya: Letters from Prison, 1982-1988*; Alamin Mazrui's *Chembe cha Moyo*, a collection of prison poems which Mazrui wrote during his two-year detention without trial, and Ngũgĩ wa Thiong'o's memoir *Detained: A Writer's Prison Diary* and the novel, *Devil on the Cross*, first published in Gikuyu as *Caitaani mũtharaba-Inĩ*.

Mentioning Ngũgĩ, Abdilatif's chief collaborator from Moi's dictatorial reign until now, gives me an excuse to search my memory and talk of Ngũgĩ and the disco girl. It must have been either a Wednesday or a Thursday when Ngũgĩ wa Thiong'o rang to ask if I was free the following Saturday to accompany an Indian professor of English literature from a Canadian university to his home in Limuru, on the eastern edge of the Great Rift Valley and some 50 km north-west of Nairobi.

Ngũgĩ came to fetch me early that evening to take me to the Boulevard Hotel where he introduced me to the Indian professor who turned out to be Govind Narain Sharma. We arrived at the hotel to find Sharma already waiting for us in the lobby. Ngũgĩ had barely introduced us when across the lobby I spotted Wanjiku (not her real name), a Gikuyu girl who I knew from the floor of Nairobi's New Florida discotheque.

Seeing me with Ngũgĩ at the Boulevard Hotel, Wanjiku became ecstatic and beckoned me over. 'Is that *Mwalimu* (teacher)?' she asked. She must have been in her early twenties. With her obedient smile, she was delightful and vivacious. But she was also articulate and informed. That notwithstanding one would have been hard put to associate her with the world of literature. At least I couldn't.

However, what followed after I had introduced her to Ngũgĩ was a very long and absorbing private tête-à-tête between them in Gikuyu. They were so engrossed in their talk that they appeared totally oblivious not only to the passage of time but also to the presence of Sharma and myself.

Ngũgĩ – ever polite – apologized and explained that they were discussing his first ever published novel in Gikuyu *Caitaani mũtharaba-Inĩ* (The Devil on the Cross). Apparently, the young lady was in the habit of reading *Caitaani mũtharaba-Inĩ* to her grandmother every day. She would read until after a while when the grandmother would say, 'Enough, stop.'

The following day the granny would recount the story from the beginning to where they had reached the previous day and would then tell her granddaughter, 'now continue.' Wanjiku told us there were a lot of phrases, words and expressions which she couldn't understand; but which were then explained to her by her granny. Apparently, they were in classical Gikuyu.

What I witnessed that evening was a fascinating encounter – what one may describe as a sporting girl engaging in a lively discourse with an author of Ngũgĩ's stature on his novel.

My contention is that it must have been the first time for Ngũgĩ to have had a direct feedback on his creative work from such a source, as a representative of the general reading public. The ordinary reader was the critic. Ngũgĩ was dangerous because he talked directly with the peasants in their mother tongue. This sent shivers of fear up the spine of the *wabenzi*.

Perhaps Wanjiku's familiarity with Ngũgĩ's work was not a one off. Perhaps Ngũgĩ did – and probably still does – have a following of sorts among ladies of the night. If he does have such admirers he will not have been alone. After all, Victor Hugo is said to have had a huge following among the Parisian prostitutes and after his burial in the Pantheon they offered themselves for free – just for that one day – to those who needed consolation.

But then Ngũgĩ is an amazing writer with amazing friends. This I found out when I visited him in Kenya immediately after his release from Kamiti Maximum Security Prison in 1979. Kamiti is hardly the best of prisons – it is dilapidated, has no reliable water system, and at the time of Ngũgĩ's and Abdilatif's incarceration, was infamous for its brutality.

Homosexuality was rampant in its cells. In connivance with senior sergeants inmates could, for a fee, get another prisoner transferred to his cell for sex. A prisoner who paid for the transfer was called a *mende* (a cockroach) and the transferred one was called a *mtoto* (a baby or wife).

Kamiti was set up by the British colonial administration to jail freedom fighters and it is where Kenya's hero Field Marshal Dedan Kimathi was hanged in the early hours of 18 February 1957, one of the 1,090 suspected Mau Mau who were hanged by the British between October 1952 and March 1958. In total the British killed more than 20,000 Mau Mau fighters in combat.

One Saturday morning in early 1979 when I was visiting Kenya, an old comrade from London, the Zimbabwean Chenhamo (Chen) Chimutengwende and I took a public bus to Limuru in search of Ngũgĩ. Chen was then working with UNESCO in Nairobi.

It was mid-morning when Chen and I set off on our journey not knowing exactly where to find Ngũgĩ. But as we alighted on a dusty patch somewhere near the Bata Shoe Factory in Limuru, a young fellow passenger on the bus from Nairobi asked us if we were looking for Ngũgĩ.

It was a surprise because we had not mentioned Ngũgĩ's name during our entire journey. We had talked about many other things but the name Ngũgĩ was uttered by none of us. Chen and I were befuddled. How did he know we were after Ngũgĩ? He directed us to Ngũgĩ's residence in Gitogothi, Limuru.

As we walked to the front of the dwelling we chanced upon Ngũgĩ in a pickup truck with his now deceased wife, Nyambura, and children driving out of their compound. They must have been setting off for a day out but when Ngũgĩ saw us he beckoned us in. I don't know how his family felt because we had obviously torpedoed their plans. We chatted for a while in his home and then he suggested that we follow him to meet some of his neighbours.

I must confess that when he said 'my neighbours' I had in mind some academic-types and was pleasantly surprised when he took us to a shack in nearby Kamirithu, his birth village.

There we found some truly amazing individuals – elderly ladies and gentlemen who were members of the Kamirithu Community Educational and Cultural Centre imbibing gourds of *muratina*, the local brew. They were a friendly lot and were elated when Ngũgĩ told them in Gikuyu that Chen and I had run an international campaign in London for his release when he was detained in Kamiti by Kenyatta.

All of them had acted mostly by improvisation in his Gikuyu play *Ngahiika Ndenda* (*I'll Marry When I Want*). I saw in them a group of democracy conscious, landless peasants but who were imbued with a sense of mission. Their consciousness was both national as Kenyans and was also a class consciousness as the have-nots.

It was obvious from their talk that they possessed an inner strength. They made it clear that *Uhuru* or formal independence from British rule had not had any meaningful impact on their lives. To them the Moi government, as the Jomo Kenyatta one before it, was neo-colonial and was as oppressive as the colonial government that had dispossessed them of their land and detained and killed their heroes. The government saw them as a threat because of these subversive views just as it had viewed Abdilatif.

We ate a lot of *nyama choma* with the Kamirithu villagers and talked till late at night, the conversation flowing and becoming more intense as they became more charitable with their *muratina*. When the village was already enveloped by darkness Ngũgĩ insisted on driving us back to Nairobi. It must have been around 11:00 p.m. when he dropped us at the New Stanley Hotel where Chen and I headed straight for the open-air bar to ponder on our experiences. Ngũgĩ, with only his thoughts for company, returned to Limuru.

It is important and certainly urgent in this age of greed that we should keep tales like these in people's memory. Traditionally in Africa, the history of the family, clan, tribe or nation gets passed down either orally or in some kind of national epic that provides a national memory. The silence of political leaders leaves a historical void, which is at best filled by academics, often foreigners, who mostly leave an imperfect remembrance. For this reason Africa is poorer because it lacks memoirs by people of the stature and experience of such luminaries as Zanzibar's Marxist leader Abdulrahman Babu, Kenya's Pio Gama Pinto and Makhan Singh, Guinea-Bissau's Amilcar Cabral or Guinea-Conakry's Diallo Telli, the illustrious former OAU secretary-general, to mention but a few.

More damaging to Africa's memory in general is the dearth of memoirs by guerilla fighters or urban underground activists. Joaquim Chissano has come out with an autobiography in Mozambique but there is none from his comrade, Marcelino dos Santos, who, like Abdilatif, is a poet and a revolutionary.

In almost all African countries, it is the victors and those who are literate who write history. This means we do not know about the optic of those who lost in intra-party struggles. These include Frelimo's Uria Simango (Mozambique) although a Mozambican academic Barnabe Ncomo has written a biography of him (*Uria Simango: Um homem, uma causa*); Unita's Jorge Sangumba (Angola); MPLA's Viriato da Cruz, another poet and revolutionary (Angola) whose heroic life has been ably captured by Francisco Soares and Moises Silva in *Viriato da Cruz: O Homen e o Mito*; and TANU's Oscar Kambona (Tanzania).

We also have a responsibility to allow those who are silent because they cannot write to speak through oral histories. These can be recorded in video and transcribed.

As a Kenyan patriot and a passionate pan-Africanist, Abdilatif has always used his poetry mostly in the service of the oppressed like Ngũgĩ's former colleagues in Kamirithu. He uses it as a weapon to fight against his country's rapacious leaders.

There are no contradictions – at least overtly — in his didactic poems between his poetic persona and his political life. He lives the life of his poetry. When he is of a philosophical bent of mind Abdilatif produces a poetry that aptly epitomizes a fusion of prosodic dexterity with rhetorical complexity. His poetry has been very much influenced by his maternal great uncle, Ahmad Basheikh bin Hussein, a conservative Swahili poetic prosodist who was his mentor in poetry. He inherited from him an unflinching commitment to traditional prosody and a penchant for the quaint *Kimvita* dialect, the everyday language of his environs.

Abdilatif's other role model in metrical composition and poetic cadences has been his older brother, Ahmad Nassir Juma Bhalo, a major poet with a very versatile style.

Politically, Abdilatif was first inspired by yet another brother, his eldest, Sheikh Abdilahi Nassir. A former publisher and former coastal politician, Sheikh Abdilahi is an author, a renowned Shii scholar and a public intellectual with a following in East Africa and beyond. It was Sheikh Abdilahi who introduced Abdilatif to nationalist politics and to radical political tracts such as Fidel Castro's 'History Will Absolve Me,' (*La historia me absolverá*), the concluding sentence and subsequent title of a four-hour speech made by Castro on 16 October 1953. The speech was in his own defence in court against the charges that were brought against him after leading an attack on the Moncada Barracks.

It is the synthesis of the poetic with the political that has enabled Abdilatif to emerge as a committed poet of the people. In this sense, the symmetry of his poetry fits in very well with his political praxis and ipso facto with the act of preserving the memory of the earlier struggle for independence and of the current — more challenging — struggle for Africa's second liberation.

## References

Abdalla, Abdilatif. 1971. *Utenzi wa Maisha ya Adamu na Hawaa,* Edited by Abdilahi Nassir. Nairobi: OUP.

Abdalla, Abdilatif. 1973. *Sauti ya Dhiki.* Nairobi: OUP.

Edmundo Melo Rocha, *Francisco Soares* & *Moisés Silva* Fernandes. 2008. *Angola : Viriato da Cruz : o homem e o mito. Luanda:* Prefácio.

Foucault, Michel. 1972 (1969). *The Archeology of Knowledge.* London: Routledge.

Itote, Waruhiu. 1967. *Mau Mau General.* Nairobi: East African Publishing House.

Itote, Waruhiu. 1979. *Mau Mau in Action.* Transafrica..

Kariuki, JM. 1963. *Mau Mau Detainee.* Nairobi/London: OUP.

Karume, Njenga & Mutu wa Gethoi. 2009. *Beyond Expectations: From Charcoal to Gold.* Kenway.

Khamisi, Joe. 2011. *The Politics of Betrayal: Diary of a Kenyan Legislator.* Trafford.

Kinyatti, Maina wa, 1997. *Mother Kenya: Letters from Prison, 1982-1988.* Vita Books.

Kinyatti, Maina wa. 2009 (1996) *Kenya: A Prison Diary.* BookSurge.

Mazrui, Alamin. 1988. *Chembe cha Moyo.* Nairobi: East African Publishers.

Ncomo, Barnabé. 2004. '*Uria Simango: Um homem, uma causa'.* Maputo: Edicoes Novafrica.

Ndegwa, Duncan. 2006. *Walking in Kenyatta Struggles*: My Story. Nairobi: Kenya Leadership Institute.

Thiongo, Ngũgĩ wa. 1981. *Caitaani mũtharaba-inĩ.* Nairobi: Heinemann Educational Books.

Thiong'o, Ngũgĩ wa. 1981. *Detained: A Writer's Prison Diary.* London: Heinemann.

Thiong'o, Ngũgĩ wa. 1982. *Devil on the Cross.* London: Heinemann African Writers Series.

Thiongo, Ngũgĩ wa (with Ngũgĩ wa Mirii). 1980. *Ngaahika Ndeenda: Ithaako ria ngerekano.* Nairobi: Heinemann Educational Books.

Wanjau, Gakaara wa. 1988. *Mau Mau Author in Detention: An Author's Detention Diary.* Nairobi: East African Educational Publishers.

# Section 2

---

## Selected Works of Abdilatif Abdalla

## Kenya Twendapi Facsimile pg 1

K E N Y A :   T W E N D A P I ?

Kwa muda wa miezi mitatu - tangu mwezi wa
July 1968 tulipotoa karatasi yetu tuliyoiita TURUUU, mpaka
hivi leo—tulikuwa tumenyamaa kimya. Kila mtu alikitafsiri
kimya chetu hicho alivyotaka mwenyewe. Moja katika tafsiri
nyingi zilizopawa kimya chetu, ni, tuliambiwa, "Mbona mu kimya
au munshatishwa?" Wale waliokuwa wakifikiri hayo twawaambia,
MUNLALA!! Sio sisi. Kitisho sicho kimfanyacho mtu kuwacha
kufanya lile aaminilo kuwa ni sawa. Bali sisi twaamini kuwa kiti
sho huzidi kumpa mtu ushujaa wa kuendelea na lile alifanyalo.
Bora awe ataliamini kisawa sawa. Kwa hivyo hata tuseme tukatish-
wa tena safari hii, pia hatutanyamaza. Mara mbili za mwanzo
tulitishwa. Lakini tangu siku hiyo badili ya vitisho hivyo kutu-
tia uwoga, vimezidi na vitazidi kututhubutishia kuwa tufanyalo
ni la haki. Kwani kama si la haki, hao wenye uwezo wa kutisha
watu wasingejipa tabu yote hiyo. Twasema tena kuwa MwENYE LAKE
HAWATI.

Katika karatasi ya mwezi huu tutazungumza juu
ya jambo moja la aibu kupita kiasi ambalo lilifanywa na sirikali ya KANU Kenya nzima, katika mwezi wa August 1968. Hatuna budi
na kulisema. Wao walifanya walivyopenda kwa kujivunia kuwa wana
nguvu za kisirikali. Jee sisi ambao twanyimwa haki zetu na ambao
hatuna hizo nguvu za kisirikali tutafanyaje hata tuzipate hizo
haki zetu? Ni njia gani nyengine inayofaa kutumiwa ili haki hizo
zipatikane maadamu njia za sawa sawa na za kidemokrasi zimetupiliwa mbali, na wala hazijaliwi na hao walio na nguvu za kisirikali? Ni jambo gani tutakalo fanya maadamu KANU yataka "kutawala" kwa nguvu, - "maisha", - bila ya idhini yetu Wananchi? Ni njia
gani tutakayopita ili tuiondoshe hii sirikali ya KANU na watawa-
wala wake wa kidikteta, ambao wameupitisha mpaka udikteta wao
kuliko hao wenyewe waliouanza? Ni njia gani Wananchi wenzetu?
Ni lipi la kufanywa? Hizo ndizo suala ambazo mtu ataka ajiuli-
ze. Sisi hatujui mutazipa jawabu gani suala hizo. Lakini upande
wetu sisi tunayo jawabu ikubaliwayo kila mahali ambapo mambo ya

dhulma namna hii yamepata kutokea. Vile vile jawabu kama hiyo
tutakayowapa, imewasaidia kila waliokuwa wametawaliwa na madik-
teta mfano kama hawa wa sirikali ya KANU. Jawabu yetu hiyo tuta-
waeleza baadaye, kwani mwanzo twataka kuwaeleza lililo tufanya
sisi kutoifikiria njia nyengine ya kuiondoshea hii sirikali ya
KANU ya kidikteta, isipokuwa hiyo tutakayo waeleza.

Bila ya shaka ndugu zetu, vile vioja vilivyo-
fanywa na sirikali ya KANU katika mwezi wa August, bado hamjavi-
sahau. Vioja ambavyo havijafanyika mahali popote katika histori
nzima ya siasa. Vioja vyenyewe ni hikima na hila ambazo sirikali ya KANU ilikutumilia chama cha upinzani - cha KPU. Chama
ambavyho ni cha halali kama kilivyo hicho cha KANU. Na ni chama
chenye wafuasi wengi zaidi kuliko KANU. Hila hizo zilifanywa
ili kutoipa KPU nafasi ya kusimamisha wajumbe wake ili kupigania uchaguzi wa Manispaa. Hila zilizofanywa (kama muliyyo sikia
na mulivyoona) ni kutozikubali karatasi za wajumbe wa KPU kwa
kuwa ATI "hazikujazwa sawa sawa kama sharia itakavyo". !!!
Sisi hapa tuna masuala machache ambayo nyinyi ndio mutakao-
hukumu. Yaingia katika akili Wananchi wenzetu, kuwa katika
karatasi za KPU "zipatazo 1800" ikawa haikupatikana hata moja
ambayo ilijazwa sawa sawa "kama sharia itakavyo"? Akili zenu
zaweza kukubali kuwa katika hizo karatasi za KANU kuwa haikupatikana hata moja ambayo ilikuwa na makosa? (Au labda zao wao
zilijazwa na Miungu-watu). Sababu namna hizi haziwezi kukuba-
liwa hata na mwandazimu!! Au walikuwa viongozi wa KPU hawaijui
hiyo sharia ya kujazia fomu? Haimkiniki! Tujuavyo sisi ni kuwa
sharia zote hutungwa bungeni. Kwa hivyo haiwezekani kuwa iwe
wajumbe wa KPU, ambao wamo ndani ya bunge, wakawa hawakuijua

## Kenya Twendapi Facsimile pg 2

sharia hiyo. Na pia haiwezekani,baada ya kuwa KPU walikuwa waki-
ijua sharia hiyo wakawa hawakuifuata,hali ya kuwa nia yao ilikuwa ni kuishinda KANU. Na hilo lilikuwa wazi kabisa. Sisi twasema kuwa KPU iliifuata sharia kama itakikanavyo. Na tutawathubuti
shia hilo tukiwaeleza yaliyotukia Machakos.

Hio ndiyo hila ya sirikali ya KANU. Baada ya
sirikali ya KANU kuona kuwa wale ambao siku zote ndio wenye,
dhamana ya    kuzipokea karatasi za uchaguzi wa Manispaa,pengi-
ne hawataweza kuzikataa karatasi za wajumbe wa KPU kwa kutumia
dhulma,badili yao waliwekwa maDC ili wawe ndio wapokeaji wa hizo
karatasi. Twasema hivyo maana tunao ushahidi kuwa Town Clerk wa
Nairobi alilazimishwa kuzifelisha karatasi za wajumbe wa KPU wa
Nairobi,lakini alikataa. Ndipo akawekwa DC wa hapo. Vile vile
tunao ushahidi wa kuonesha kuwa Town Clerk wa Mombasa pia alilazimishwa afanye hivyo. Kwa moyo wake mdogo hakuweza kurudi nyuma
na kuonyesha ushujaa wa kukataa kama mwenzake wa Nairobi. Na
matokeo yake muliyaona ndugu zetu. Hapa yataka tukumbushane
jambo moja kuhusu hao maDC waliowekwa kuwa wawe ndio wapokeaji
wa karatasi za uchaguzi. Tarehe 27 July 1968,kulikuwa na mkutano
mkubwa wa viongozi wote wa KANU uliofanywa Nakuru. Katika mkutano huo maDC na maPC wote wa Kenya waliitwa kwenda kuhudhuria.
Vile vile hapa twataka tufahamishane kuwa maDC na maPC ni Watumishi wa Raia (Civil Servants). Na Mtumishi wa Raia yoyote hana
ruhusa kuingilia mambo ya siasa,wala kusaidia chama chochote
cha siasa. Hata kama ndicho kilichounda sirikali. Hii ni dasturi ya kidemokrasi katika kila nchi ambayo ina vyama vya siasa
zaidi ya kimoja. Ikiwa ni nchi yenye chama kimoja tu cha siasa,
hapo huwa ni lazima watumishi wa Raia kukisaidia chama hicho kwa
kila njia. Sasa ni vipi basi,ikawa sirikali ya KANU ambayo yaji-
dai kuwa yafuata demokrasi ikawa itatumia watumishi wa Raia
kuwapelekea shughuli za chama chao cha KANU? Bila ya shaka musha-
pata kuwaona PC wa Pwani na DC wa Mombasa walivyojitia katika
siasa siku hizi. Sasa wamekuwa ni kama Organising Secretary
wa KANU na msaidizi wake. Vituko vikubwa hivi!! Demokrasi ya
sampuli gani hii? Hamusemi kweli!?

Basi huko Nakuru ndiko walikokwenda pawa
amri maDC kuwa ni lazima wazifelishe karatasi za KPU kwa njia
yoyote itakayowezekana. Ili kuwathubutishia kuwa maDC walipawa
amri hizo huko Nakuru, tutawapa mfano mmoja tu,katika mingineo
mingi tuliyonayo. Kwa mfano: karatasi za wapiganiaji uchaguzi
wa Machakos zilipokelewa kabla ya huo mkutano wa Nakuru. Kwa
kuwa mkutano huo ulikuwa haujafanywa,karatasi za wajumbe 32 wa
KPU zilikubaliwa. Kwa hivyo zilijazwa "kama sharia itakavyo",
kwani zisingepasishwa. Baada ya DC wa hapo kurudi huko mkuta-
noni Nakuru,alizifelisha hizo karatasi zote 32 ambazo yeye
mwenyewe ndiye aliyezipasisha kabla ya kwenda Nakuru. Yakifika
hapa husemwaje? Mwaziona namna dhulma zilivyotumika?

Ndugu zetu. Hayo ndiyo yaliyofanywa na
sirikali ya KANU ambayo ATI yaongozwa na Muafrika. Na walio-
fanyiwa hayo ni Waafrika sawa na hao waioongozao sirikali. Hawa-
kupungukiwa na chochote katika Uafrika wao. Mambo yafikapo
namna hii,ndipo mtu asemapo maneno ambayo moyo wake haupendi
kuyasema. Ndugu zetu tumemuona Muingereza alipokuwa ametutawala.
Muingereza si Muafrika mwenzetu. Na juu ya uovu wake wote alio-
tufanyia na kutudharau kwake kote kupita kiasi,pia hakusubutu
kutenda kama haya tutendwayo na Waafrika wenzetu. Wakati huo
wa Muingereza,karatasi za uchaguzi zilikuwa hazifelishwi kwa
kutoandikwa sawa sawa. Na ilikuwa iwapo umefanya makosa ulikuwa
ukioneshwa makosa yako na ukaruhusiwa kuyasahihisha. Na juu
ya yote hayo,halafu karatasi hiyo ilikuwa ikipasishwa.
Jambo lililokuwa likisababisha kukataliwa karatasi yako ya
uchaguzi lilikuwa ni iwapo umeipeleka baada ya saa zilizowekwa
kwisha. Ikiwa mambo ni namna hii,basi"afadhali ya Firauni

Kenya Twendapi Facsimile pg 3

- 3 -

kuliko ya Musa". Ndipo hapa mtu asemapo jambo asilo lipenda
kuwa, "ni afadhali wakati wa Mkoloni". (Mgala muuweni ma haki
mpeni). Na mambo yafikapo hapa ndipo yaoneshapo uchungu zaidi-
kumuona Muafrika yuwamtenda visa Muafrika mwenzake ambavyo hata
Muingereza asietujua mwanzo wala mwisho hakututendea. Lakini
MWISHO WA MBIVU NI KUOZA. Hakuna zaidi ya hapo.

Sirikali ya KANU ilikitumilia chama cha KPU
dhulma hizo, maana bila ya shaka KANU ingeula wali mkavu. Sirikali
ya KANU yajua kuwa watu wamechokeshwa na sirikali hii. Watu wamechokeshwa na vitendo vya kishenzi vifanywavyo na sirikali hii.
Na kwa sirikali ya KANU kukitumilia KPU dhulma hizo imesababisha
kuwanyima wananchi haki yao ya kupiga kura. Haki hii ndiyo impayo Mwananchi nguvu za kumchagua yule amfikiriye kuwa ndiye atakaye kuwa ma manufaa naye. (Sio hivi yalivyofanywa, - kuja mtu
akatoa amri kuwa fulani na fulani kuwa wawe ndio).Vile vile haki hii
ya kupiga kura ndiyo impayo Mwananchi nguvu za kuiondoshea
sirikali asiyoitaka, - kwa amani bila ya kutumia nguvu. Lakini
leo mutaona kuwa haki hii wamenyimwa Wananchi na imechukuliwa
na sirikali ya KANU,kwa kujipa idhini ya kinguvu nguvu,ya kuwa-
chagulia Wananchi wajumbe wasio wataka. Wajumbe ambao wamewekwa
ili kulifanyia kazi kabila fulani ili lizidi kudhulumu makabila
mengine. Hii ndiyo demokrasi ya sirikali ya KANU ya kikaburu.

Mwanzo mwanzo wa karatasi hii,suala ya pili
tuliyo iuliza ni hii, "Ni njia gani nyengine inayofaa kutumiwa
ili haki hizo zipatikane maadamu njia za sawa sawa za kidemokrasi zimetupiliwa mbali na wala hazijaliwi na hao walio na nguvu
za kisirikali?" Tuliwaahidi kuwa sisi tutaijibu. Mwanzo twape-
nda tufahamishane yafuatayo:- Ikiwa kweli kwa dhati ya nyoyo
zenu,mwaionea uchungu na kuipenda nchi ya Kenya, (ikiwa mtu
yuwaamini kuwa hapa ndipo kwao na hana pengine pa kwenda),na
ikiwa mwapenda usawa na ubinaadamu ufanyike Kenya na dhuluma
ziondoke, (kama tuaminivyo kuwa hakuna akubaliye kuonewa wala
kudhulumiwa), basi yasikizeni sana haya tuwaambiayo na muyatie
akilini mwenu. Sisi (WASIOTOSHEKA) twafahamu kuwa siku zote hizi
twafuatwa. Na twafahamu kuwa haswa safari hii,kwa kuwa tumesema
maneno haya,tutatafutiwa kila njia ya kunyamazishwa ili tusi-
ndelee kufunua watu macho zaidi. Vile vile twafahamu kuwa safari
hii utakuwako mpango mwengine wa kutuzamisha (mpango huu umeja-
ribiwa mara mbili zilizo pita), lakini nyoyo zetu hazitarudi
nyuma hata chembe,maadamu twaamini kuwa tufanyalo na tusemalo
ni haki na ni sawa. Vile vile twafahamu kuwa kila atakaye kuwa
akikubaliana na sisi kwa maneno yetu tusemayo, pia naye atapa-
tishwa tabu. Lakini nyoyo za binaadamu zikiungana ili kufanya
walilo kusudia,hakuna kiwezacho kuzishinda. Licha kifungo hata
kifo. Ndiyo dasturi ya kila mahali duniani,kuwako watu ambao
wako radhi kupata tabu wao,lakini wawasalimishe wenzao watakao
bakia. Kwa moyo mmoja, kwa fikra moja, na kwa imani moja,bila
ya shaka tutafaulu. Hata mara toja hatutakubali kunyamaza kimya
kwa kuogopa kuadhibiwa,maadamu sirikali ya KANU yaendelea kuwa
fanyia watu dhulma namna hii. Kadhalika twawaomba Wananchi
wenzetu wasikubali kufunga mikono yao nyuma kwa kutarajia kuwa
mambo yatabadilika bila ya sisi wenyewe kufanya bidii na kuya-
badilisha. Wala tusikubali kuwa na tabia kama ile ya watu wengine,ya kusema kuwa, "Mngu atatuondoshea". Ni kweli kuwa si
kazi kubwa kwa Mngu kufanya hilo;lakini yeye mwenyewe Mngu
amewaambia binaadamu kuwa hatawabadilishia hali yao mpaka mwanzo binaadamu wenyewe wajibidiishe kuibadilisha.

Wananchi. Jawabu ya suala tuliyoiuliza hapo
mbele ni hii. Maadamu njia ya amani ya kuiondoshea sirikali,
- yaani ya kupiga kura,yaanza kuuliwa na sirikali ya KANU,

..... /4

# Kenya Twendapi Facsimile pg 4

- 4 -

kabla ya uchaguzi mkubwa wa 1970, na maadamu sirikali ya KANU
ina vitendo vichafu kama hivi tuvionavyo, basi hakuna dawa wala
njia nyengine ya amani ya kuiondoshea sirikali hii. Lakini kabla
ya kuwa na uwezo wa kutumia hiyo njia isiyokuwa ya amani, ni lazi
ma mwanzo tuwe na IMANI (siyo ya kumhurumia mtu), bali ni IMANI
ya kuamini kuwa tutakalo fanya ni haki na ni sawa. IMANI namna
hii hii ndiyo iliyowapa nguvu Wakikuyu ("MAU MAU") kuingia misi-
tuni na kupigana na Muingereza kwa kupigania ardhi na mashamba
yao waliyokuwa wamenyang'anywa. IMANI namna hii hii ndiyo iwasa-
idiayo watu wa Vietnam ya Kaskazini. IMANI namna hii hii ndiyo
iliyowasaidia ndugu zetu wa Zanzibar mpaka wakafaulu. Na IMANI
kama hii ndiyo iliyo wapa nguvu na ushujaa, jimbo la Nigeria lililo jitenga - Biafra - wakawa mpaka leo bado waendelea kupigana.
Na IMANI kama hiyo ndiyo itakayotupa nguvu sisi, na ushujaa wa
kuwaondoshea hawa watawala wa kidikteta wa sirikali ya KANU.
watawala ambao ngozi zao na nyuso zao ni za Kiafrika, lakini nyoyo zao na vitendo vyao ni vya Kikaburu. Hatukuwaondoa Makaburu
weupe ili tuweke Makaburu weusi. Wakati wa "viongozi majina" sio
tena huu. Sasa twataka "viongozi vitendo".

        Ni kweli kuwa kutumia njia hiyo si kazi ndo-
go wala si rahisi. Ni jambo ambalo litatubidi tutoe jasho letu,
ikiwa twataka tufaulu. Hakuna jambo liwezalo kumsalimishirubina
damu na kifo. Kila penye utetezi na ukombozi, ni lazima kuwe na
vifo. Watu wote ni lazima kufa, lakini kuna daraja mbili za kifo.
Kama alivyosema mtetezi mmoja mkubwa kuwa, "Ingawa kifo kitam-
fika kila binaadamu, lakini kuna kilicho kizito kama jabali na
kuna kilicho chepesi kama unyoya." Siku bado zikaliko. Tuyangoje
ya 1970 tuyatizame. Ikiwa mwendo utakuwa ni kama ulivyokuwa
August mwaka huu, na kama ulivyokuwa 1966, basi ni hapo......!

              "HAKI INAYO CHELEWESHWA KUTIMIZWA,
              AU DHULMA ZIENDELEAZO KWA MUDA
              MREFU, HUSABABISHA KUTUMIWA NGUVU
              ILI KULETA NAFUU".

                        —— J.B.

NOVEMBER 1968.

                    W A S I O T O S H E K A.
                    . M O M B A S A .

# Abdilatif Abdalla

## Wajibu wa Mshairi Katika Jamii Yake[26]

Hakuna Fasihi hata moja ulimwenguni ambayo imechimbuka na kuendelea kuishi katika ombwe tupu. Fasihi yoyote iwayo itakuwa imeupata uhai wake, miongozo yake, na hata maudhui yake, kutokana na hali ya kitamaduni, ya kisiasa na ya kiuchumi ya jamii hiyo iliyochimbukana nayo.

Uhusiano huu wa Fasihi na hizi tanzu nyengine za maisha ni uhusiano ambao haufai kupuuzwa - haswa katika hizi nchi zetu za Afrika ambazo kwa muda mrefu fasihi zake zilikuwa zimepandikizwa miche iliyokusudiwa kuudumisha udhalimu wa aina mbalimbali za ubeberu na ukoloni. Na jamii yoyote itakayojaribu kuupuuza uhusiano huu wa fasihi na utamaduni, siasa na uchumi haiwezi kufaulu; kwani itakuwa yajidanganya na kujifunga kizuizui.

Kwa vile fasihi ya jamii yoyote ndiyo kioo cha utamaduni (maisha) wake, na kwa vile fasihi zetu zilikumbwa na athari hizo kwa miaka mingi (na mpaka hivi leo bado athari hizo zingali zaendelea kuziathiri jamii zetu), basi hapana budi kwamba tamaduni zetu hazikusalimika na kumbo hizo za kitamaduni, za kisiasa na za kiuchumi za hao waliokuwa wametutawala. Na mara tu athari kama hizo zipandikizwapo katika maisha ya watu na zikanyweshezewa maji mpaka zikakita na kusitawi vilivyo katika mabongo na nyoyo za watu hao, basi utamaduni wa watu hao huwa hauwezi kujiepusha na kuutumikia mfumo huo uliowapagaza. Ifikapo hadi hiyo, mabongo na nyoyo za watu hao huwa hazina hiari tena, wala hazingojei kuamrishwa na hao waliowapagaza, bali zoo zenyewe hujikuta zikitekeleza matakwa na haja za hao watawala.

Uhusiano wa fasihi na hizo tanzu nyengine za maisha haufai kupuuzwa wala kutenganishwa kwa sababu fasihi ni sanaa; na sanaa haiwezi kuwako bila ya msanii; na vile vile sanaa yenyewe ni tukio la kijamii la msanii huyo; na msanii ni kizalia cha jamii, ambayo haiwezi kuwako bila ya utamaduni, siasa na uchumi. Kwa hivyo, fasihi ina fungamano kubwa na jamii. Hakuna fasihi ambayo haikuathiriwa na jamii, na vile vile hakuna fasihi ikosayo kuiathiri jamii - kwa uzuri au kwa ubaya. Kwa ufupi, kuna uhusiano mkubwa baina ya mwanafasihi na jamii yake.

Lakini uhusiano huo wa mwanafasihi na jamii yake si uhusiano wa kujikakatia nao. Yaani si uhusiano ambao siku zote hubakia kuwa ni mzuri. Hauwezi kuwa hivyo daima kwa sababu ni uhusiano baina ya viumbe vyenye uhai na fikira, vyenye matamanio na malengo tafauti, na vyenye tabia ya kutaka mabadiliko. Na muda kunapotokea mabadiliko fulani katika jamii, basi mahitaji yake, nyendo zake, maadili yake na utaratibu wa maisha, navyo pia hubadilika. Hali kama hiyo itokeapo huwa si lazima - na haimkiniki - mwanafasihi na jamii kuiona hali hiyo kwa jicho hilo hilo moja, wala huwa si lazima hali hiyo ikubalike na pande zote mbili bila ya kuwako hitilafu za

---

[26] Haya yalikuwa ni mazungumzo yaliyotolewa tarehe 23 Oktoba, 1976, katika mjadala uliotayarishwa na Idara ya Kiswahili, Chuo Kikuu cha Dar es Salaam. Yalichapishwa na *Lugha Yetu*, Vol. 30, October 1977.

maana ya mabadiliko hayo au namna ya kwenda nayo. Yaani uhusiano huu huenda ukibadilika kulingana na nyakati ambazo jamii hiyo inazipitia na pia kulingana na mazingira yake. Kwa hivyo una matatizo yake.

Katika historia ya Fasihi ya Kiswahili, hakuna fani ambayo imeitumikia sana jamii kama fani ya ushairi. Na mshairi wa Kiswahili amekuwa na uhusiano wa aina mbalimbali na jamii yake. Yaani kumepata kutokea washairi waliokuwa wakitunga mashairi yenye kueleza hisia na mahitaji ya jamii zao - maliwaza yao, masikitiko yao, itikadi zao, bidii zao, matatizo yao, maadili yao, na kadhalika. Vile vile kuzisemea na kuzitetea jamii zao hizo dhidi ya uonevu na dhuluma za wakoloni waliopata kuwafikia, na pia dhidi ya watawala waovu wa kienyeji.

Na pia kumepata kutokea washairi ambao walikuwa ni vibaraka vya wakoloni au watawala waovu wa kienyeji, na wavunjifu na wasaliti wa jamii zao. Hawa waliutumia ushairi kuwaunga mkono watawala wa aina zote mbili, na kwa hivyo kuwapa nguvu za kuzidi kuwakandamiza na kuwadhulumu wenzao.

Aina ya tatu ni ya kundi la washairi waliokuwa wakitunga mashairi yasiyopinga wala kuunga mkono tawala hizo, lakini yaliyokuwa na maudhui yaliyohusiana na hisia na mambo ya kibinafsi kama vile mapenzi, wasifu na kadhalika. Hata hivyo, marehemu Shihabuddin Chiraghdin[27] asema kuwa shairi kama hilo huwa si hisia tena za kibinafsi za mtunzi huyo maana shairi hilo likishatolewa hadharani huwa ni la kila mtu kwa vile huwa laeleza jambo ambalo laweza kumfika mja yoyote na katika wakati wowote. Lakini pia yawezekana, kama alivyosema Mugyabuso M Mulokozi[28], kwamba walikuwako baadhi ya washairi waliotunga mashairi ya aina hiyo kwa makusudi ya kutaka kujikimbiza na harakati za kumpinga mkoloni, kwa mfano, na wakati huo huo wakawa hawataki kujidhihirisha kwamba wanamuunga mkono.

Ijapokuwa haiwezekani kila msanii kuwa na msimamo au mwamko wa kisiasa, lakini pia ni jambo lisilokanika kwamba si washairi wote walio na msimamo wa kuzitetea jamii zao au kupinga wazi wazi dhuluma inapotendeka. Imani yangu ni kuwa mshairi aogopaye kufanya hivyo hali ya kwamba yuwajua kwamba litendekalo ni ovu na lina madhara kwa jamii nzima, ni mtu mwenye moyo dhaifu[29]. Kwa mfano, katika hilo kundi la waliokuwa wakijipendekeza kwa watawala wa Kiarabu, au wa Kijerumani au wa Kiingereza, kulikuwa na washairi ambao tungo zao zilikuwa zikiwatukuza wakoloni hao na wakijinasibisha nao. Ni kama alivyosema Frantz Fanon[30], kwamba ukiziangalia tungo au maandishi ya wenyeji (watawaliwa) wa Afrika katika nyakati za mwanzo mwanzo za

[27] Utangulizi wake katika *Malenga wa Mrima:* Diwani ya Mwinyihatibu M. Amiri, Oxford University Press, Nairobi, 1977, uk. 2.

[28] Mulokozi, M M, *Revolution and Reaction in Swahili Poetry*, katika KI-SWAHILI, jarida la Taasisi ya Uchunguzi wa Kiswahili, Chuo Kikuu cha Dar es Salaam, 1975, Toleo la 45, uk. 46-65.

[29] Imani yangu hii yatokana na kauli ya Mtume Muhammad (saww) isemayo kuwa:"Yoyote katika nyinyi atakayeuona munkari (jambo ovu) basi naaliondoe kwa mkono wake; asipoweza kufanya hivyo, naaliondoe kwa ulimi wake (yaani aseme na kulipinga); asipoweza kufanya hata hivyo, basi (alipinge) moyoni mwake (yaani asononeke na kuona vibaya); na hiyo (hali ya kulipinga moyoni tu bila ya kutumia mkono au ulimi) ni udhaifu wa chini kabisa wa imani."

[30] Frantz Fanon, *The Wretched of the Earth*, Mac Gibbon & Kee, London, 1965, uk. 179. Kitabu hiki, ambacho mwanzo kiliandikwa kwa Kifaransa, kimetafsiriwa kwa Kiswahili na Clement Maganga na G. Ruhumbika na kuchapishwa na Tanzania Publishing House, 1978. Tafsiri ya Kiswahili yaitwa *Viumbe Waliolaaniwa*.

ukoloni, utaona jinsi wanavyojitolea ushahidi wao wenyewe katika tungo zao kwamba wameigiza nyendo na fikira za watawala hao na kuzifanya ni zao, na kwamba hata hupata ilhamu ya kutungia tungo zao kutokana na yale mambo yenye asili ya watawala wao.

Lakini, kama ilivyo kawaida, katika historia ya ushairi wa Kiswahili hakukupata hata mara moja kutokea kukawa na mashairi yenye kuunga mkono tu tawala za kikoloni, bali papo hapo kulikuwako pia na mashairi ya kupinga kutawaliwa na kudhulumiwa - mengine yakipinga wazi wazi na mengine kwa kufumba. Na kila uchao, idadi ya mashairi haya ya kupinga ilikuwa ikiongezeka kutokana na mwamko wa kisiasa. Hasara moja kubwa tuliyonayo hivi leo ni kwamba mashairi mengi ya zamani yaliyopinga ukoloni hatunayo au hatuyajui. Hilo linatokana na sababu mbili kubwa:

Sababu ya kwanza ni kwamba tungo nyingi za zamani zilikuwa zikitungwa na kuimbwa papo kwa papo katika ngoma au shughuli mbalimbali[31]. Kwa mfano, katika sherehe fulani ya ngoma alikuwa akisimama manju au mngoi aimbe wimbo au atongoe shairi lake, na waliohudhuria walipokee; nao wakiondoka hapo na kwenda zao majumbani kwao waondoke nao wimbo huo au shairi hilo. Baada ya muda utungo huo huwa umeenea katika sehemu mbalimbali za kijiji, na hata ng'ambo zake, kwa kupokezanwa kwa midomo na kuhifadhiwa nyoyoni. Kwa hivyo, kwa vile tungo hizo hazikuwa zikiandikwa, zikawa hazitaweza kubakia mpaka tuje kuzikuta sisi - baadhi zilikufa muda waliozihifadhi walipokufa, na nyengine zikafa na wakati.

Sababu ya pili (na hii yahusiana na tungo zilizotungwa kwa kuandikwa kwanza au kuhifadhiwa kwa maandishi badala ya kutolewa hadharani tu) ni kwamba baada ya kuja hati za Kiarabu pande za Pwani ya Afrika ya Mashariki, kulikuwako washairi waliotunga tungo zao kwa kuziandika. Lakini tungo hizi hazikuwa na bahati ya kutangaa kwa vile hakukuwako na vyombo vya habari kama ilivyo hivi leo. Kwa hivyo tungo hizo sana sana zikiwafikia watu wachache tu, pengine marafiki na jamaa za mtunzi mwenyewe. Na pia zile tungo zilizokuwa zikipinga tawala hizo za kigeni, watawala hao walikuwa wakijaribu kuzifunikiza ili zisiwafikie watu wengi. Hali kama hii vile vile imezikumba tungo zilizotungwa mwanzoni mwa karne hii ya ishirini (baada ya kuingia hizi hati za Kirumi). Lakini baadhi ya tungo hizo zilisalimika na zikawa zikichapishwa magazetini kwa sababu nyingi kati ya hizo zilikuwa zikitungwa kwa lugha ya mafumbo.

Kwa ufupi, ni kwamba kuna baadhi kubwa ya washairi wa Kiswahili waliojifunga masombo kuzitetea jamii zao katika wakati mgumu na wakawa hawako tayari hata mara moja kukengeushwa na msimamo wao huo.

Ili mshairi, au mwandishi yoyote yule, awe na manufaa kwa jamii yake ni lazima awe na msimamo madhubuti: asiwe kitatange - leo yuko huku kesho yuko kule. Na ili kuwa na msimamo madhubuti, mwanzo ni lazima awe yuwaifahamu

---

[31] Ndipo kukawa na msemo wa Kiswahili usemao, "Wimbo hutokea ngomani."

vilivyo jamii yake. Na hawezi kuifahamu vyema jamii yake mpaka aitwalii kwa
kuishi nayo, yaani awemo katika maisha ya jamii yake na awe ni mshiriki wala
asiwe kama mtu kando. Akishafanya hivyo, asiishie katika kuyaishi  maisha
hayo kwa ajili tu ya kuyaishi au kwa ajili tu ya kutaka kuonekana au kusifiwa
kwa kuambiwa kuwa naye yuwashiriki, bali afanye hivyo huku akijua kwamba
huo anaoufanya ni wajibu wake wala si kwamba yuwaifanyia fadhila jamii hiyo.
Akishajiweka katika hali hiyo na akawa yuwayafanya hayo kwa dhati ya moyo
wake na kwa nia ya kutaka kuifanyia kazi jamii wala si kwa maaribu mengine
yoyote, basi hapana shaka kwamba athari atakayoipata hapo itamfanya aikabili
sanaa yake kwa mkabala tafauti. Mkabala huo hautamkubalia kuikabili sanaa
kama kwamba ni kitu kilicho kando na jamii, bali utampa uangavu wa kuzieleza
hisia za jamii yake, kuyashangilia mafanikio yake, kuyaonyesha matatizo yake
na kushirikiana na jamii katika kutafuta njia za kujitoa katika matatizo hayo.

Nimesema kwamba mshairi wa Kiswahili anayetaka kujinasibisha na jamii
yake na kuifanyia kazi ni lazima awe na msimamo wa kuitetea jamii. Pengine
kutaulizwa: aitetee na kuilinda jamii kutokana na nini au na nani? Wako baadhi
ya watu ambao hwenda wakauliza swali kama hilo baada ya kuona kuwa nchi
zote za Afrika ya Mashariki (ambako kwa hivi sasa ndiko kuliko na washairi
wa Kiswahili, na ndiko Kiswahili kisemwako zaidi) ziko huru, na kwa hivyo
hakuna tena ile hali ya kumtaka mshairi huyo aendelee kuwa na msimamo huo.
Au pengine atakuwa ameliangalia bara zima la Afrika na akaliona kuwa zaidi ya
asilimia 95 ya nchi zake zimeshatokwa na wakoloni na hivi sasa walioshikilia
madaraka ya kuziendesha serikali za nchi hizo ni watu wenye ngozi nyeusi
kama zetu. Lakini sote twafahamu, na wala hapana haja ya kuelezana kwa
urefu, kwamba kuondokewa na wakoloni si sawa na kwamba zile dhuluma
na maovu yaliyokuwako wakati wa ukoloni hayaendelei kutendwa hivi leo
na Waafrika wenzetu walioshika nafasi zilizokuwa zimeshikwa na wakoloni.
Maana kilichobadilika ni rangi za ngozi za wanyonyaji na madhalimu lakini
vitendo ni vile vile: Tumetoka kufiwako tumekwenda kuliwako nyama! Kwa
hivyo mapambano lazima yaendelee. Na mapambano ya sasa ni magumu zaidi,
maana tunapambana na jinsi yetu wenyewe.

Jamii kama hiyo huwa ni jamii ambayo ina tabaka dogo linalonufaika kwa
jasho la walio wengi, na hao wengi wakabakia katika hali duni kwa kuzidi
kunyonywa na kukandamizwa. Katika jamii ya aina hii, mshairi wa jamii ni
lazima aweko upande wa hao wengi wanaonyonywa na awapige vita wanyonyaji
hao kwa kila namna. Mshairi huyo hana budi kukata shauri hilo ikiwa kweli
nia yake ni kutaka hali za walio wengi ziwe bora na wafaidike kulingana na
jasho lao wanalolitoa. Hapa huwa hakuna swala la kuwa kati na kati. Ni moja
kati ya mawili - aitumikie jamii au awatumikie wanyonyaji na madhalimu.

Halafu kuna aina nyengine ya jamii - jamii ambayo imekubaliana kufuata
mfumo fulani wa kisiasa na wa kiuchumi ambao wanautakidi kwamba
utawaletea wengi wao manufaa na maendeleo. Tuchukue mfano wa Tanzania
na mfumo wa siasa ya Ujamaa na Kujitegemea. Katika jamii ya aina hii pia,

mshairi ana wajibu wa kuyalinda na kuyatetea maslahi ya tabaka la wafanyakazi na wakulima; na hata kuzipiga vita ishara zozote za kutaka kuudumisha ubepari na unyonyaji, na pia kumfichua kila anayefanya mambo au kutekeleza siasa hiyo kwa njia mbaya ili mfumo huo usifaulu kwa makusudi ya kuutaka umma uanze kuuchukia mfumo huo kwa kuona kuwa unawaletea shida tupu.

Huenda kukatokea malalamiko kwamba twamlazimisha mshairi huyu kutunga tungo zenye maudhui ya kisiasa. Jambo la kwanza ambalo lafaa lifahamike ni kwamba hakuna sehemu yoyote ya mwanaadamu ambayo haikuingiliana na siasa kwa njia mojawapo au nyengine. Na ukweli ambao haukataliki ni kwamba hata tukataka kuiepusha siasa na maisha tunayoishi - jambo ambalo ni muhali - yoo siasa yenyewe haitakubali hata kidogo kupuuzwa au kujitenga na maisha yetu. Isipokuwa kitu muhimu cha kukumbuka na kutahadhari nacho hapa ni kutomshikilia mshairi kutunga mashairi ya kisiasa au yenye kuimba "ujamaa na kujitegemea" na hali ya kwamba moyoni mwake hamna hata chembe ya imani ya hayo ayasemayo katika tungo zake. Kufanya hivyo itakuwa ni kuindoa ile nafsi ya itikadi yenyewe; maana itikadi yoyote haiwezi kupachikwa kijuujuu katika fasihi bali yataka itokane na mwenyewe mtunzi kwa hiari yake baada ya kuijua, kuikubali na kuiamini itikadi hiyo. Hapo ndipo utungo wake utakapokuwa na athari kubwa kwa wausomao au wausikiao. Kwa hivyo, jambo muhimu la kufanywa na jamii ni kumuelimisha mtunzi huyo mpaka aifahamu vyema siasa ya mfumo huo na halafu yeye mwenyewe kwa hiari yake - bila ya kuambiwa na mtu - atakuwa akitoa tungo zitokanazo na imani yake.

Lakini mshairi aliyekata shauri kuwa mtetezi na mlinzi wa maslahi ya jamii yake hana budi na kufahamu kwamba haiachi haibudi atakabiliwa na matatizo, vikwazo na dhiki zenye makusudi ya kumvunja nguvu na kumwangamiza ili asipate kuutekeleza wajibu wake. Yatamfika hayo kutokana na watu au vijopo fulani vya jamii hiyo ambavyo vyajua kwamba kufanikiwa kwa mapinduzi ya jamii hiyo kutakuwa ni maangamizo yao. Na mara nyingi vijopo hivyo huwa vina nguvu za kitawala katika jamii. Kwa hivyo, mshairi huyo ni lazima akate shauri tangu mwanzo kwamba hata mbingu zikishuka hataacha kupigania haki! Na pia itambidi afahamu kuwa hakuna jambo lolote la maana lipatikanalo bila ya misukosuko. Na pia itambidi asivunjike nguvu wala kukata tamaa hata akijiona kwamba amesimama peke yake, kwani nguvu zake zatokana na jamii. Kama alivyosema Jean-Paul Sartre, yeye ni "mtu miongoni mwa watu[32]."

Hapa sasa ndipo panapoingia swala la uhuru wa mwandishi au mtunzi katika jamii yake. Yaani anao uhuru au hana? Na kama anao, uhuru huo ni upi? Uhuru huo una mipaka au hauna? Hivi leo tutaligusia swala hili kwa ufupi tu maana hili ni swala kubwa linalohitaji nafasi yake pekee[33].

---

[32] Angalia *Marxists on Literature: an Anthology*, (mhariri, David Craig), Penguin Books Ltd, London, 1975, uk. 458.

[33] Swala hili lilijadiliwa kwa urefu katika Kongamano lililotayarishwa na Chama cha Kiswahili, Chuo Kikuu cha Dar es Salaam, tarehe 16 Agosti, 1974. Angalia jarida *Zinduko*, Chama cha Kiswahili, Chuo Kikuu cha Dar es Salaam, 1974.

Hapana shaka kwamba mwandishi au mtunzi ana haki ya kuwa na uhuru wa kutoa fikira zake, kukosoa, kusahihisha na kuipendekezea jamii yale aonayo kuwa yataaletea faida. Lakini wakati huo huo jamii nayo ina haki yake kwa msanii huyo; na wakati mwengine humdai msanii kwamba asende kinyume na yale yaliyokubaliwa na kukatiwa shauri kwa njia zinazokubalika na jamii hiyo. Chembelecho Fidel Castro[34], "mwandishi ana kila haki ya kuyaendeleza mapinduzi lakini hana haki yoyote ya kuyapinga." Kwa maoni yangu, kusema hivi hakuna maana ya kwamba mwandishi awe akiitikia "Amin!" kwa kila lisemwalo, au kazi yake iwe ni kusifu tu kila hatua ichukuliwayo kwa sababu tu imeambiwa kwamba hatua hiyo ni ya kimapinduzi. Bali atakiwalo kufanya ni kufunua macho yake na bongo lake na kuchunguza kama hayo yasemwayo ni sahihi. Akatikiwapo kwamba hivyo sivyo, basi ni wajibu wake kusema vile aonavyo. Asipofanya hivyo, atakuwa ni mnafiki. Yaani uhuru wa mwandishi si uhuru wenye maana ya kwamba jamii imuachilie ajiandikie atakayo hata kama anayoyaandika yanakwenda kinyume na maadili ya jamii hiyo au ni ya kuivunja na kuizuilia kufikia lengo lake. Kwa hivyo, kama yalivyo mambo mengine ya kilimwengu, uhuru huo una mipaka yake. Kinyume cha hivyo ni kwamba mwandishi huyo hatakuwa huru bali atakuwa ni mtumwa wa uhuru.

Jambo la mwisho ni kwamba nataka kusisitiza kuwa katika jitihada zake hizi za kuitumikia jamii, mshairi mwenye msimamo madhubuti hafai kukata tamaa kwa matatizo yatakayomkumba, au kwa kuona kuwa kila alisemalo katika tungo zake halitiwi maanani au halizuii kutendeka kwa maovu na dhuluma zitendwazo na baadhi ya walioshika hatamu za uongozi wa jamii. Badala yake yamfalia awe na imani na kujitia moyo kwamba, kama alivyosema Bertolt Brecht[35] wakati alipokuwa akipinga utawala wa Kifashisti ukiongozwa na Adolf Hitler, Ujerumani: „Sikuwa na kubwa nililoweza kufanya. Lakini matumaini yangu yalikuwa ni kwamba lau sikuwako (yaani lau nisingekuwa nikisema) watawala hao wangekuwa na uhuru zaidi" (wa kuendelea kufanya waliyokuwa wakifanya).

Na, kama alivyosema Shaaban Robert katika shairi lake liitwalo 'Kweli', "Kweli itashinda kesho, kama leo haitoshi[36]."

---

[34] *Radical Perspectives in Arts,* (mhariri, Lee Baxandall), Penguin Books Ltd, London, 1973, uk. 276.
[35] Kama 6 hapa juu, uk. 483.
[36] Shaaban Robert, *Masomo Yenye Adili*. Dar es Salaam: Nelson, 1968.

# Abdilatif Abdalla

## Matatizo ya Mwandishi wa Jamii Katika Afrika Huru[37]

Katika mwezi wa Februari, 1967, huko Stockholm, Sweden, kulikuwa na mkutano wa waandishi wa Afrika na wa Skandinavia. Baadhi ya waandishi wa Afrika waliohudhuria mkutano huo walikuwa ni Kofi Awoonor-Williams, Dennis Brutus, Eldred Jones, Alex La Guma, Ezekiel Mphahlele, John Nagenda, Wole Soyinka, Ngũgĩ wa Thiongʼo, na wengineo.

Mwisho wa mkutano huo wa siku nne, kulipitishwa azimio ambalo sehemu yake yasema:

> *...Ni kwa sababu ya kuwa sisi ni waandishi ndio tumekutana hapa, na kwa kuwa kwetu waandishi ndio haswa tumeingiwa na hamu ya kwamba kuweko na uhuru wa mwanasanaa kutoa mawazo yake, na uhuru wa kila mwanaadamu kuweza kutoa mawazo yake bila ya kukandamizwa. Kwa sababu hiyo, hivi leo twalani ukandamizwaji wa waandishi, na haswa kupigwa marufuku kwa waandishi na maandishi, kunakofanywa na utawala wa kibaguzi wa rangi kusini mwa Afrika... Kadhalika tunatoa kauli kwamba waandishi wa kila mahali wapinge vikwazo vyote vinavyowanyima uhuru waandishi, mahali popote yanapotokea haya[38].*

Bila ya shaka sisi tuliokutana hapa si waandishi pekee, bali kuna na wengineo pia. Lakini lililotukutanisha leo ni mmoja miongoni mwa hao waandishi waliohudhuria huo mkutano uliofanyika Stockholm – yaani Ngũgĩ wa Thiongʼo. Na zaidi ni kwamba haya yaliyomfika Ngũgĩ hivi karibuni, yalingana na yaliyosemwa katika azimio hilo.

Kuna methali moja ya Kiswahili isemayo kuwa: 'Fisi akila muwele, mzima funga mlango.' Yaani umuonapo fisi yuwamla mtu mgonjwa, basi wewe uliye mzima funga mlango maana akishammaliza huyo, atakuwa ashapata nguvu za kukujia wewe uliye mzima. Na nafikiri kufunga mlango kwetu ni huku kuja kukutana hapa tukayazungumza haya na kujadiliana.

Baada ya riwaya yake iitwayo *Petals of Blood* kutoka, Ngũgĩ wa Thiongʼo aliulizwa na mwandishi wa habari kama alikuwa na hofu yoyote kwamba kitabu hicho kitawafanya wakuu wa serikali ya Kenya kumtia matatani. Ngũgĩ akajibu:

> *La! Sina hofu hata kidogo kwa sababu naamini kuwa kuzikosoa taasisi za jamii zetu ni jambo la maana sana... Iwapo waandishi wa sehemu yoyote ulimwenguni hawatakuwa wakilifanya hili, basi watakuwa wanakwenda kinyume na wajibu wao. Naamini kwamba kuambiana na kukosoana wazi wazi ni jambo la maana sana katika jamii yoyote iwayo[39].*

Lakini hivyo alivyodhania na kuamini Ngũgĩ, sivyo yalivyokuwa.

---

[37] Mazungumzo haya yalitolewa katika Kongamano la *Usiku wa Ngũgĩ wa Thiongʼo*, lililotayarishwa na Chama cha Kiswahili, Chuo Kikuu cha Dar es Salaam, tarehe 30 Januari, 1978, na yamechapishwa na Lugha Vol. 3, 1984.

[38] Per Wästberg *(mhariri), The Writer in Modern Africa,* The Scandinavian Institute of African Studies, Uppsala, Sweden, 1968, uk. 119.

[39] *Sunday Nation*, Nairobi, tarehe 17 Julai, 1977, "On the Carpet".

Katika Afrika ya leo, ambayo sehemu yake kubwa yaambiwa kuwa nayo iko huru, mwandishi aliyejifunga masombo kuitumikia na kuihami jamii yake dhidi ya madhalimu wa nje na wa ndani, amezungukwa na matatizo kadha wa kadha. Lakini kwa ajili ya mnasaba wa hadhara yetu mahususi ya usiku huu, nitajaribu kuzungumza kwa jumla tu juu ya matatizo mawili ambayo mimi nayaona kuwa ndiyo vipingamizi vikubwa kwa mwandishi wa jamii katika Afrika huru.

Tatizo la kwanza ni kutokuwa na uhuru kamili wa kutoa mawazo yake, ambayo huwa ni ya kuifaidi sehemu kubwa ya jamii, lakini ambayo huwa yapinga maslahi ya madhalimu na wakandamizaji wachache wa jamii hiyo – madhalimu ambao mara nyingi huwa ndio wenye nguvu za kiserikali. Na tatizo la pili ni jinsi ya kuyafikisha mawazo yake hayo kwa sehemu ya jamii aliyoikusudia.

Kwa kuwa hii Afrika tuliyonayo leo yatokana na mlolongo wa matukio na mabadiliko ya Afrika ya jana na ya juzi, hatuna budi kumtizama mwandishi huyo katika hizo hatua ambazo Afrika imezipitia, kwa sababu yeye ni kizalia cha Afrika. Kwa hivyo, tukitaka kumfahamu vizuri huyu mwandishi wa jamii ya Afrika ya leo – na tukitaka kujua kwa nini yu hivi alivyo, na kwa nini akakumbwa na matatizo haya – ni lazima tumhusishe na mwandishi wa Afrika ya jana na ya juzi. Kwani hapana budi kwamba kuwa kwake hivi alivyo leo kwatokana na athari za hayo matukio yaliyopita, na nyakati zilizomtangulia. Haswa kwa vile huyu mwandishi wa Afrika ya leo ndiye huyo huyo mwandishi wa Afrika ya jana na ya juzi – isipokuwa amekuwa akiandika kulingana na matukio ya kila wakati ambao Afrika imeupitia.

Kuna kipindi fulani ambacho mwandishi wa Afrika alijishughulisha na kueleza katika maandishi yake, jinsi bara hili lilivyovamiwa na wageni wa mwanzo mwanzo kutoka sehemu mbalimbali za ulimwengu, kwa madhumuni ya kuja kutawala na kudhulumu. Kadhalika, akaja akaungana mkono na mwanasiasa katika kuulani ukoloni na kuupigania uhuru kwa kutegemea kwamba ahadi zote zilizokuwa zikitolewa na mwanasiasa huyo kwenye majukwaa, zitatimizwa wakati uhuru utakapopatikana. Na zaidi ni kwamba mwandishi huyo alikuunga mkono huko kupigania uhuru kwa sababu – mbali na kuwa ukoloni ukimnyonya na kumnyima haki za kujitawala na kuyaongoza maisha yake vile aonavyo mwenyewe ndivyo – ukoloni pia ni ukandamizaji; na mwandishi wa sawa sawa ni kiumbe ambacho hakipendi, na hakikubali, kuminywaminywa na kunyimwa uhuru wa kutoa mawazo yake. Kwa hivyo, hili nalo likazidi kumpa nguvu za kuupinga ukoloni na kutaka kuutokomeza, huku akitarajia kwamba uondokapo ukoloni na uminywaji wa kutoa mawazo na ukandamizwaji wa kusema kweli, pia navyo vitaondoka.

Hapana shaka kwamba matumaini ya mwandishi huyo, pamoja na ya wanajamii wenzake, yalikuwa ni makubwa sana. Kwani waliamini kwamba huyo mkoloni ndiye sababu ya ukorofi, udhalimu na dhiki zote zilizokuwa zimewakumba; na kwamba akitokomezwa huyo mkoloni, na madaraka ya nchi yakawa mikononi mwa mwenyewe Mwafrika, huu ukorofi, udhalimu na dhiki pia vitatokomea naye; na kwamba uhuru ujapo utawaletea manufaa wananchi wote. Hatimaye, uhuru uliokuwa ukipiganiwa kwa jina la uananchi, jina la Uafrika, na jina la utaifa, ukaanza kupatikana katika nchi baada ya nchi ya Kiafrika, na usukani wa nchi hizo ukawa umeshikwa na wale viongozi walioisaidia jamii kuungana pamoja na kuwa silaha kubwa ya kupigania vita hivyo.

Lakini uhuru huo uliopatikana ulikuwa ukipatikana baada ya wakoloni kuwa na hakika kwamba hao watakaoshika usukani huo watakuwa saa zote wako tayari kutii amri za mabwana zao waliokuwa wamewatawala, na kwamba mfumo wa uchumi utakaotumiwa na hao washika usukani wapya hautawadhuru wakoloni hao na maslahi yao. Kwa hivyo, mkoloni aliyeondoka alikuwa ni mkoloni jina tu lakini kivuli chake kilibakia na kikawa chaendelea kuyafanya yale yale aliyokuwa akiyafanya zamani.

Kama nilivyotangulia kusema, mwandishi wa jamii naye alikuwamo katika kuzinyweshezea maji harakati za mapambano hayo ya uhuru kwa kutarajia kwamba uhuru ujapo utakuwa ni uhuru wa kweli. Mapambano hayo yalipokwisha, na uhuru ukapatikana, mwandishi huyo naye akaanza kuushangilia kwa kuutungia tungo mbalimbali. Naye alikuwa na kila haki ya kuushangilia! Akautumia umbuji wake wote na nguvu zake kwa kuandika juu ya mapambano yaliyotokea, na huku akiwasifu na kuwatukuza viongozi wa mapambano hayo kuwa ndio wakombozi wa watu wao. Akausifu uhuru uliopatikana huku akiwa na yakini kwamba huu ndio mwisho wa safari na kwamba sasa lililobakia ni kila mtu kuanza kuufaidi uhuru wenyewe kama ilivyoahidiwa wakati huo.

Ndipo katika kipindi hicho kukawa kwamiminika maandishi yenye dhamira za kuutukuza na kuuonyesha utamaduni wa Mwafrika na thamani yake. Vile vile maandishi hayo yakawa yanaonyesha jinsi jamii ya Kiafrika ya zamani ilivyokuwa (yaani historia yake), wakati mwengine bila ya kuichambua historia hiyo bali ukawa unaonyeshwa upande mmoja tu – upande wa uzuri. Basi mwandishi huyo akawa ana hamu ya kukidhihirisha kila cha Mwafrika wa hapo kale ambacho ni kizuri na cha fahari, kiasi cha kuifanya hiyo kale ya Mwafrika - kabla ya kuja kwa mkoloni – kwamba ilikuwa ni pepo tupu, haina matatizo. Na hali hii ilitokana na kwamba mkoloni alipotaka kumtawala Mwafrika kwa urahisi, alimjaza fikira potofu bongoni mwake kwamba yeye (Mwafrika) ni duni, si sawa na wanaadamu wengine; kwamba hakuwa na historia yoyote kabla ya kuja kwa majambazi ya Kizungu (waliokuwa wamejivika ngozi ya "wavumbuzi"); kwamba hakuwa na utamaduni wala ustaarabu wowote, wala hakuchangia chochote katika maendeleo ya ulimwengu.

Basi mwandishi huyo, baada ya kuzipata nguvu za huo uhuru, akafanya ghera na akapania kutaka kumthibitishia mkoloni huyo - na kuwathibitishia Waafrika wenzake - kwamba hayo yote yaliyosemwa na mkoloni si ya kweli. Kwa hivyo, mwandishi huyo akawa ni mwalimu wa historia ya Mwafrika pia. Katika kipindi hicho – kwa madhumuni ya kutaka kuisahihisha historia yake iliyopakwa tope na mkoloni – akawa yuwajishughulisha na ya jana na ya juzi tu badala ya wakati huo huo kujishughulisha na yatendekayo katika jamii yake ya wakati alipokuwa akiandika. Na mwandishi huyo alifika hadi ya kuingia katika hatari kubwa ya kusahau kwamba hiyo jamii yake ya zamani airembayo hivyo katika maandishi yake, haiko tena na kwamba ya hivi leo imebadilika kabisa! Na pia akasahau kwamba kujifahirisha kwa yaliyopita zamani hakuwezi kuisaidia jamii yake ya leo kutoka katika matatizo yanayoikabili.

Wakati mwandishi huyo wa jamii alipokuwa amelala katika huo usingizi wa utamaduni na historia (baada ya kuhimizwa na mwanasiasa kwamba aufufue utamaduni wake), huyu mwanasiasa mwenyewe alikuwa ameshughulika na jinsi ya kuishi maisha yake ya sasa, na kuyatayarisha maisha yake ya baadaye. Kwa hivyo, mwanasiasa aliyatumia hayo madaraka mapya aliyoyapata, kutokana na jasho na damu iliyomwagwa na wengi wakati wa kuupigania uhuru, kwa kujinufaisha yeye binafsi na wale walio karibu naye zaidi. Akaingilia kukusanya mali kwa wingi na kujitajirisha upesi upesi bila ya kujali. Akajisahaulisha kabisa kuwa ahadi zilizotolewa wakati wa harakati za kupigania uhuru zilikuwa ni kwamba uhuru ujapo utainufaisha sehemu kubwa ya watu wala si kikundi kidogo tu cha watu maalumu. (Kisa hiki cha mwandishi wa jamii na mwanasiasa huyu ni sawa na kisa cha ule msemo wa Kiswahili usemao, "Mwana kuku lala, kipanga yuwaja")!

Haya yametokea katika nchi zetu nyingi za Afrika kwa sababu baadhi kubwa sana ya viongozi waliokuwa wakipigania uhuru wa bendera na wimbo wa taifa hawakuwa na mipango thabiti ya kwendea kwenye uhuru wa kweli (wa uchumi) na kuutumia uchumi huo kwa faida ya wengi. Kwa sababu mtu akiziangalia kwa makini nchi kama hizo, ataona kwamba hakukuwa na mipango madhubuti ya kuutoa uchumi wa nchi hizo kutoka kwenye makucha ya wakoloni na mabepari wa kimataifa na badala yake kumilikiwa na umma kwa manufaa ya taifa lote muda wakoloni watokomeapo. Nchi nyingi katika hizo hazikuwa zikijua zitautendaje uhuru huo wakati upatikanapo, wala hazikuwa na habari kamwe juu ya uchumi wao na mbinu zitumikazo kuunyonya[40]. Bali katika nchi hizo, wale viongozi waliowangoza wenzao katika vita hivyo vya uhuru, mabongoni mwao walikuwa na mipango yao maalumu ya kibinafsi. Hamu yao ilikuwa ni kuitekeleza mipango hiyo mujarabu wa kupatikana uhuru: mipango ya kuyarithi yale yote waliyokuwa nayo wakoloni – tangu vipato mpaka tabia pia!

Mwandishi wa jamii alipokuja zindukana kutoka kwenye usingizi aliokuwa amelala, akayakuta mambo yamekwenda kinyume kabisa na matumaini ambayo jamii ilikuwa nayo. Akaja akatanabahi kwamba baadhi ya watu waliitumia ile nafasi ya kutokuwa kwake macho kwa kujiimarisha barabara mpaka wakawa wamekita mizizi, hawatikisiki; ikabakia "Domo kaya samli kwa mwenye ng'ombe." Na mwandishi huyo alipougeuza uso kuwaangalia

---

[40] Kwa mfano, tazama jinsi Frantz Fanon alivyoitabiri na kuieleza vizuri sana hali hii katika kitabu chake, *The Wretched of the Earth,* kwenye sura iitwayo "The Pitfalls of National Consciousness", McGibbon & Kee, London, 1965, kurasa 121 – 163. Kitabu hiki, ambacho mwanzo kiliandikwa kwa Kifaransa, kimetafsiriwa kwa Kiswahili na Clement Maganga na G. Ruhumbika, na kuchapishwa na Tanzania Publishing House, 1978. Tafsiri ya Kiswahili yaitwa *Viumbe Waliolaaniwa.*

wananchi wengine (ambao ndio wengi, na ambao ndio nguvu zilizosababisha uhuru huo upatikane) akawaona kuwa hali zao hazikuwa na tafauti yoyote zikilinganishwa na zilivyokuwa wakati wa ukoloni.

Ndipo wote (mwandishi na hiyo sehemu kubwa ya jamii) wakadhihirikiwa kwamba kumbe huo uhuru wa bendera walioupata haukuleta mabadiliko zaidi ya kuwa ule mlingoti ambao zamani ukipepea bendera ya mtawala wa kikoloni, sasa wapepea bendera iitwayo kuwa ni ya nchi huru; na kwamba mahali palipokuwa pakifanywa unyonyaji na udhalimu na wakoloni na mabepari wao, sasa panafanywa hayo hayo na ndugu zao wenyewe waliokuwa wakiwaamini kwamba ndio wakombozi wao. Yaani, kwa mfano, mahali pa setla wa kikoloni kuzihodhi peke yake ekari elfu kumi za ardhi, sasa pakaingia setla wa Kiafrika kuzihodhi yeye pekee ekari hizo hizo elfu kumi (kama hakushikwa na tamaa ya kuziongeza nyengine) na hali ya kwamba kuna mamilioni ya wananchi wasiokuwa na hata ngwe moja ya kulima ili wapate cha kuwapelekea mbele maisha yao. Na ardhi ndicho kitu kimojawapo muhimu kilichopiganiwa uhuru.

Kwa hivyo, mabadiliko yaliyopatikana katika nchi zetu nyingi za Afrika yakawa ni mabadiliko ya kubadilisha rangi za ngozi tu; lakini yale mambo na vitendo vilivyowasababisha watu kujitwanga na kujifua, na wengine wakahitari kuzitoa sabili roho zao ili watokane na unyonge, njaa, unyonyaji na dhuluma, vikabakia papo hapo. Uchumi wa nchi nzima ukawamo mikononi mwa watu wachache ambao hukubali kuwa viboi na vibaraka vya mabwana zao mabepari wa kimataifa. Na kinyang'anyiro hicho hufanywa kwa kisingizio cha "kuutia uchumi wa taifa mikononi mwa wananchi." Kwa ufupi, hivyo ni vikundi vya wanyonyaji na madhalimu waliopata ulinzi wa serikali hiyo hiyo inayojidai kuwa yawatumikia wananchi wote.

Mambo yalipofika kiwango hiki, mwandishi wa jamii akaanza kujiuliza - na kuiuliza sehemu ya jamii anayoiandikia - maswali kama vile, Uhuru ni nini? Uhuru umewaletea faida gani wananchi walioupigania? Kuna tafauti gani za msingi baina ya wakati wa mkoloni na huu wakati wa uhuru? Maswali kama haya yakawa ni chanzo cha matatizo ya mwandishi wa jamii katika Afrika huru. Kwa hivyo, mwandishi huyu akatambua - naye akawatambulisha wenzake - kuwa jamii yake imesalitiwa na wale wale walioaminiwa kuikomboa jamii kutokana na ukoloni, na kuiongoza kwendea kwenye uhuru wa kweli.

Mwandishi huyo alipoona kwamba hata baada ya mkoloni kuondoka zile dhuluma zilizoambiwa kwamba nazo zitaondoka, bado zingaliko na zinaendelea kufanywa na wale wale walioahidi kuondoka kwake, ndipo akafahamu zaidi - naye akawafahamisha wanajamii wenzake - kuwa kumbe tatizo halikuwa ni "mtu mweupe" (Mzungu) kwa dhati ya weupe wake, bali tatizo haswa lilikuwa ni mfumo mzima wa uchumi uliotumiwa na mweupe huyo na ambao sasa umerithiwa na "mtu mweusi" (Mwafrika), ambaye ni kibaraka cha mtu mweupe huyo. Kwa hivyo, yule nyoka aliyedhaniwa kwamba ameuwawa kumbe bado alikuwa angali hai, au kwamba kile kilichokatwa kilikuwa ni kimojawapo tu miongoni mwa vichwa vyake vingi.

Lakini huyu mwandishi wa jamii yumo katika kundi mojawapo tu kati ya makundi mbalimbali ya waandishi wa Afrika. Kwa jumla, kumetokea makundi mane:

Kundi la kwanza ni la waandishi ambao maandishi yao yaliunga mkono kuendelea kuwako kwa hali hiyo ya watu wachache kuhodhi njia zote kuu za uchumi wa nchi. Kundi la pili ni la wale ambao hawakubaliani na hali hiyo na waamini kwamba inafaa ikomeshwe, lakini wamekosa ujasiri wa kujitokeza na kusema hivyo kwa sababu ya kuogopa kuingia matatani; kwa hivyo hunyamaza kimya ingawa wasononeka moyoni. Kundi la tatu ni la waandishi ambao wamejikimbiza kabisa kuieleza hali halisi ya mambo yanayotukia katika jamii na badala yake wanakwenda kujificha katika kwapa za kuandika juu ya mambo yasiyolingana na ukweli wa jamii hizo, au kuandika maandishi ambayo si muhimu katika kuendeleza mbele maisha ya wanaadamu. Kisha katika kundi la nne ndimo alimo huyu mwandishi wa jamii. Yeye, kwa vile yuwaujua wajibu wake kwa jamii yake, huwa hakubali kuyapa mgongo na kuyakimbia matatizo haya bali husimama pamoja na jamii yake hiyo akayakabili kwa kuueleza ukweli na kuieleza jamii jinsi ilivyosalitiwa na kikundi cha watu wanaoidhulumu na kuinyonya kwa jina la uananchi na utaifa.

Sasa, mwandishi huyo ajaribupo kuieleza jamii yake ukweli huo - kwamba tatizo walilonalo ni la kitabaka wala si la rangi ya ngozi, na kwamba jamii ni lazima itafute njia za kulitatua - basi milango ya magereza na vizuizi huwekwa wazi ikimngoja kumfungia ndani. Au akionekana kwamba hata huko gerezani atakuwa bado ni hatari kwa kikundi hicho, hupelekwa ambako hataweza kurudi tena - kuzimu! Au, kabla ya kufanyiwa hayo mawili, hunyamazishwa kwa njia nyengine ambayo mimi naiona kuwa ni mbaya zaidi kuliko kifungo au kifo. Nayo ni kutafutiwa mbinu mpaka akaingizwa katika huo mfumo anaoupinga. Na atetelekaye akakubali kuiramba asali, akishairamba huwa hairambi mara moja!

Basi kikundi hicho kinapoona kwamba jamii imeshatambua kuwa hicho ndicho adui wao, hutumiwa hila nyengine (kama iliyotumiwa na mkoloni wakati wa utawala wake) - ya kuigawanya jamii kusudi isiungane na kuwa kitu kimoja. Kwa hivyo, huyachukua hayo yanayoitwa 'makabila' wakayagonganisha vichwa ili kila mojawapo lione kuwa adui wake mkubwa ni kabila jengine wala si hicho kikundi cha wanaotawala. Kwani kikundi hicho kinajua kwamba wanajamii hao watakapojiunga kitabaka wataondoa utengano wa kubaguana kwa makabila yao, au sehemu wanakotoka, au dini zao; na kwamba hawatadanganyika watakapohimizwa waungane kwa jina la utaifa pekee. Kwani katika ulimwengu kuna mataifa mawili tu - taifa la wenye nacho na taifa la wasio nacho.

Tumetangulia kueleza kwamba tatizo la kwanza la mwandishi wa jamii katika Afrika huru ni kutokuwa na uhuru wa kutoa mawazo yake, ambayo yanaeleza hisia na matakwa ya jamii ya kuondoa dhuluma na unyonge. Lakini mawazo hayo huwa yenda kinyume na maslahi ya hicho kikundi cha watu wachache ambao lengo lao huwa si kuinufaisha jamii hiyo bali ni kujinufaisha nafsi zao. Katika hali kama hiyo, mwandishi mwenye msimamo wa kuitetea na kuisemea jamii yake hukabiliwa na mambo mawili: Abakie nchini na atoe mawazo yake bila ya kuogopa, na kwa hivyo awe anasumbuliwasumbuliwa na kuminywaminywa, au atoke ende akaishi nje ya nchi yake ili aweze kuandika wazi wazi na bila ya vipingamizi kuhusu yale yatendekayo katika jamii yake.

Na jambo hili la mwandishi kuminywaminywa husababisha kiwango cha fasihi iandikwayo katika jamii kama hiyo, kuteremka chini. Maana, kama nilivyopata kusema mahali kwengine[41], fasihi au sanaa yoyote ya maana haiwezi kuchanua na kuendelea katika nchi au taifa ambalo bado limo katika minyororo na ambalo halimruhusu mtu kusema vile aaminivyo, au kupendekeza marakibisho ya yale yatendekayo. Na mwanasanaa yoyote wa maana hawezi kuivumilia hali hii ya utumwa, kwani utumwa wa mawazo ni aina nyengine ya mauti kwa mwanaadamu. Mwanasanaa akishanyimwa uhuru huu, na yeye akanyamaza kimya na akakubali, basi huwa amekubali kujiua mwenyewe. Mwandishi wa maana na mwenye msimamo wa kupigania haki ni lazima aupinge utumwa huo kwa kila namna. Asipofanya hivyo atakuwa ni kikaragosi tu. Hataweza kuandika chochote cha maana wala kilicho na asili ya mawazo yake, kwa sababu ataogopa kuikiuka mipaka aliyowekewa na hao wachache ingawa kuikiuka mipaka hiyo kutaileta jamii nzima faida. Fasihi haiwezi kukua na kushamiri katika taifa lolote lenye watumwa wa mawazo. Na ujumbe wa mwandishi ambaye yuwakubaliana na hali kama hiyo ya unyonge huwa ni ujumbe wa kuwakubalisha watu maonevu; ni ujumbe wa kuwakatisha watu tamaa; ni ujumbe wa mauti.

Kwa bahati nzuri, katika Afrika huru tunao waandishi ambao wamekata shauri kuzitumikia jamii zao na kuzilinda na dhuluma zinazowafikia. Nao hufanya hivyo kwa kuufichua uovu na ufisadi utendekao, wakawafichua hao wautendao, na mbinu wazitumiazo, na sababu zinazowapelekea kutenda hayo, ingawa kwa kufanya hivyo huwa wanajitia katika hatari kubwa. Hata hivyo, sidhani kama huku kuishilia katika kuyafichua hayo na kuilalamikia hali hiyo kwa maandishi pekee kwatosha. Bali, kwa maoni yangu, ni lazima waandishi hao vile vile watafute njia nyengine za kutumia ili kuitokomeza hali hiyo. Kwani kuitumia njia moja tu - ya maandishi - hakutaisaidia sana jamii wala haitawafanya hao wayatendao hayo kutoendelea kuyatenda. Chembelecho Waswahili, "Maneno matupu hayavunji mfupa", wala "Maji ya moto hayachomi nyumba." Kwa hivyo, huko kusema na kulaumu pekee hakuwezi kuwatisha hao wanaodhulumu. Bali wakishindwa kumpuuza mwandishi kama huyo watasema kwamba kulaumu ndiyo kazi ya pekee ambayo wasomi wanaijua[42]. Ni kama mfano wa paka na panya alioutoa yule mwandishi maarufu wa China,

---

[41] Angalia "Utangulizi" katika *Shaaban Robert: Uhakiki wa Maandishi Yake*, cha T. S. Y. Sengo, Longman, Tanzania, 1975.

[42] Kwa mfano, Wole Soyinka alipokuwa akizungumza na mwandishi wa habari na akaambiwa (Soyinka) kwamba viongozi wa kisiasa wasema kwamba kulaumu ndiyo kazi pekee ambayo waandishi wanaijua, Soyinka alijibu, "mpaka mwenye bunduki afanye ia kufanya ili kuyasahihisha makosa yanayotendwa (na hao viongozi) ndipo inapokubaliwa. Lakini mwandishi akijaribu kuyasahihisha makosa hayo hayo kwa kusema tu na akawa hana bunduki mkononi, basi huambiwa (yuwafanya hivyo) kwa sababu ya kuwa ni msomi". Mahojiano haya yalichapishwa katika jarida liitwalo Afrika (toleo la Kiingereza), Vol. xviii, No.4, Afrika Verlag, Ujerumani, 1977, kurasa 14-15.

Lu Hsun[43]. Kwamba paka amshikapo panya kusudi kumla, panya hupiga kelele
ili paka apate kumwachilia; lakini hizo kelele za panya huwa hazimsaidii kitu
panya, kwani paka huendelea kumtafuna tu. Kwa hivyo, nionavyo mimi, ni
kwamba jambo ambalo waandishi wa jamii wafaa kulifanya ili lisaidiane na
hayo maandishi yao, ni kuyakata makucha ya paka huyo na kuyang'oa meno
yake badala ya kulalamika tu. Kwani malalamiko matupu huzidi kumpa
mkandamizaji nguvu za kuendelea kukandamiza.

Tatizo la pili lililomkabili mwandishi wa jamii katika Afrika huru, ni jinsi ya
kuwasiliana na sehemu ya jamii ambayo ameikusudia ujumbe wake. Na tatizo
hili lina vitanzu viwili: Kitanzu cha kwanza ni chombo kitumiwacho kuufikisha
ujumbe huo; na kitanzu cha pili ni lugha inayotumika kuupelekea ujumbe huo.

Waandishi wengi wa Afrika ambao katika maandishi yao huwa wanajadili
na kuyahakiki matatizo mbalimbali yanayohusiana na jamii zao, wasema
kwamba waandikapo huwa wawaandikia "watu wa chini", yaani makabwela.
Lakini ni jambo lililo wazi kabisa kwamba mpaka hivi sasa maandishi ya
fasihi yaliyoandikwa na waandishi wa Kiafrika na yanayozihakiki jamii zetu
kwa kina kirefu, yameandikwa kwa lugha za kigeni: Kiingereza, Kifaransa au
Kireno - lugha ambazo hao waliokusudiwa ujumbe huo hawazifahamu. Na
hiki sicho kiini cha tatizo lenyewe, bali kiini cha tatizo ni kwamba fasihi hiyo
imo vitabuni, yaani *imeandikwa*. Maana hata kama ingekuwa *imeandikwa*
kwa lugha ambazo hao waliokusudiwa wanazifahamu, bado tatizo lenyewe
lingebakia papo hapo kwa sababu sehemu kubwa sana ya hao makabwela
hawajui kusoma wala kuandika. Kwa hivyo, lengo la mwandishi kama huyo
huwa halijatimia, wala hiyo kauli yake ya kuwa yuwaiandikia sehemu hiyo ya
jamii huwa haina ukweli.

Tatizo hili ndilo lililompa yule mwandishi maarufu wa Senegal, Sembene
Ousmane, akabadilisha njia ya kuifikisha sanaa yake kwa jamii yake. Badala
ya kuendelea kuandika vitabu, sasa yuwashughulika zaidi na kufanya filamu
kwa lugha ya jamii hiyo - Kiwolof. Sembene amekata shauri kufanya hivyo
baada ya kumthibitikia kwamba hayo maandishi yake huwa hayana athari kwa
hao aliowakusudia, na kwamba huwafikia watu wachache sana wajuao kusoma
(au tuseme "wasomi"), na ambao mara nyingi huwa si watu wa kutegemewa
sana katika kuleta mabadiliko ya kuinufaisha sehemu kubwa ya jamii. Na
nimeelezwa kwamba tatizo hili hili la mawasiliano ndilo limkeralo sana hivi
sasa mwandishi mwengine maarufu wa Afrika, Ayi Kwei Armah, wa Ghana.

Kutokana na hali hiyo, mwandishi wa jamii hata angajitahidi vipi, athari ya
ujumbe wake kwa hao anaowakusudia ni ndogo sana. Basi labda suluhisho ni
kutumia fani ambazo msanii ataweza kuwasiliana na hadhira yake moja kwa
moja, na papo kwa papo. Yaani kutumia mbinu za Fasihi-Simulizi. Athari ya
kuwasiliana namna hii ni kubwa sana kuliko ya maandishi. Maana, kwa mfano,
mtu awapo yuwasoma riwaya, au tamthilia, au diwani ya mashairi, huwa ni

---

[43] Katika hotuba yake, "Literature of a Revolutionary Period", aliyoitoa kwenye Chuo cha Kijeshi cha
Huangpu, tarehe 8 Aprili, 1927. Hotuba hii imechapishwa katika jarida Chinese Literature, No. 9, Foreign
Languages Press, China, 1977, kurasa 3-9.

yeye pekee na kitabu akisomacho. Lakini iwapo ni sanaa ambayo inawakusanya watu wengi kwa pamoja, na halafu sanaa hiyo ikatongolewa au kuigizwa hadharani, huwa ni rahisi kuwatia hamasa na kuwaathiri hao waliohudhuria na ujumbe kuweza kupenya nyoyoni mwao kwa wepesi zaidi - haswa iwe sanaa hiyo ni kwa lugha ifahamiwayo na watu hao.

Tuchukue mfano wa huyu mwandishi aliyetukutanisha hapa usiku wa leo, yaani Ngũgĩ wa Thiong'o. Hivi majuzi, tamthilia iitwayo *Ngahiika Ndenda*, aliyoiandika kwa Kikikuyu pamoja na mwenzake, Ngũgĩ wa Mirii, iliigizwa hadharani katika sehemu ya Kenya iitwayo Kamiriithu ambako wengi wa wanaoishi huko ni wasemaji wa lugha hiyo. Tamthilia hiyo iliwatetemesha wakuu wa serikali ya Kenya na hatimaye wakaipiga marufuku. Lakini riwaya ya mwandishi huyo huyo, *Petals of Blood*, haikuwatia shughuli wala wasiwasi kwa sababu wanafahamu kwamba ujumbe uliomo humo (ingawa unaikosoa serikali ya Kenya) hautawafikia Wakenya wengi kwa sababu, mosi, ni maandishi (na wengi hawajui kusoma), na pili, maandishi yenyewe ni kwa lugha ya Kiingereza (ambayo yapunguza zaidi idadi ya wasomaji).

Basi haya, kwa ufupi, ndiyo matatizo mawili makubwa – miongoni mwa mengi - yaliyomkabili mwandishi wa jamii katika Afrika huru. Mkusanyiko ulioko hapa usiku wa leo wafaa ujiulize: Ni lipi la kufanywa ili tuepukane na matatizo haya?

# The Right and Might of a Pen[44]

**Abdilatif Abdalla, a broadcaster and Swahili poet of eminence, relives the agony of incarceration in a Kenya maximum security prison**

## May 12, 1969

Four days ago, the Mombasa High Court increased my sentence to three years' imprisonment after the Attorney General appealed against the earlier sentence of 18 months as inadequate. Today, I'm transferred from Shimo la Tewa Prison, Mombasa, to Kamiti Maximum Security Prison, near Nairobi. I arrive in Kamiti at 7pm. What a dark night this is! Very heavy rain, lightning and thunder greet me.

Immediately after setting foot in the prison, the gate-keeper asks of me: "Who is this devil?" After being told of my "offence", another warder picks it up and asks sarcastically: "So he is the one who asked, 'Kenya Twendapi?' (Kenya: Where Are We Heading To? Referring to the pamphlet I wrote, published and distributed and which I was convicted of). "We'll show you where it is heading to", I'm assured by another. But I already know where it is destined. That's why I'm posing this question for the benefit of those who wield the power, lest they are blinding by it. I sure know where it is heading to. All the signs on the road it is travelling on indicate very clearly that it is heading towards tyranny and repression. Is it a crime to warn of the imminent danger?

I'm escorted by two warders to Isolation Block and locked in Cell No.1. My only 'companions' are a pair of tatty almost transparent blankets as my bedding, a plastic mug, a plastic pot – my handy 'lavatory'. I'm left alone in my cell shivering, cold and wet.

Am I alone in this whole block? Two different voices call out from two widely separated cells and welcome me: "Karibu ndugu! Jela ni ya wanaume!" (Welcome! Prison is for men!) Later on the voices ask me what my name is. The voices shout out their names too: "Israel Otieno Agina!" "Field Marshal John Okello!" They say that when they heard, through a warder, about my "offence", conviction and sentence they were sure of my joining them in Kamiti Maximum Security Prison and especially in Isolation Block.

## May 13, 1969

Today I was taken to be presented to the Senior Superintendent of Prison (SSP), the Officer-in-Charge of the prison, as is the procedure for the new admissions. Now I've a new prison number on my chest (KAM/285/69/LS). That is I'm the 285th prisoner to be admitted to Kamiti so far in the year 1969 and that the sentence I'm supposed to serve is a long one – hence the abbreviation LS at the end.

---

[44] First published in *Africa Events*, 1985.

Once again I'm reminded by the officer allocating the numbers to prisoners that as from now on I'll always have to remember my number – whenever it is called. Reduced to a mere number! I'm no longer my name! Stripped of my freedom (although in a cell and circled by three long and thick walls, my cell door is permanently locked except for three brief times when my meals are brought in). Stripped of my privacy (the warder peeps every now and then through a specially made hole on the door to see what I do. In fact I have to be on the opposite side of the door so that I can be easily seen. Yes, even when I'm shitting!)

Stripped of my dignity and humanity and bared to occasional insults and rudeness. There's one instance when my mother was insulted for no sound reason, and once one of the warders made very rude remarks about the Quran when I mentioned that it is my guidance. Perhaps it was just to provoke me so that they get an excuse to beat me up.

And now I'm stripped even of my name! I'm no longer me. Just a mere breathing, walking thing!

Two well-built warders escort me. Nearing the SSP's office, I'm sandwiched between the two warders – one in front and one at the back of me. I'm ordered to quick march like a soldier. "Right turn!" it was the husky voice of Sergeant 'Masharubu' (nick-named so because of his long whiskers of which he was very proud) commanding the three of us. Now I'm face to face with the SSP who is seated about three feet away from where I stood and in between us, his desk.

"Attention!" I tell myself that by the time I finish my prison term, I'll be an accomplished prison, police or army officer. The two warders stand behind me. The SSP gives me a hard stare and then goes through my record file on his desk. He looks at me again.

"So you're the one who asked Kenya Twendapi?", he asks me sarcastically. Oh no, not through it again! I've been asked this same question time and time again. I'm sick of it now. What's so spectacular about it?

"Yes, *afande*", I reply.

"So you think you're cleverer than Kenyatta and his government?"

What is he expecting me to answer?

In the course of this interview, I make a mistake of forgetting to add the word "afande" (Kiswahili word used in forces to mean "sir") while answering one of his questions. The SSP calls out: *Amsha yeye!* (broken Kiswahili for "wake him up"). Before I had time to digest these words and make out what they were specifically supposed to mean, there was a sudden and sharp pain in my both ears caused by a heavy blow which left them blocked for a while, not being able to hear a thing. I saw stars. I first thought that my ear drums had ruptured.

The SSP then gave an order that I remain in solitary confinement in the same "Isolation Block." That means I remain quarantined in my small cell throughout the 24 hours with only ten minutes' sunshine in the small courtyard in front of the block I'm held in.

### July 23, 1969

I'm moved from Isolation Block to G Block: from the frying pan to the fire. So, at last, here I am in the G Block which some of my friendly warders told me horrifying stories about: that G Block is the most punitive block in the whole Kamiti Prison; nay, in the whole of Kenyan prison system. The block that even the hardcore prisoners dread. I was told stories of how prisoners are straight-jacketted and left in that condition for days; stories of how prisoners get beaten up by warders; stories of how some prisoners are left naked in their small cold cells and even semi-starved for several days; stories of how some of them smear their bodies with their own excrement and even eat it! Of how some are left in water-logged cells to freeze; of how some of them become incapable of withstanding such treatment that they ultimately end up in mental hospitals. When I was in the neighbouring Isolation Block, I used to hear their voices of agony and despair. Now, here I am where the 'action' is and where (as the warders keep in intimidating me) the 'real' prison is!

Here I am now, not only to hear those voices of agony and see with my eyes and heart what is taking place in this block but to undergo some of these "horrifying" experiences myself. I hope that my conviction in what I believe will sustain me and give me enough courage and strength to persevere. That even if they manage to tear and break my external body, my conviction will guard the rest of me so that they won't get to that very important spirit in my chest – in the heart.

For when I started writing and publishing my very first pamphlet (Kenya: Twendapi? being the seventh) I was warned that imprisonment was my likely fate if I continued with what I was doing; and yet I accepted that fate.

I received intimidations from some of the Mombasa politicians. I was summoned at the Coast Provincial Commissioner's office and warned to cease writing the pamphlets or I'd end up in prison. And when I refer to my book of guidance, the Quran, it teaches me not to sink that low but to defy such warnings when it is the truth and justice which one is fighting for. For instance, what was Nabii Yusuf's reply when he was threatened with imprisonment when he wouldn't do what the king's wife wanted him to and which he, Yusuf, believed was wrong and unjust? This was his reply: "O my Lord! The prison is more to my liking than that to which they invite me…" (Quran 12:33)

I'm locked in Cell No. 3, which is one of the four cell situated in the ground floor of G Block. These four are separated from the rest of the ground floor cells by a door which is always locked. The place is dark and cold. As usual, the first thing in the morning is to strip naked before three or four warders who come to inspect the cells in case you are in possession of "marufuku", that is something that goes against prison regulations. After stripping, you're ordered to bend, open your mouth, put their fingers between the hair to continue the search. Then, the two blankets are taken out of the cell where they remain until about six in the evening.

## March 18, 1970

A few weeks ago I learned from the officer-in-charge of the prison that he had got instructions from the Ministry of Home Affairs that I should not benefit from the usual one-third remission given to almost all prisoners. That means I'll now have to do the full three-year term instead of two.

I've completed one year today. Two more years to go. I'm still in solitary confinement under the same conditions. My several requests to the Officer-in-Charge to allocate me some work to while away the time have been to no avail. It is so boring and tiring to be locked in a cell with nobody to talk to or with nothing else to do except lie down on a cold cement floor and when tired stand up, or do some exercises in the cell to keep the body warm. Idleness is more a punishment than hard work.

The few days I spent in Kamiti Medium Prison – before being sent back to Mombasa High Court for the sentence to be extended – splitting stones, were more bearable than the idle moments in this cell. I had dislocated my wrist in the course of doing that hard labour, but I still would prefer that to this idleness and solitary life. Were it not for the fact that I still believe that what I did, speaking out, was right, I would be insane by now. Thanks to my 'friends' for toilet paper which eases my suffering a bit by writing poems on it.

The routine of the day: after emptying my pot of the night's outpour of urine, I'm given a mug of sugarless and saltless maize flour porridge. At eleven in the morning, two plastic bowls are pushed into the cell – one containing *ugali* (maize meal) and the other *mboga* – boiled greeny water with three of four leaves floating and sometimes 'spiced' with insects. That is supposed to be lunch. At about 3.30pm, one plastic bowl is shoved in containing what is supposed to be supper – another portion of *ugali* topped with dry boiled *maharagwe* (beans). During the first few weeks of my prison term, I used to stay hungry, but now I finish the whole portion and then lick my fingers!

## May 22 1970

A sudden, frenzied and unusual search in my cell. I didn't know exactly what they were looking for. But they found leaves of toilet paper I had written a poem on. They confiscated all the 14 verses of my poem "Kamliwaze" (Go and Comfort Him). It's a pity I've lost it, especially that I had memorized only the first four stanzas of it. The rest is now gone and lost. Fortunately, they couldn't find the other three poems (*Nshishiyelo ni Lilo*, *Tuza Moyo* and *Jipu* which I had wrapped in a plastic paper and tossed them in my urine pot for 'safe custody'; and also the two poems ("Siwati" and "Mamba" which were dangling on a blanket thread outside my cell window. But I doubt if they will be able to make out the meaning of the poems. Even if they will, I have 1001 alternative interpretations for each one of them.

# Section 3

Contexts

# Sheikh Abdilahi Nassir

## Hope and Despair in Kenyan Politics
## During and After Independence

The subject given to me is political: Hope and Despair in Kenyan Politics During and After Independence. This is a very political and sensitive subject. I will try as much as I can to see that I do justice to it.

To appreciate this, we have to go back in history. Was there Kenya before the coming of Europeans? Yes, there was; but not as it is demarcated today. Kenya, as it is, came about in 1896 following the Partition by the then Western Colonial Powers. Before them were the Arabs of Oman, who were largely confined to the coast of East Africa, with their headquarters in Zanzibar.

When Kenya was created by the British, with the present-day boundaries, its coast was accepted to be the Sultan's, with whom the British entered into an agreement for them to administer it on the Sultan's behalf. This was known as Kenya Protectorate, distinct from Kenya Colony.

Kenya Colony was all British. The British 'owned' it. They were free to do whatever they liked with it, but not so fully with the Protectorate. With it they agreed to share its ownership with the Sultan – nominally though – with all other powers vested with Britain. Thus, unlike in the Colony, we had an Arab Administration (Liwalis and Mudirs) answerable and subservient to the Colony's Provincial Administration (all British) as well as a Chief Kadhi and several other Kadhis subservient to the colony's Chief Justice, under Kenya Colony's Judicial Service Commission.

However, here we need to realize one factor which was common with both rulers – the Omani Arabs as well as the British. Both were outsiders, not indigenous. They came from distant lands. Using force and trickery, they occupied and ruled over it. They marvelled at the fertile land that was there in plenty, invited their fellow countrymen to come, stay and exploit that land for their own benefit; not for the benefit of the *mwananchi* (citizen). Britain devised legislative means of legalizing ownership of that land to the exclusion of the indigenous people. In fact the indigenous people were chased away from their own land, the land of their forefathers. Put simply, and in plain language, they were dispossessed.

What was most disturbing, however, was that not only were they dispossessed of what they owned, they could not even preserve what remained of their land by the very means legalized for the settlers to own 'their land'. They could not own it individually; it had to be a communal reserve. A trust. No title deeds for African individuals.

As to the produce of White settlers' farms, e.g. coffee, tea, etcetera, the Africans were not allowed to cultivate and sell for their benefit. It was illegal. Yes, they could only cultivate it for their 'masters', in their masters' farms, for the masters to export.

Besides this, was the humiliation they suffered, particularly in Nairobi, where Africans had to carry lanterns come 5 o'clock in the evening; could not wait for their masters at the railway platform wearing shoes; could be shot at for fun by the settlers when passing by at the Muthaiga Railways Club in Nairobi; or stripped apart – again for fun – by tying one leg to one horse, and another to the other horse, and have the two horses run in opposite directions! Hard to believe! Yet true.

Here we need to pose and ponder over this simple and straight-forward question: how on earth could foreigners come from distant lands and do what the colonialists did in Kenya, and not expect Kenyans to react as they did? It is unimaginable, particularly after a number of Africans had participated (conscripted) in both World Wars, where they could see that what the colonialists could do in the battle fields, the Africans could do too, if not much better! That participation too gave them the opportunity to see the outside world and get exposed to the sufferings of their colonized colleagues in other lands with whom they compared notes.

This emboldened them. Hence, on their return from the battlefields, and in cooperation with those who were left behind, they organized themselves to fight for their human rights, with land issues in the forefront. In the beginning, it was by pure word of mouth, i.e. political agitation. But later on, following the colonialists' violent reaction, it turned into an armed struggle, organized and directed from the forests – best known in history as Mau Mau – which lasted for around seven years.

While in the beginning the struggle was confined to land issues, following developments in other parts of the world – particularly after the two World Wars – it later turned to *uhuru* (independence). Africans not only wanted their lands back. They wanted colonialists to leave their country and leave them to rule themselves. They wanted *uhuru*, complete Independence.

Of course, the colonialists would not accept this voluntarily. After all, that was not what they came to Africa for. Seeing the pressure of the armed struggle ever mounting, and the resultant loss of lives ever increasing, they were forced to accede to the *wananchi*'s demands – but not before they had stifled it and rendered it harmless to their permanent interests. To do this, they resorted to the famous tactic of the colonialists: divide and rule. To fight the freedom fighters, they enlisted the support of their own brothers, sisters, cousins and nephews – the loyalists. They called them Home Guards.

To win their support and collaboration with the colonialists, they were 'well-rewarded' by being appointed chiefs with adequate powers to suppress the freedom fighters. Facilities were given to them to enrich themselves, relatively speaking, thus creating a class of the haves who would exploit the plight of the have-nots when they came out of the forests, with neither land nor any properties – destitute!

Education for Home Guards' children was generously provided, not only at primary level, but up to university level. This equipped them, not only to administer, but to manage and rule over the country as their benefactors would want to.

With Kenya divided so blatantly along tribal lines, those of the freedom fighters who were not in the forests, but were waging the fight politically in the cities and rural areas, realized the need for a hero – a rallying point – around whom the struggle would be centered. At that point they could think of none other than Jomo Kenyatta, who was in prison with five others convicted as leaders of the Mau Mau. Kenyatta was held by the colonialists as the head.

At that point in time, Ghana had attained its independence – the first country in Sub-Saharan Africa to do so. South Africa, on its part, was boiling with the non-whites there fighting for their independence, and against apartheid, with the freeing of Nelson Mandela from prison as their rallying cry – a cry that united them.

Realizing that Kenyans were so divided among themselves, with various political groups having different political agendas, with no one leader around whom they could converge, and so solidify their struggles, Dr Kwame Nkrumah approached Tom Mboya. Mboya was then the Secretary General of the then strongest political party in the country, i.e. Kenya African National Union (KANU), and a prominent trade unionist himself. Nkrumah urged him to declare Kenyatta as the leader of Kenya's national movement for independence. Mboya, with his own ambitions of course, would hear none of it.

Undeterred, Nkrumah next approached Jaramogi Oginga Odinga, who was the Vice President of KANU, with the same suggestion. Jaramogi, whom the colonialists regarded to be a leftist and a communist, accepted the hint without reservation. As soon as he got the opportunity – and this was in the Legislative Council – he declared it unequivocally, to the consternation of the entire Council.

Understandably, the white settlers Members of Legislative Council (MLC) and the Government's representatives were up in arms against the declaration. But to the dismay of *wananchi*, who believed their MLCs were with them as their leaders, all the MLCs disowned Jaramogi. In their list were leaders of both major parties – KANU as well as Kenya African Democratic Union (KADU). On realizing that Kenyatta was a 'reinvented' hero while in prison, the KADU would, however, on his release, embrace him and accept him as their leader.

When out of prison and detention, and in appreciation of the tumultuous welcome and support of the masses, Kenyatta came up with his famous statement of 'Let us not forget, but let us forgive'. By this statement, the Africans thought that he had directed it at the white settlers who were apprehensive about him, holding him responsible for the loss of their lives and properties as a 'manager' of Mau Mau. Hardly did they imagine that it also covered 'the privileged Home Guards and the favoured colonial chiefs who stole the independence dream and transformed infant Kenya into an ugly replica of imperial theft, plunder, repression and exclusion.' (Daily Nation, 23 April, 2011). In the process, he not only forgave, but forgot as well, thus laying the foundation stone of what brother Ngũgĩ calls in one of his texts, 'a history of amnesia.'

Kenyatta minced no words when it came to the return of the land to the rightful owners. He told the veterans and former detainees that nothing was free. If they wanted their land back, they would have to buy it like everyone else. Once, admonishing a congregation that he addressed, he said: 'We are determined to have independence in peace, and we shall not allow hooligans to rule Kenya […] Mau Mau was a disease which had been eradicated and must never be remembered again.' (Kenyatta 1968: 189).

With such statements, he opened the doors for European investors and most wealthy loyalists to buy the land that was sold to the Kenya Government. He also, through his show of magnanimity, allowed former loyalists to wield political clout to consolidate their own interests and power. That was how, immediately after independence, the former Home Guards dominated bureaucracies that had been the preserve of the British colonial officers – powerful posts like Provincial Commissioner and District Commissioner. Thus, the nature of governance did not change much with Independence.

This was when hopes were dashed, prompting nationalists like Odinga to say NOT YET UHURU, and J.M. Kariuki to describe Kenya of the 1970s as a Kenya of 10 millionaires and 10 million paupers. Bildad Kaggia, who was Kenyatta's fellow prisoner and detainee, disclosed that

> Kenyatta was not one of us in prison. He had married a woman whose father was a Chief, and because of that when we went to prison, he was often on the side of the conservatives and the Government. I became the leader of the group in his place, though we were all disappointed. (Elkins 2010: 197).

And my younger brother, Abdilatif Abdalla, asked, Kenya: Twendapi? (Where is Kenya heading?), condemning Kenyatta's dictatorial rule in a critical pamphlet in November 1968.

The tragedy is that our successive leaders have only succeeded in making the situation worse! Exit Kenyatta, enter Daniel Arap Moi. True to his word, on his ascension to power after undergoing all forms of abuse and humiliation from Kenyatta's loyalists, he coined his policy as Nyayoism, i.e. following the footsteps of his predecessor. And follow he did, by replicating what Kenyatta did during his reign.

Immediately upon coming to power, he gradually replaced Kenyatta's provincial administrators with his own, largely from his Kalenjin community, as well as other loyalists from other communities. Using these administrators, he made sure he had his own clientele of wealthy supporters using land as their milking cow.

While serving as Kenyatta's Vice President, he closely watched the game of forest allocations and how these were used by favoured political allies to establish lucrative farms or make instant mega-millions from their sales. Hence, when he rose to the presidency he made sure he made good use of these lessons and, in the true spirit of *Nyayoism*, continued with degazettements.

Like Kenyatta, Moi did not brook any opposition to his instructions. Those who did so lived to regret it. Witness what happened to Kenneth Matiba, Charles Rubia, Martin Shikuku, Ngũgĩ wa Thiong'o, Charles Njonjo, Raila Odinga, Koigi wa Wamwere, Wangari Maathai, to name just a few. He had his own 'Black Hole of Calcutta' in the form of the infamous Nyayo Chambers or cells in the Nyayo House.

With this type of policies and leadership, Kenya has grown to be one of the most unequal societies in the world, where the rich and privileged have become richer and more privileged while the poor and the depraved are left to wallow in their indigence; a country that Mwalimu Julius Nyerere, the late President of Tanzania, once aptly described as that of 'man-eat-man' society.

For more than three years now, the IDPs (internally displaced, as well as, internally dispossessed people) of today are just as neglected and impoverished as the survivors of the colonial detention camps. Both sets of survivors emerged from their respective camps to be met with political manipulation, contempt and indifference. As one of the readers, in his letter to the editor of one of Kenya's dailies, the *Kenya Star*, put it, 'How sad to see the lack of support from the Kenyan Government who at the very same time were squandering public resources on a foolish political junket 5,000 miles away in The Hague.' (18 April 2011).

Unless our Government tackles impunity, negative ethnicity, poverty and joblessness, there is likely to be a repeat of the sort of violence that brought Kenya to the brink of collapse three years ago. This is a fact that cannot be gainsaid: that whatever befalls Kenya will not be spontaneous; it will be the result of an accumulation of grievances; and not all of them will be political.

Finally, let me end my talk with a quotation from a recent editorial (April 21) of the *Daily Nation* newspaper, Kenya's leading daily, where it is stated that

> *While the country might stand out as a modern oasis of prosperity and development, that facade hides a ticking time-bomb. We still hold the dubious distinction of being one of the most unequal societies in the world.*
>
> *The high crime rate is a direct consequence of poverty and unemployment. It is what fuels the fire for organized criminal gangs to thrive in urban slums and rural townships. When that pent-up anger is directed outwards from the slums towards the middle class upwards, it might become unstoppable.*
>
> *Politicians and senior civil servants who enjoy armed protection at taxpayers' expense might not be safe from the wrath of the people. Nor will the upper classes that imprison themselves behind high walls, iron gates, razor wire, 'burglar proof' doors and windows, and private security guards.*

*The warning signs are there. The government must move speedily to*
*design and implement policies that will give all an equal chance to prosper.*
*This is a discourse, however, that must be conducted soberly, not infused*
*with political points-scoring as witnessed with the debate in Parliament.*
(Daily Nation, 2011, April 21st)

Briefly, and generally, given the time at my disposal, this is what Kenyans hoped for before independence, and how – as a result of their successive leaders' betrayal – they have been pushed to a point of despair. All the same, it is inspiring to note, from the current activities in the country, a true reflection of the Kiswahili saying: *Kuinamako ndiko kuinukako* (where it bends, it rises).

## References

Elkins, Caroline 2010. *Imperial Reckoning. The Untold Story of Britain's Gulag in Kenya.* New York: Henry Holt.

Kenyatta, Jomo 1968. *Suffering Without Bitterness. The Founding of the Kenyan Nation.* Nairobi: East African Publishing House.

# Alena Rettová

## Existentialism and Swahili Literature[45]

### Introduction

Since Euphrase Kezilahabi introduced existentialism into Swahili literature in his two novels, *Kichwamaji* (Hydrocephalus, 1974[46]) and *Dunia Uwanja wa Fujo* (The World is an Arena of Chaos, 1975), there has been a tendency in literary criticism to apply the label of 'existentialism' to every Swahili novel which shows an inclination towards philosophy. Also the two latest prose works by Kezilahabi, *Nagona* (proper name, 1990) and *Mzingile* (Labyrinth, 1991), in spite of being analyzed as 'postmodern' (Bertoncini 2001, Gromov 2004, Khamis 2005), 'experimental' (Rettová 2007a) or 'magical realist' novels (Khamis 2003 and 2005, Tarrant 2014) or called 'Kezilahabi's metaphysics' (Wamitila 1991), have been subjected to a reading within the conceptual framework of existentialism (Wamitila 2002, Diegner 2005). This classification is endorsed by arguments that point out the thematic focus of the novels, such as death and the meaning of life, or the structure and formal components of the narratives, such as the journey motif as a depiction of the search for knowledge (Wamitila 2002: 121). It is only recently that the complex relationship between existentialism and the philosophy of postmodernism has been analyzed in less reductive ways. Jason Taffs (2009), for example, suggests that postmodernism and existentialism manifest themselves in Kezilahabi's narratives as the opposition between deconstruction as an act of intellectual comprehension and destruction as an ontological act of violence.

After an investigation of the theoretical presuppositions of existentialism and of existentialist literature in Swahili and in Shona (Rettová 2007a, 2007b, and 2008), the present article examines the relationships between existentialism and Swahili literature from another angle and in a more comprehensive manner. The paper is subdivided into five sections. I will first elucidate the foundations of the philosophy of existentialism. Then I will expose novels that programmatically rely on existentialism. Thirdly, I will speak of implicitly existentialist works. The following section will interrogate the potential of existentialism as an analytical framework. Finally, on the basis of what Swahili literature tells us, I will raise the question of authenticity in more general terms.

---

[45] This article was first published in French as 'L'existentialisme et la littérature Swahili', in: Virginia Coulon & Xavier Garnier (eds.). *Les Littératures africaines. Textes et terrains.* Paris: Karthala, 2001, pp. 427-442. I thank the editors for allowing me to publish this English version.
[46] None of the works quoted in this paper has been translated into English, except for *Kiu*, which has been translated as *The Thirst* by William Mkufya; however, the translation was never published. The titles in the brackets are translations of the titles only.

## Existentialism as a Philosophy and as a Literary Programme

Historically, existentialism is a philosophical and artistic movement which started in Western Europe in the 1920s. It was developed by thinkers such as Martin Heidegger, Jean-Paul Sartre, and Karl Jaspers, and it served as an intellectual foundation to many writers, film-makers and other artists (Crowell 2010). The movement drew its power from the traumatizing historical events of the first half of the 20th century, especially the world wars. After the WWII, existentialism gradually lost its momentum in Western Europe, but it gained new vigour in the totalitarian régimes in Eastern Europe, where the political and social situation continued being oppressive (Řehák 2007).

As a philosophy, existentialism is, in the first place, a reversal of perspectives. Before existentialism, philosophy conceptualized the human being as one amongst others, one creature amongst others, one thing amongst others, even if endowed with certain characteristics that made the human being superior to those others. The human being is defined through his/her difference to other beings. The classical definitions of the human being correspond to this view: the human being is a 'featherless biped', a definition that the tradition places in Plato's mouth. Aristotle defines the human being as a *zôon logon ekhon* - an animal having reason and speech. These definitions see the human being as one animal among others, distinguished from the other animals through certain features. Philosophies influenced by religions, such as Christianity or Islam, see the human being as part of a plan larger than him/herself, a divine project of Creation. In the same spirit, in a philosophy like Hegel's, humanity is in the world in order for the Absolute to become conscious of itself. Human history is the culmination of the development of Nature, and philosophy is the apex of the intellectual progress of history. The exciting consummation of the original purpose of the totality of Being was, according to Hegel, taking place in his very era, in his own philosophy. Marxism, a negative image of Hegelian idealism, places at the end of history the inevitable victory of communism.

These philosophies operate with transcendence: something outside of human existence, be it God or another arrangement projected upon the universe, through which human existence is given meaning. Humans are not seen as individuals; they are reduced to instantiations of a transcendent essence. Existentialism radically reverses this perspective. It rejects a meaning of human life conferred by a project larger than the individual and enters directly into the human mind to look for the meaning of existence there; it takes its point of departure in subjective human experience. What are the reasons and what are the consequences of this reversal?

Existentialism is an anti-metaphysical movement. Metaphysics is the duality of being and its transcendent source, which defines it, which is truer and has a higher value than that being itself. The rejection of such thinking leads the existentialists to a profound reevaluation of being - of immanence. The existentialist programme starts with a rigorous critique of subjective experience

- a methodological procedure drawn from phenomenology - and proceeds to elaborate a radically new conception of the human being as an individual. The focalization on subjective experience gives a very different image of the world: the world shows in diverse perspectives; things are endowed with meanings which do not exhaust themselves in their exterior and objective characteristics; the human being is in the world with emotions originating in the human body, such as hunger and thirst, fear, warmth and cold, joy and sadness. These emotions are not an 'addition' to objective reality, but they participate in a fundamental manner in the very constitution of this reality.

This also gives a very different definition of humanity from the one we cited before. The human being finds him/herself situated in the world and this experience precedes - indeed, determines - all 'objective' self-definition and perspective on him/herself. As Jean-Paul Sartre famously stated: 'existence precedes essence' (Sartre 1946: 17ff.). Before I - a subjective being - define myself through my job, the colour of my eyes and hair, my height, my role in society, etc., I already know myself and understand myself on the basis of my existence in an environment (in space), through my physical experience of hunger, of warmth and of joy, etc. Certainly, I *also* have all those objective characteristics pertaining to my body, my social roles, etc.; but they are not more important than the subjective characteristics of my existence and, especially, they *never* exhaust who I am. Even if a being with an infinite capacity of knowledge and memory knew all that I have ever done, every cell of my body, even all that I have ever thought and said, I could still *be different*: this is guaranteed by my freedom.

That is then the 'essence' of the human being: not to have an essence, always to be free to be different; and it is highly important to preserve this freedom - not to forget it or give it up. Living freely is very difficult and from time to time the human being *likes* to renounce his/her freedom. But to renounce it equals to a loss of the very meaning of humanity, a fall into the world of things. When that happens, the human being fails to live in authenticity.

The loss of authenticity can take place in several ways: one can define oneself through the collective morality of the crowd, adopting it without questioning and unthinkingly; one can also identify oneself with the commands of other individuals, becoming an instrument of their life projects. But even when one projects one's life freely and lives by one's own projects, even these very projects are only things, and if a person identifies with his/her projects to the extent of losing freedom and self-determination, the capacity to rethink his/her life and to decide whether these projects are still good, this also is a fall into the world of things. Fortunately or not, the human being cannot continue living an unauthentic existence infinitely. The moment comes, sooner or later, when s/he becomes aware of the fact that s/he is not a thing among other things and that s/he cannot escape the responsibility for his/her self-determination and his/her choices. When this moment arrives, it is often accompanied by a feeling of anxiety, because, all of a sudden, the entire world of things loses its habitual meaning. It appears stripped of meaning, futile, or, as the existentialists say, absurd. If one has invested oneself in it with all of one's energies, perhaps spending one's whole life in the pursuit of a goal which derives its importance from the world of things (riches, education, etc.), one may come to the conclusion that one's life lacks a meaning.

This is then another concept connected to existentialism: the meaning of life. If the objective world shows itself suddenly deprived of meaning, where can the human being draw the meaning of his/her life? In other words, what is authentic life? How can one live in a way that does not lead to the highly unsettling conclusion that life has no meaning? How can one avoid living life that is estranged from one's own existence? How can one avoid the loss of one's self in alienation? If the existentialists reject all meaning given from outside, the meaning of human life must be sought within this very existence, in the immanence. The search for the meaning of life is thus the heavy task of the human being on earth. This meaning cannot be given by others, it also cannot be found and kept once for all times; it's an endless journey.

Let us now examine how Swahili writers present this situation in their writings.

## Existentialist Writing in Swahili Literature

Existentialist writing was introduced into Swahili literature by the Tanzanian author, Euphrase Kezilahabi, who admitted to being influenced by European existentialists, such as Camus and Beckett (Bernarder 1977: 49). Kezilahabi's first existentialist novel was *Kichwamaji*, published in 1974. The title plays with the double meaning of the word *kichwamaji*. On the one hand, *kichwamaji* means hydrocephalus: the pathological retention and accumulation of cerebrospinal fluid in the ventricles of the brain. In children, this leads to excessive growth of the head and to a range of neurological problems. If the condition is left untreated, about 50% of hydrocephalic children die. On the other hand, *kichwamaji* refers to a person who is maladapted in his/her environment and society. In the novel, Kezilahabi uses hydrocephalus as a medical condition (there are children who suffer from it) but also as a metaphor for the alienation of contemporary East African intellectuals from their societies and traditions.

The plot focuses on two intellectuals, Kazimoto and Manase, confronted with a very complicated situation. Manase rapes the younger sister of Kazimoto, Rukia, and impregnates her. Rukia dies at childbirth. Kazimoto decides to revenge on Manase by seducing his sister, with the intention of impregnating and jilting her. But when two people want to do the same, it is never the same. The older sister of Manase, Sabina, is Kazimoto's senior and, at 26 years of age, she has already lost the hope of finding a husband. When Kazimoto shows interest in her, she is only too happy. Moreover - against his own intentions - Kazimoto falls in love with her, and the two get married. At the same time, Manase marries an urban woman, Salima. The young couple buys a large house and a beautiful car, provoking the admiration of Kazimoto and Sabina when they visit the rich newly-weds. Manase and Salima live a life of luxury until the day when they give birth to a monstrous child with an enormous head. Kazimoto and Sabina pay a second visit to Manase and Salima's mansion after their own child dies at childbirth, because it had an excessively large head that could not pass through the birth canal. They find the once luxurious house dilapidated and bats hanging in the corroded car. In the talks between the two couples, it is revealed that the two men slept with the same prostitute, Pili, and contracted from this woman a venereal disease. In turn they infected their wives, who then gave birth to hydrocephalic children. Unable to bear the guilt for the destruction of his family, Kazimoto kills himself.

He leaves behind a short note to say good-bye:

*Nimejiua. Siwezi kuendelea kuzaa kizazi kibaya. Pia sikuona tofauti kati yangu na mdudu au mnyama. Akili! Akili! Akili ni nini? Pia nikiwa duniani sikupata kukutana hata siku moja na mtu anayeamini kwamba kuna Mungu. Watu wanaoogopa kufa na kwenda motoni hao nimewaona, tena wengi sana. Mtu ye yote asilaumiwe kwa kifo changu. Mimi, kabla ya kufa, ninaungama mbele ya ulimwengu kwamba nilimwua mdogo wangu ingawa sikumgusa.* (Kezilahabi 1974: 217)

> *I have killed myself. I cannot continue giving birth to a bad generation. I also did not see a difference between myself and an insect or an animal. Reason! Reason! What is reason? Additionally, when I was in the world, I did not meet even one day a person who believed that there was God. People who are afraid to die and go to hell, I've seen those, and many of them. No one should be blamed for my death. I, before dying, confess before the world that I have killed my younger brother although I did not touch him.*

The letter shows how Kazimoto eventually loses the meaning of his own life - a typically existentialist topic. He has doubts about human reason, as well as about the privileged status of the human being among the other beings in the world: he sees no difference between the human being and animals, even insects. Next to the philosophical discussions between the characters of the novel, Kazimoto's observations about the world (Diegner 2002), and the question of guilt and remorse, the novel ends on an explicitly existentialist note in pointing out the question of the absurdity of life.

The other existentialist novel by Euphrase Kezilahabi is called *Dunia Uwanja wa Fujo* (The World is an Arena of Chaos, 1975). Chaos – again, a word that evokes a lack of meaning, the absurdity of the world - derives from the social and economic situation during the era of *ujamaa* (Tanzanian socialism). The main character, Tumaini, loses all of his possessions during the nationalization. He takes revenge on the party functionary responsible for the nationalization in Tumaini's district and kills him. In the final scene, in prison, Tumaini is waiting for execution and analyzes the economic and political situation: a state of chaos that he does not manage to understand.

Thirty years later, in 2004, a third Swahili existentialist novel was published. The book written by the Tanzanian novelist, William Mkufya, is called *Ua la Faraja* (A Flower of Consolation). The main character of this novel, James Omolo, is an existentialist thinker. He asks about the meaning of everything, including sexual attraction. He decides not to have relationships with women. In spite of his determination, he is seduced by a rich lawyer, Queen, who is later diagnosed with AIDS. Fearing he might have been infected with HIV, Omolo regrets even more the fact he betrayed his principles and failed to avoid women and sex. Many characters in the novel suffer from AIDS, are seropositive or anguished they might be, fearing the blood test. The disease of AIDS leads to profound questioning of the meaning of life. If one knows that one is seropositive, why live on? What meaning does life still have if one knows that one will die after a limited period of time?

All three novels exhibit an oppressive condition - an illness or an illness used as a metaphor for a more complex phenomenon (such as alienation, colonization, etc.) or the political and social situation as such. It is this oppressive condition that leads to the existentialist questioning: how can life have a meaning if there are so many problems and limitations?

### Existentialism without Programme: Swahili Poetry

All the works covered so far are, so to say, 'programmatically existentialist': their authors know the philosophy of existentialism and they have been inspired by it. However, there are also works which do not explicitly profess existentialism, but they nevertheless share the tendency towards immanence - towards the reevaluation of human experience instead of external or objective characteristics of the human being. These texts express the ideas of existentialism without an explicit reference to it.

The Kenyan poet Abdilatif Abdalla is one of the most famous contemporary poets of the Swahili language. Because of his political engagement, he was sentenced to three years in prison (1969-72). During this time, he wrote poems that were secretly smuggled out of the prison by one of the guards and published in 1973 in the collection *Sauti ya Dhiki* (A Voice of Agony). This collection brings together poems on a range of topics: politics, love, and also philosophical themes, such as the perfection of the human being. The perfection of the human being, *mja*, does not consist in the fact that a person has legs, a stomach, a chest, arms, a chin, a mouth, teeth, a tongue, a nose, ears, eyes or a head. While a human being can never achieve the utmost perfection - which is reserved to God, there is a type of perfection that applies to humanity, as the poet explains:

> *Aiyelewe duniya, kwa marefu na mapana*
> *Azipite zile ndiya, za miba mitungu sana*
> *Avuke bahari piya, zilo na virefu vina*
> *Hiyo ni yangu maana, ya mja kukamilika*

*Akishafikwa na hayo, si kwamba ndiyo akhiri*
*Lazima awe na moyo, wa kuweza kusubiri*
*Kuyasubiri ambayo, yote yatayomjiri*
*Kama huyo 'tamkiri, ni mja mekamilika*
*(Abdalla 1973: 14)*

[the meaning of perfection/completeness of the human being is]
That he/she may understand the world deeply and broadly
That he/she may pass those paths full of very painful thorns
That he/she may also cross the oceans which have unfathomable
  depths

That is my concept of the perfection of a human being
Once he/she has been affected/struck by these, that is not the end
[The person] must also have a heart capable of patience
To persevere those things that will happen to him/her
To one like that I will admit he/she is a complete human being

This concept of humanity is based on experience. It defines the human being through the existential aspects of life, explicitly rejecting a definition through external and objective characteristics.

In the same collection, another poem describes a never completed journey:

*Bado safari ni ndefu, wasafiri tusichoke*
*Natusiwe madhaifu, twendeni hadi tufike*
*Tusafiri bila hofu, wenye nazo ziwatoke*
*Huu ndiwo mwanzo wake, siwo mwisho wa safari*
*[...]*
*Twendeni tukifahamu, kila mtu akumbuke*
*Safari yetu ni ngumu, si rahisi ndiya yake*
*Kuna miba yenye sumu, tunzani tusidungike*
*Huu ndiwo mwanzo wake, siwo mwisho wa safari*
*[...]*
*Kusafiri ni lazima, tukitaka tusitake*
*Wale waliyo wazima, maguu nayanyosheke*
*Na aliye na kilema, naabebwe na mwenzake*

*Huu ndiwo mwanzo wake, siwo mwisho wa safari*
*(Abdalla 1973: 67)*

The journey is still long, travellers, do not let us feel tired
And let's not be weak, let us go until we are there
Let us travel without fear, those who are afraid should stop
This is the beginning, it is not the end of the journey
[...]
Let us go and know, everyone should remember
That our journey is difficult, its course is not simple
There are poisonous thorns, let us pay heed not to get hurt
This is the beginning, it is not the end of the journey

[...]

It is necessary to travel, whether we want to or not
Those who are healthy should straighten their legs
And the disabled one may be carried by his fellow
This is the beginning, it is not the end of the journey

The poem can be read as a metaphor for political struggle, but it can also be understood as referring to human life as such.

These poetic texts introduce new oppressive conditions and, with them, new understandings of authenticity or of authentic life. In political poetry the oppressive condition is dictatorship. Consequently, the fight against this oppression leads to authenticity, often characterized as 'true humanity'. The loss of authenticity is identified with a loss of political consciousness, of the awareness that what is presented by the undemocratic government is not the truth. In another poem, *Mama Ye tu Afrika* (Abdalla 1973: 36-41), Abdilatif Abdalla identifies the loss of authenticity with the dehumanizing effects of racism: slavery and colonialism have negated the humanity of Africans on the grounds of the colour of their skin.

## An Existentialist Reading of Swahili Literature

A third possibility exists to see the relationship between existentialism and Swahili literature: existentialism can be employed as a theory that generates concepts serving as analytical tools to critique literature in general, not only literature that is explicitly or implicitly existentialist. This means that reading a literary work in an existentialist way does not necessarily presuppose having a piece of existentialist writing[47]. It is especially the concept of authenticity, derived from existentialist philosophy, that yields a particularly productive reading of Swahili literature.

This reading was pioneered by Ida Ragnarsson, who read two Swahili novels, *Kiu* (The Thirst, 1972) by Mohamed Suleiman and *Njozi Iliyopotea* (Lost Dream, 1980) by Claude G. Mung'ong'o, through the prism of existentialism. In *Kiu* all the characters lose themselves in one way or another. A young girl, Bahati, loses herself in her love for Idi, who, on his part, loses himself in his avidity for money; because of this, he prostitutes Bahati to a rich old man, Mwinyi, who, himself, is lost in his sexual desire. Bahati regains control of her life when she leaves Idi and returns to her mother. Later on, having talked to the domestic servant Mwajuma, she claims her rights and demands divorce and a part of the money that the couple gathered together. Authenticity is here linked to issues of gender: to the claim for women's rights.

*Njozi Iliyopotea* describes a young agronome Kiligilo, who is in love with Nyalindele. Nyalindele is also the object of the desire of Ndugu Lupituko, a

---

[47] It has to be emphasized that this approach is clearly different from that mentioned in the introduction, where a work is initially qualified as existentialist and only then does literary criticism look for the presence of existentialist ideas in it, in particular the search for the meaning of life, the awareness of death, the journey as a metaphor of life, etc.

corrupted functionary of TANU (Tanganyika African National Union, the only party of the socialist Tanzania). Lupituko kills Nyalindele's mother for having refused to give him a jar with their ancestor's skull. Finally, he also kills Nyalindele in an attempted rape. The skull of the ancestor, *fuvu la babu*, symbolizes here authentic life, manifest in the adherence to traditions and opposed to modern, corrupted life represented by the *ujamaa* politics (Ragnarsson 2008/09).

Ragnarsson's penetrating analysis of these two novels opens the possibility to interpret in a similar way also Mohamed Suleiman's second novel, *Nyota ya Rehema* (Rehema's Star, 1976), which also offers an interesting insight regarding the question of authenticity. Rahma was the oldest daughter of a rich Arab land-owner. Her father rejected her at birth, because her skin tone was darker than both his own and her mother's. In fact, the girl resembled her grandmother, but the Arab maintained that she was fathered by another man. She is mistreated in the house of her father, especially after he marries a second wife and Rahma's mother dies of a broken heart. Rahma's name is pronounced Rehema by the domestic servants among whom she lives. Eventually Rehema decides to leave home. She goes to the city, but gets lost in the forest, where she nearly dies. She is saved and healed by Sulubu, a black African. Having recovered her forces, Rehema leaves for the city, where she leads a promiscuous existence. Finally, she sees no meaning in such lifestyle and starts searching for 'true love'. She remembers Sulubu, finds him and proposes to him. In the meantime, Rehema's father regrets having driven away his daughter and leaves her a part of his possessions as inheritance. After his death Rehema and Sulubu, by now a married couple, install themselves at the farm Rehema has inherited and life seems, at last, to take a turn for the better. However, a relative of Rehema's visits their farm and claims the property. He maintains her inheritance is invalid. At this moment, Sulubu lifts his axe and kills the relative by one powerful strike. He is sentenced to death, but the 1964 revolution and the subsequent amnesty save his life.

In this novel Rehema, like the characters of *Kiu*, is disoriented: she is rejected by her own father for racial reasons and lives a loose life in the city. She finds 'true love' with Sulubu and with it a certain 'authenticity', in their peaceful existence in the country. As Xavier Garnier notes, Sulubu represents the earth, the soil, reality - he is 'a presence'[48]. The character of Sulubu, like that of Mwajuma in *Kiu*, is read as one of the rare entirely positive characters in Mohamed Suleiman's prose.

---

[48] 'Rehema (...) trouve en Sulubu une presence.' (Garnier 2006: 151) The rendition of this sentence in the newly published English translation of Garnier's book reads: 'Rehema (...) finds a place at Sulubu's side.' (Garnier 2013: 119). Unfortunately, this translation dilutes the message of this key sentence in Garnier's chapter, which is based on reading Mohamed Suleiman's novels through a dynamics of 'presence' and 'absence' (the very title of the section where the 'presence' of Sulubu is discussed is called 'The presence of the real', pp. 119 ff.) and through exploring the link between 'presence' and 'reality'. Replacing 'finds a presence' with the idiomatic expression 'finds a place' not only weakens Garnier's central argument; it also shifts the attention from the description of Sulubu as an embodiment of 'the real' to a focus on Rehema's feelings: she is comfortable, feels at ease by his side.

Yet, according to the interpretation of Said Khamis[49], Sulubu raped the girl when he found her in the forest, before he took care of her. It is an act that Rehema does not remember nor did she, at the time it happened, have the concepts to understand it. As a consequence of the violent act being focalized through Rehema in the novel, the rape itself is described in a veiled and ambiguous manner:

> *Baada ya hapo, jambo jingine alilohisi Rehema lilikuwa sauti ya mbwa iliyodhofu ikitoka mbali shimoni. Tena mara aridhi ilisukasuka na yeye akajiona akinyanyuliwa na kuanza kupaa juu, kashikwa hodari na kitu asichokijua, miti ikimfukuzia, na mawingu yakilewalewa juu yake. Alitaka kujitikisa ili kuiamsha fahamu yake, lakini hakuweza. Alikuwa kapooza, hana udole. Alifumba tena macho yake na kujaribu kukumbuka... hakuona kitu. Aliyafumbua na kuangaza, akaiona tena miti yenye kila sura na umbo ikielea katika mawimbi huko angani na kumpita kwa kasi. Aliangalia kwa mastaajabu hata pale mwishowe gome liligubika juu yake na kujiona akitelemka moja kwa moja chini hadi akabwatika juu ya kitu kigumu. Kimya kifupi, na mara alianza kuona misukosuko isiyotambulikana ikimpitia huko sehemu ya miguuni. Musuli zake zikikuchuliwa na kukandamizwa; vinyama vikimtambaa. Akajikamua kupiga kelele ukomo wa nguvu zake, lakini sauti haikutoka. Alikihisi hasa kinywa chake kikifunuka chote; na hata pumzi hakuzisikia kutoka. Na sasa mitikisiko ikipanda juu mapajani, tumboni, kifuani... Maumivu makali, ya ghafula yalimpitia chini ya mbavu, akajipinda, na yoe likakwamuka katika koo lake. Tena hapo maumivu shadidi yalifumka na kuanza kuvikeketa viungo vyake... Kufunua macho, alikiona kiwiliwili cha mtu, kirefu, cheusi, kimemwinamia. (Suleiman 1976: 25)*

After this [running in the forest, falling and fainting] what Rehema heard was the weak sound of a dog's barking. Then suddenly the earth shook and she felt herself lifted and she started going up, held firmly by something she did not recognize, the trees distanced themselves from her and the clouds were swinging above her. She wanted to shake herself in order to come to senses, but she could not. She was paralyzed, without power. She closed her eyes again and tried to remember… she could not see anything. She opened her eyes and looked and she saw again trees of every appearance and shape floating in waves in the sky and moving past her rapidly. She watched with surprise the bark that was covering them and she felt she was coming straight down and fell on something hard. A brief silence and suddenly she started feeling an unknown shaking that

---

[49] An interpretation confirmed to Khamis by the author himself of the novel; the interpretation was presented in Professor Khamis's course of Swahili literature, Bayreuth University, 2005/06.

went over her legs. Her limbs were rubbed and kneaded; tiny animals crept over her. She strived to scream from all her forces, but the voice did not come out. She felt her mouth was fully covered; even her breath could not be heard. And now the shaking went up her thighs, stomach, chest... Suddenly an accute pain shot under her sides, she doubled up and a cry rose from her throat. Then a strong pain grasped her again and started gnawing on her body... When she opened her eyes, she saw the body of a man, tall, black, bent over her.

According to this interpretation, even the apparently positive character of Sulubu has a shady side. In this way, authenticity, whether understood as finding 'true love' or as living in the country and working on the land, is a mere illusion. The character of Mwajuma, in *Kiu*, apparently a fully positive character, equally remains ambiguous and obscure. She manipulates Bahati to desire the money of her husband, which she did not care for initially, and the final tragedy of *Kiu* takes place entirely under Mwajuma's direction: she acts as a messenger between Idi and Bahati, she mediates all the information that the reader is given. It is Mwajuma who appears menacing and deadly in Bahati's prophetic dream.

### Conclusion: Literature in Search for Authenticity

Based on the analysis of the search for authenticity in Swahili literature, it is possible to pose questions about authenticity in general. Swahili literature exposes several different origins of authenticity: tradition (*Njozi Iliyopotea*); or the act of keeping intact one's conviction and resisting at any cost injustice and oppression (political poetry). But Swahili literature also shows us how authenticity is deceitful and even impossible: Rehema only finds her 'authentic love' thanks to the fact that truth remains hidden in the depths of the unconscious and of oblivion (*Nyota ya Rehema*).

The question of authenticity in *Kichwamaji* is complex: Kazimoto is alienated to traditions and alienation implies a loss of authenticity, but do African traditions - rural life - represent authenticity in Kezilahabi's novel, somewhat like in 'Njozi Iliyopotea? The answer has to be 'no'; traditions are no longer a source of authenticity for Kazimoto as a contemporary intellectual. Observing these traditions would be equal to a fall into the world of things, of reified, objectified morality exterior to his true being. They are the morality of the crowd and Kazimoto has become an individual in the modern sense of the word. The authenticity that Kazimoto seeks is both beyond his Western education and his African traditions. He needs a third way - one that he fails to find. It is for these reasons that he sees no future for himself - and ends in suicide.

It was also said that existentialism, whether explicit or implicit, flourishes in oppressive situations. In view of the historical conditions to which Africa has been exposed and from which modern African literature is born, it is not surprising that the major part of its literature has been written with the desire to find authenticity, an 'African truth'. But as Kezilahabi incisively criticizes in his doctoral dissertation of 1985, authenticity has been understood by many African authors in the sense of a fixed essence. He clarifies:

> African writers [...] constantly struggle to construct an African mundus with a center of its own. As Mircea Eliade has observed, it is the center that 'renders orientation possible'. African writers seem to hold the same view. We argue that it is the very idea of the center that must be destroyed. There is no center of knowledge. The 'center-and-penumbra' structure of understanding is a mystification of knowledge. It is the idea of the center that has made African literature an easy target for structuralist analysis. It is the center that makes combinations possible. Thus African narratives, novels, and plays are dismantled and reassembled around an axis operandi. This mechanical reproduction is what has come to pass in disguise as scholarly analysis. The center that 'renders orientation possible' is nothing less than essence. (Kezilahabi 1985: 237)

Literary criticism informed by existentialism shows the pitfalls of this project and elaborates the concept of authenticity on the basis of existence, distinguishing it from the static concept of essence. It exposes the protean nature of the authenticity of the human being: the truth remains an elusive phantasm of the quest that is human life - a motor of literature.

## Bibliography[50]

Abdalla, Abdilatif. 1973. *Sauti ya Dhiki*. Nairobi, Dar es Salaam: Oxford University Press.

Bernarder, Lars. 1977. Ezekiel (sic!) Kezilahabi – Narrator of Modern Tanzania. *Lugha* 1: 46-50.

Bertoncini-Zúbková, E. 2001. Topical Trends in Swahili Literature. In: L. Kropáček & P. Skalník (eds.). *Africa 2000: Forty Years of African Studies in Prague*. Prague: SET OUT, 243-248.

Crowell, Steven. 2010 (2004). Existentialism. In: Edward N. Zalta (ed.). *The Stanford Encyclopedia of Philosophy* (Winter 2010 Edition). http://plato.stanford.edu/archives/win2010/entries/existentialism/.

Diegner, Lutz. 2002. Allegories in Euphrase Kezilahabi's Early Novels. *Swahili Forum* 9: 43-74.

Diegner, Lutz. 2005. Intertextuality in the Contemporary Swahili Novel: Euphrase Kezilahabi's *Nagona* and William E. Mkufya's *Ziraili na Zirani*. *Swahili Forum* 12: 25-35.

Garnier, Xavier. 2006. *Le roman swahili. La notion de « littérature mineure » à l'épreuve*. Paris: Karthala. English edition: *The Swahili Novel: Challenging the*

---

[50] All the internet sources were retrieved on 20th May 2014.

*Idea of 'Minor Literature'*. Transl. Rémi Tchokothe Armand and Frances Kennett. London: James Currey, 2013.

Gromov, Mikhail D. 2004. Nagona and Mzingile - Novel, Tale or Parable? *Afrikanistische Arbeitspapiere* 55: *Swahili Forum* 5: 73-78.

Kezilahabi, Euphrase. 1974. *Kichwamaji*. Dar es Salaam: East African Publishing House.

Kezilahabi, Euphrase. 1976 (19751). *Dunia Uwanja wa Fujo*. Kampala, Nairobi, Dar es Salaam: East African Literature Bureau.

Kezilahabi, Euphrase 1985. *African Philosophy and the Problem of Literary Interpretation*. Unpublished doctoral dissertation. Madison: University of Wisconsin.

Kezilahabi, Euphrase. 1990. *Nagona*. Dar es Salaam: University Press.

Kezilahabi, Euphrase. 1991. *Mzingile*. Dar es Salaam: University Press.

Khamis, Said A. M. 2003. Fragmentation, Orality and Magic Realism in Kezilahabi's Novel Nagona. *Nordic Journal of African Studies* 12, 1: 78-91.

Khamis, Said A. M. 2005. Signs of New Features in the Swahili Novel. *Research in African Literatures* 36, 1: 91-108.

Mkufya, William E. 2004. *Ua la Faraja*. Dar es Salaam: Mangrove Publishers.

Mohamed, Mohamed S. 1972. *Kiu*. Dar es Salaam: East African Publishing House.

Mohamed, Mohamed S. 1976 *Nyota ya Rehema*. Nairobi: Oxford University Press.

Mung'ong'o, Claude G. 1980. *Njozi Iliyopotea*. Dar es Salaam: Tanzania Publishing House.

Ragnarsson, Ida. 2008/09. Existentialism as an Interpretive Tool: A Reading of Mohamed Suleiman's *Kiu* and Claude Mung'ong'o's *Njozi Iliyopotea*. Unpublished term paper. London: School of Oriental and African Studies.

Rettová, Alena. 2007a. *Afrophone Philosophies: Reality and Challenge*. Zdeněk Susa: Středokluky.

Rettová, Alena. 2007b. Lidství ni Utu? Ubinadamu baina ya Tamaduni. *Swahili Forum* 14: 89-134.

Rettová, Alena. 2008. 'The horns of my thoughts are fastened together in a knot': Transformations of 'Humanity' in Swahili and Shona Literatures. In: Oed, Anja & Uta Reuster-Jahn (eds.). *Beyond the Language Issue - The Production, Mediation and Reception of Creative Writing in African Languages*. Cologne: Rüdiger Köppe, 263-274.

Řehák, Vilém. 2007. Kazimoto and Meursault: 'Brothers' in Despair and Loneliness. Comparing Kezilahabi's *Kichwamaji* and Camus' *L'Etranger*. *Swahili Forum* 14: 135-151.

Sartre, Jean-Paul. 1946. *L'existentialisme est un humanisme*. Paris: Editions Nagel.

Taffs, Jason. 2009. *Towards a Postmodern Reading of Nagona*. Paper presented at the 22nd Swahili Colloquium, Bayreuth, 22nd May 2009.

Tarrant, Duncan I. 2014. *To What Extent Can E. Kezilahabi's Nagona Be Considered a Magical Realist Novel?* Paper presented at the 27th Swahili Colloquium, Bayreuth, 9th June 2014.

Wamitila, Kyallo. W. 1991. *Nagona* and *Mzingile*: Kezilahabi's Metaphysics. *Kiswahili* 54: 62-67.

Wamitila, Kyallo W. 2002. *Uhakiki wa Fasihi. Misingi na Vipengele Vyake.* Nairobi: Phoenix Publishers.

# H. Ekkehard Wolff

Language in Africa Between the Local and the Global: How Political are 'Dialects'?

## Introduction

In order to address the special occasion of this symposium, I would like to begin by paying homage to the man who is honoured by it: Abdilatif Abdalla. For almost the whole 15 years that I was privileged to hold the Chair of African Languages & Literatures at this university, he was on our team as an outstanding colleague, both in personal and professional terms. Abdilatif Abdalla was an ever reliable comrade and fellow-activist in the struggle to maintain, at this university, an adequate academic representation of the genuine voices of Africa – both in terms of the linguistics of the indigenous African languages as well as with regard to the literatures and oratures in these languages, i.e., genuine African verbal art whether encoded in writing or transmitted through exclusively oral channels.

Abdilatif Abdalla and I were one in the conviction that the study of the indigenous languages and literatures is the ideal way towards intercultural learning and understanding whenever and wherever Africa and the 'Western World' meet. This approach has a long tradition in this country. One of the very early metaphors used in German *Afrikanistik* at the turn of the 19th to the 20th century was that of 'language as the key to understanding Africa and the African peoples and their cultures'. As a matter of fact and in this perspective, Abdilatif Abdalla was the perfect person to have 'on board' as a teacher, co-researcher, and intellectual representative of his home country and continent in an academic institution devoted to '*Afrikanistik*' which looks back on 125 years of African linguistics under this particular German paradigm.

Intercultural learning is not a one-way street. Taking the study of African languages and literatures seriously, this also helps towards our own emancipation from ideological positions such as *Eurocentrism* and *Orientalism* (in the sense of Edward Said's still controversial book of 1978). Early missionary and colonialist activities in Africa and elsewhere had infested us with *Eurocentrism*, and the shackles of largely anti-Islamic *Orientalism* still tie us Europeans down to the perpetuation of much prejudice and stereotype. Both *Eurocentrism* and *Orientalism* also blur our view on Africa, its peoples, their cultures, languages, their literary and oratory productions. I would like to quote here from Chinua Achebe's recent book *The Education of a British-Protected Child* (2009), where he says

> If you are going to enslave or to colonize somebody, you are not going to write a glowing report about him either before or after. Rather you will uncover or invent terrible stories about him so that your act of brigandage will become easy for you to live with.

If Chinua Achebe was right in this book, and I am deeply convinced that he is, then

*... it is not necessary for black people to invent a great fictitious past in order to justify their human existence and dignity today. What they must do is recover what belongs to them – their story – and tell it themselves.*

And, one would hasten to add that they can and must do this in their own languages. Or should they not? Here we are getting to one of the core issues: How can the vast majority of Africans do this, i.e., *tell their own story*, and be heard, when 80% - 90% of them exclusively use their African mother tongues, and many of us, i.e., intellectuals outside Africa, don't even care to listen even if given the opportunity to do so?

We are here, at this symposium, in German-speaking academia, where a crucial distinction comes into play, namely that of language-focused *Afrikanistik* on the one hand, and largely language-indifferent *Afrikawissenschaften* on the other. Classic German *Afrikanistik* was established as an autonomous academic discipline in the heyday of colonialism in Berlin (1885), Leipzig (1900), and Hamburg (1908), not to forget similar developments in Vienna at about the same time. It deals with all issues concerning language in Africa and is best translated into English as *African linguistics* in a very broad sense. German *Afrikawissenschaften*, on the other hand, is a copy of Anglo-American *African Studies*. It came about in the 1960s and 70s. It deals with almost anything except languages in Africa, and the term best translates back into English as *African Studies*. There are representatives of this type of *African Studies* in this country, even at this university, who would claim that it is not at all necessary to take notice of what African people say or write in their own languages, because anything worth knowing about Africa was available in English or French anyway! This truly fulfils the mockery which goes round in intellectual circles in Africa, and which I picked up at the University of Cape Town in South Africa only the other day: *African Studies is anything that you can read about Africa in English*!

German academia, therefore, prides itself, and suffers from, the competition and rivalry between two rather different yet complementary approaches to the study of African affairs and realities. The theoretical foundations of German *Afrikanistik* involve a perspective from within; the focus is on endogenous factors of language, communication and culture. The *Afrikawissenschaften/ African Studies* approach, on the other hand, would be more concerned with the impact of external factors on African societies and cultures. The *Afrikanistik/ African linguistics* approach, therefore, links up neatly with the notion of 'Deep Language' as invoked in the overall topic of this symposium.

## What is 'Deep Language'?

There is reference in the title of this symposium to 'deep language'. Obviously, 'deep language' in this particular context and on this particular occasion of honouring Abdilatif Abdalla, is used to render the Kiswahili expression *lugha ya ndani*. This expression refers to a kind of deep level linguistic and cultural competence, a kind of trademark of being a native speaker and referring, as it was said in the invitation to this symposium, to 'one of the cornerstones of being Swahili'.

This notion of 'deep language' is, of course, something entirely different from what psychologists and theoreticians of learning call 'deep language' in some of their expert discourse. It is even different from the deceivingly similar term 'deep structure of language' which figured so prominently in early Chomskyan models of transformational grammar which have had and still have a tremendous impact on 20th and 21st century Western thinking.

In J. W. Oller's (1983) 'hierarchy of learning', for instance, *deep language* is equated with 'language as intelligence'. It constitutes the primary level of a hierarchy which entertains an as yet poorly understood dialectical internal relationship with the intermediate level of *natural language* that we as general or theoretical linguists are concerned with. This intermediate level in turn relates to the general skills of listening, speaking, reading and writing as well as to the deeper cognitive skills that are learnt through these four modes of language (cf. Gamaroff 1995).

## Oller's Hierarchy Of Learning

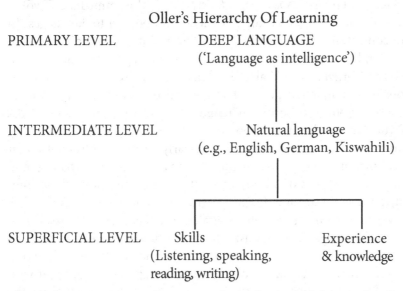

PRIMARY LEVEL — DEEP LANGUAGE ('Language as intelligence')

INTERMEDIATE LEVEL — Natural language (e.g., English, German, Kiswahili)

SUPERFICIAL LEVEL — Skills (Listening, speaking, reading, writing) — Experience & knowledge

Oller's and Gamaroff's perspectives neatly link up with what Konrad Ehlich calls the fundamental *gnoseological* dimension of language, in addition to the *teleological* and the *communitary* dimensions (cf. Ehlich 2009). The *gnoseological* dimension of language is intimately related to aspects of knowledge acquisition, knowledge transfer, and 'deep learning'. It is this gnoseological dimension which tends to be overlooked in most discourse on language, be it among linguists or social and cultural scientists. Hence much of the ignorance when it comes to understanding the interrelationship between patterns of language use and 'development', in particular with reference to the African 'mother tongue' languages vis-à-vis the imported 'official' languages of mostly European provenance. As a matter of fact, it is not too long since this issue has become focal in some subfields of sociolinguistic research in Africa under the new 'language as resource' paradigm that prevails in much of the professional sociolinguistic discourse since the 1990s (cf. Wolff 2012).

Linguistics as much as literary and oratory studies are concerned with natural human language. So is African linguistics. In the old *de Saussurian* terms we are dealing with *langue* and *parole*, most of all, and only marginally, if at all, with *langage* (or: *faculté de langage*), i.e., the human ability to have natural language, which again links up with Ollert's and Gamarof's 'deep language'.

Therefore, talking about 'deep language' in purely linguistic discourse could be misleading, to say the least. But it remains an interesting notion in terms of cultural and political aspects of language use, and as such I will continue to use it occasionally – at least in the subsequent sections of this presentation.

## Are 'Dialects' Political – or rather: How 'Political' Can Dialects Be?

'Deep language' in the context of this symposium as based on the Kiswahili expression *lugha ya ndani* would surely involve the whole gamut of linguistic variation within a given natural language, what we would simply call language variants (in terms of *dialects, sociolects, idiolects*, etc.). This immediately evokes the question of status for, for instance, 'dialects' as opposed to 'languages'. In the African context, in particular when the African situation is looked at from the outside (and by embracing distortions and misrepresentations due to *Eurocentrism* and *Orientalism*), 'dialect' is often used as a discriminating term for instantations of human language which are regarded as 'inferior', in particular when compared to our own European 'languages'. Such discrimination of 'folk languages' (or: 'vernaculars') as opposed to 'standard languages' has a long tradition in European thought systems. It clearly relates to essentially *non-linguistic* features of language use, namely standardization and writing, and subsequently the existence of a body of written literature. Along these lines of thought, even German and English were once considered inferior folk languages, vernaculars or mere dialects, which were automatically associated with absence of writing, analphabetism, lack of sophisticated education, and, therefore, inferior levels of civilization. Does that sound familiar when looking at the African context? Clearly, the colonial masters spoke and brought with them proper 'languages' in the above sense, which became imposed on the local 'dialects' or 'vernaculars' or 'tribal idioms' of the African populations in the colonized territories. Until today, African languages still carry the stigma of being essentially connected to absence of writing, analphabetism, lack of sophisticated education, and inferior levels of civilization. Can such languages, or even dialects of such languages, have sophisticated verbal artistry, beauty, and relevance for all humankind? Can African languages, in addition to outstanding verbal artistry, indeed perform even all teleological and gnoseological functions, in addition to their obvious communication functions, in the same way as we would assume that long-standardized languages of European provenance do? We, as *Afrikanists*, know they can. But who outside the narrow circles of linguistic experts is likewise convinced of it, given the fact that even a vast majority of African intellectuals themselves, not to speak of politicians and decision makers when it comes to designing appropriate educational policies for their societies, are not convinced? Are not large sections of African societies traumatized by the colonial experience and irrespective of individual levels of formal education, convinced that only the languages of the former colonial masters would guarantee quality education, upward social mobility, and prosperity – the lip-service paid to the promotion of, for instance, Kiswahili to 'national official language' (only alongside English, of course!) notwithstanding?

Where does that place a poet and political activist, like Abdilatif Abdalla, who insists on performing his poetry in his native 'dialect' *Kimvita*, and who is known for his resistance when it comes to have his poetry 'written', and who would flatly refuse to have it written in any kind of standard variety of Kiswahili? Is this barely a whimsical feature of an individual African intellectual, or is this a conscious act in terms of a political statement? What, may we ask, makes 'choice of a dialect' – as opposed to using the available standard variety of the same language – so eminently political? What does 'use of a dialect' stand for, as opposed to the symbolic value of using the available standard variety?

Interestingly from a general sociolinguistic perspective, Abdilatif Abdalla's conscious linguistic choice in the aftermath of colonialism, motivated by deep reasons of biography and political struggle, relates to emerging features of language use among a rebellious youth in African mega-cities and urban agglomerations today. I am referring to the use of so-called 'new urban vernaculars' which dynamically spread from the ghettos of juvenile delinquency and street gangs into the better quarters of students at secondary schools and universities. I am talking about 'new languages' like *Sheng* in Nairobi, *Nouchi* in Abidjan, *Flaaitaal* or *Totsitaal* in Johannesburg, *Franlof* in Dakar, *Camfranglais* in Yaounde, and others. Research has shown that this too has to do with politics, namely with acts of more or less conscious rebellion and resistance. By grossly manipulating the matrix languages, be it Kiswahili as in the case of *Sheng*, or French as in the case of *Nouchi*, and enriching it constantly – playfully as much as competitively – by creative lexical innovation and borrowing from any other language in the neighbourhood, be it an African or a European language, these emerging and blatantly non-standard forms of speech have gained high symbolic value for their users. In these cases, 'deviant patterns of language use' symbolize:

- Resistance against the hegemonic impact of the official language, be it ex-colonial as in the case of *Nouchi* and French, or be it African as in the case of *Sheng* and Kiswahili;
- Rebellion against the older generation of speakers of African languages who use varieties that were standardized in the colonial days by (largely expatriate) missionaries, and which have become associated with a rural origin in the sense of backwardness, acceptance and internalization

of colonial standards, and early missionary impact on more or less traditional lifestyle;

- Propagation of a free and modern urban lifestyle ('Hip-Hop') of youth which oscillates freely between local and global trends in fashion, music, and other behavioural patterns.

These 'emerging languages' (of still undetermined future) of urban African youth definitely qualify as 'non-standard', if not 'anti-standard' language varieties; they are clearly social 'dialects' (or rather: 'sociolects', some would refer to them with good reason as 'lifestyle registers') – but of which 'language'? In any case, they are politically charged language varieties which convey, among other things, anti-establishment sentiments and transport grievances with the sociocultural environment that its users live in.

Sociolinguistic analysis reveals that the conscientious usage of non-standard varieties of language can be a highly subversive and, therefore, political act, and often is meant to be! This is the case, as I understand it, of Abdilatif Abdalla's conscientious use of *Kimvita*, the local Kiswahili variety of Mombasa, in his poetry. The lesson to be drawn – spanning from Abdilatif Abdalla's days in prison after Kenyan independence to present day rappers and street fighters in African urban settings – is that language use, if not language itself as a symbol, is highly political and subversive. This is the reason why the new African political elites who have taken over the colonial states ('black faces in white places') are so reluctant to allow the empowerment of African languages. They are well aware of the fact that, by empowering somebody's language, one would, quite naturally, of course, also empower its speakers. Their expatriate advisors and consultants from Europe heavily support this basically anti-democratic position (but for their own and different hidden agenda which would be worth another paper at another occasion). The more surprising remains the fact that language issues, particularly relating to the empowerment of indigenous languages and their potential role in the fostering of democratic societies and emerging global markets, plays so little, if any, role in Western development discourse on Africa.

## Language in Africa between the Local and the Global

It is a well-established fact that most modern African states and societies are characterized by highly complex landscapes of communication. By 'landscape of communication' I like to refer to the multi-layered coexistence of 'communicative spaces' that are defined by *individual* or *institutional language use*. These communicative spaces are organized in a hierarchical manner, which allows us to speak of 'linguistic strata' which, to complicate the matter further, are structured in terms of power and prestige that are associated with them. In sociolinguistic terminology, this power hierarchy is referred to as *diglossia*, or even *triglossia*. Apart from the power-game, these linguistic strata are moulded into interlocking systems of territorial, individual, and institutional multilingualism. There are up to 5 such linguistic strata that can be identified by choice of language (cf. diagram further below).

I would like to claim that multilingualism in Africa, widespread as it is, reflects a universal human strategy which links the local with the global. Individual as much as institutional multilingualism (i.e. institutionalized multilingualism as the result of language policy, whether explicit or implicit) is able to bridge the communicative spaces between highly localized language varieties ('dialects'), across sociolectal and idiolectal varieties of standardized African languages (such as Kiswahili), to reach expressions in so-called *International* (or, as I would prefer to call them: *Intercontinental*) *Languages of Wider Communication* (ILWC) such as English, French, Portuguese, Spanish, Arabic, or what have you. Given the power hierarchy (or, as Ngũgĩ wa Thiong'o has called it during this symposium: 'feudalism') of languages, it comes as no surprise that Abdilatif Abdalla attributes such high value to his *Kimvita* variety of Kiswahili. By this he is able to feed his thoughts and grievances (at the same time also as voicing the concerns of the 'common people') into what finally will become – up the language hierarchy ladder, so-to-speak, through translation – part of global discourse. Thereby he leads the way, as I see it, and in an *avantgarde* fashion, to allow genuine African voices to be heard from the grassroots to the higher intellectual quarters – at least eventually, and provided, I hasten again to add, that there are people out there, involved in global discourse who care and are prepared to listen!

The highly complex African situation in terms of communication landscapes is graphically represented by the following diagram.

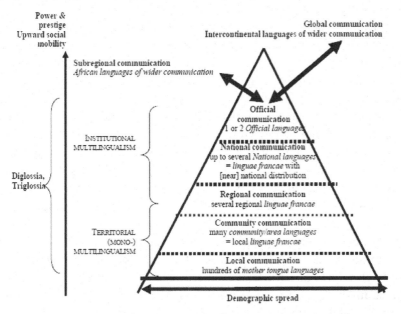

In African multilingual settings, therefore, the local and the global are not necessarily adverse positions, but form a kind of natural cline of language choices along a hierarchically structured continuum of linguistic resources. It is largely the European mind-set that tends to enforce monistic (if not monomaniac) ideological positions of the kind *one state – one nation – one language*. Under the impact of this Eurocentric position, Africa's inherited quasi natural linguistic and cultural diversity becomes sacrificed on/at (???) the altar of 'national unity'. 'Homogeneity' is the new fetish which is worshipped by imposed patterns of language use, namely through the use of a so-called 'neutral' language which, bluntly, is 'nobody's language' – with the exception of the ex-colonial masters and members of the new political elites who, by now and to no little extent through these patterns of language use, have successfully created a new elitist class. Because of dramatically underperforming systems of formal education, the masses are kept away from upward social mobility, and thus away from access to power and control of the national resources. Mastering English, for instance, is widely glorified as the gateway to educational and professional success. The poor way in which English is used in African educational systems, however, turns out to be an effective means of blocking the underprivileged masses from getting access to good education, and, thereby, to upward social mobility and, finally, to political power in a truly democratic political environment.

Until today, particularly so in terms of educational systems, African governments have opted for becoming 'copies' of the ex-colonial masters and their models of education. They are overlooking the fact that 'copy and paste' cannot work for already one simple reason: the European models are made to fit the needs of a linguistically rather homogenous society and thus operate in the mother tongue of most of the learners. The situation in Africa is completely different: The societies are heavily multilingual, and only small minorities enjoy the privilege of receiving education through the mother tongue. As a rule and in most African countries, a foreign (often ex-colonial) language is imposed on non-speakers of this language by inadequate language policies. In terms of language policies in education, therefore, the vast majority of Africans are thus made foreigners in their own countries! This cannot work; it has not worked in the past, and it will not work in the future – much to the prevailing detriment of the masses who remain dramatically under-educated, and to the effect of slowing down the emergence of civil society. The dramatic negative effects on the effectiveness and efficiency of education in Africa become immediately obvious: 'Most language models used in African education are designed to fail students.' (Heugh 2007: 52).

Furthermore, wrong language policies foster retardation in societal and political modernization as well as stagnation in economic development. In the words of my late South African colleague Neville Alexander, they cement individual mediocrity, create neo-apartheid, and maintain the hegemonic power impact of foreign donors on Africa.

Since imposed foreign languages turn out not to achieve what their propagators hope for, namely (a) neutralize internal ethno-linguistic rivalries to the detriment of national unity, and (b) open the 'window to the world' for people who, under the colonial trauma, perceive of themselves as marginalized and crippled by assumed deficiencies of their own languages, there would appear to be only one way out: Comprehensive use of the African languages as teleological, gnoseological, and communitary resources – in complementary addition to the use of languages of wider and international communication – for purposes of individual and sociocultural 'modernization' as well as for political and economic 'development'. This would and should encompass the full range of dialectal, sociolectal, and idiolectal varieties to be used in such process of empowerment and 'intellectualization' of hitherto under-challenged mother tongue-languages which, at the same time, would bring the process of decolonialization to its natural end by creating a respected communicative space for genuine African voices to be heard – like Abdilatif Abdalla's through the medium of the *Kimvita* dialect of Kiswahili. How much more 'political' could a dialect get?

Let me close with a lesson to be learnt by development theoreticians and practitioners – something to write into their autograph books: *For education as much as for development in Africa in general: language is not everything, but without language everything is nothing.*

### References

Ehlich, Konrad. 2009. Sprachenpolitik in Europa – Tatsachen und Perspektiven. In: Anthonissen, Christine & Carlotta von Maltzan (eds.): *Special Issue: Multilingualism and Language Policies in Africa. Sonderausgabe: Mehrsprachigkeit und Sprachenpolitik in Africa.* Stellenbosch University: Dept of Linguistics, 26-41.

Gamaroff, Raphael. 1995. Deep Language, Intelligence and Language Proficiency in (Academic) Learning. *Proceedings of the Linguistic Society of South Africa Conference.* University of Port Elizabeth.

Heugh, Kathleen. 2007. Implications of the Stocktaking Study of Mother-Tongue and Bilingual Education in Sub-Saharan Africa: Who Calls Which Shots? In: Cuvelier, Pol, du Plessis, Theodorus, Meeuwis, Michael & Lut Teck (eds.): *Multilingualism and Exclusion. Policy, Practice and Prospects.* Pretoria: Von Schaik Publishers, 40-61.

Oller, John W., Jr. 1983. *Issues in Language Testing Research.* Rowley, Massachusetts: Newbury Publishers.

Wolff, H. Ekkehard. 2012. Sociolinguistics in the African Context: History – Challenges – Prospects. In: Brenzinger, Matthias & Anne-Maria Fehn: *Proceedings of the 6th World Congress of African Linguistics, Cologne, 17-21 August 2009.* Cologne: Rüdiger Köppe, 93-106.

# Section 4

---

## Congratulatory Texts

### *Kongole*

# Irmtraud Herms

## Kwa Abdilatif Abdalla[51]

Mara ya kwanza nilikukuta TUKI[52]
Ambapo ulinipa kitabu hiki[53]
Ilikuwa mwaka sabini na nane
Ikafika mwaka tisini na nane

Ndipo tukaanza kushirikiana
Tulifanya kazi pamoja sana
Kufundisha lugha yetu pendwa
Kwa wanachuo wasiohesabiwa

Hukuwa mfanyakazi mwenzangu tu
Bali na rafiki muda wote huu
Tulikaa ofisi moja miaka mitano
Islamu na Mkristo bila mvutano

Tuligawana furaha na huzuni
Hata tulicheka pamoja kazini
Kicheko chako ni cha kuambukiza
Kinachofurahisha kila baraza

Wewe ni msaada mkubwa kwangu
Katika kuboresha kamusi yangu
Kwani msamiati wako mpana sana
Unajua maelfu maneno na maana

Kiswahili, Kiarabu, Kiingereza
Hizi ni lugha tatu unazocharaza
Kijerumani kuzungumza wajitahidi
Miaka iliyopita zaidi na zaidi

Lahaja yako ya mama ya Kimvita
Kwangu inanipa shida na matata
Hata nikishafahamu maneno yote
Bado shairi ni fumbo mahali pote

Kwa msaada wako machache nimefasiri
Kutoka hazina ya yako mashairi
Mungu akujaaliye afya, nguvu, heri
Upate kuchapisha zaidi mashairi

---

[51] Kwa ajili ya Kongamano la Kumwenzi Abdilatif Abdalla kwa sababu ya kustaafu kwake, Leipzig 5-6 Mei 2011.
[52] Taasisi ya Uchunguzi wa Kiswahili, Chuo Kikuu cha Dar es Salaam.
[53] *Sauti ya Dhiki*, Oxford University Press, Nairobi.

# Jasmin Mahazi

## Kumsherehekea Abdilatif Abdalla

Chwambe bisumila na niya kutiya
Tumuombe sana Moliwa Jaliya
Atupe majaza ya kuitungiya
Na hini ni ada tungo kuanziya

Tatueni fumbo nimewafumbiya
Kama mu wajuzi tanifunuliya
Tega masikio mpate sikiya
Huo nd`o mwando wa kufwata ndiya

Si wangi kama'ye katika duniya
Walo na busara na roho swafiya
Nazo swifa zake nikiwaambiya
Fumbo hili mara litawaeleya

Ni kama Liyongo na Muyaka piya
Ni shaha wa tungo na wa siyasiya
Wananti wenzi akiwateteya
Na kutuonyesha ndiya ya  kwekeya

Ni mtaalamu alosuluhiya
Mwenye umahiri wa kuineneya
Kwa Kiswahili na Kimombo piya
Hutamka *truth without fear*

Na kuno kunena ndani memtiya
Alishishiyelo hakuliwatiya
Kwa neno la haki si la kuziwiya
Khaswa kwenye dhiki lipate eneya

Baada ya dhiki na nyingi udhiya
Tabasamu yake usoni tapowa
Leo tuko hapa twasherehekeya
Dhalimu mwenyewe tuzo alitowa

Mui wa Mvita ndo alikozawa
Na Amu na Faza akajisomeya
Wa Londoni na Leipzig kuelezeya
Tamaduni zetu za kujivuniya

Na shairi hapa nitalikomeya
Yeye kumsifu na kumuombeya
Dua njema nyingi na kumsomeya
Mungu ampe nguvu na pia afiya

Nyingi tawfiqi tunamuombeya
Ili asichoke na kuendeleya
Yaliyo mazuri kutuandikiya
Na mawazo yake akitupatiya

Kila lenye kheri akupe Jaliya
Kiumbe rahimu tena maridhiya
Mwenye mwendo mwema mswafi wa niya
Memayo yadumu katika duniya

-Amin-

# Gudrun Miehe

**Dear Abdilatif, dear friends and colleagues, ladies and gentlemen.**

At the beginning, let me say a few words in English. Originally, the organisers and me had in mind to deliver this laudatio in English. However, going through my memory, trying to put my thoughts together, I realized that nothing is more appropriate than using Swahili for my small contribution, which has been our (common) language of communication since Abdilatif and me met at the University of Dar es Salaam, thirty-five years ago.

Furthermore: Since everybody can get informed about Abdilatif's merits, his work and his (official) career from numerous web-sites, I restrain today from repeating his long list of publications, papers, awards etc., rather than sharing with you some facets taken from my own memory. I will do so in picking up the three times or periods when we met, and I will take them as reference points of my more personal annotations on Abdilatif, and about what he was doing during that time, or about the role he played within the scientific Swahili community at the time in question. By doing so, my paper falls into three parts: the time in Dar es Salaam in 1976, the short encounters during conferences in the eighties (of the last century), and the longer period since Abdilatif started to teach Swahili in Leipzig. However, let me do this in Swahili.

Mpendwa Abdilatif, wakati tulipokutana mara ya kwanza, mwaka wa 1976, huko Dar es Salaam, katika Taasisi ya Uchunguzi wa Kiswahili, sisi wawili tulikuwa bado vijana, tukilinganishwa na wazee kama Mohamed Burhan Mkelle au Hamisi Akida. Wakati huo, George Mhina alikuwa mkurugenzi wa Taasisi.

Hata hivyo, wewe ulikuwa mmojawapo wa 'wachunguzi waandamizi' watatu waliotunga ile Kamusi maarufu ya *Kiswahili Sanifu* (1981). (Wawili wengine walikuwa Hamisi Akida na Canute Temu). Nakumbuka vizuri wakati lile jopo lilipoandaa kamusi hiyo: kila mwanajopo alitoa maoni yake kuhusu maana ya maneno na vilevile juu ya yaliyomo na miundo ya vitomeo vya kamusi. Rajmund Ohly alikuwa ameshatengeneza orodha ya maneno aliyoyapata kutoka katika kamusi nyingine za akina Johnson, Sacleux au Krapf, na kila mmoja miongoni mwenu alitoa fikra zake na maoni yake.

Lakini, nafikiri, kazi hii ya kutunga kamusi haikuwa lengo lako kuu! Kwani: Mwishowe, wewe ni mzaliwa wa Mvita. Mvita, ule mji muhimu kabisa miongoni mwa bandari nyingine za mwambao wa Uswahili.

*"Mvita nda mwenda p'ole, mwenda kwa haraka hukuwaa dole"*

Mvita is for the man that goes gently, the man that goes hastily hurts his big toe by stumbling.

William Taylor aliyetuhifadhia msemo huo katika kitabu chake *African Aphorisms* (1891), unaotueleza vizuri tabia ya wenyeji wa Mombasa, ameongeza tena lile shairi maarufu la Muyaka, linaloanza na ubeti ufuatao:

*K'ongowea ya mvumo, maangavu maji male*
*Haitoi lililomo, Gongwa isingenyemele*
*Msiotambua ndumo, na utambaji wa kale*
*Mwina wa chiza mbwichile, mtambuzwa hatambuli*

K'ongowea is a roaring (surf), in dead calm (and) at spring-tide
It vents not forth what it is in it - Gongwa would not be quiet
Ye who know not its war-cries, and its gait of old
The abyss of that deep gloom even he that is caused to know it, knows not.

Hasa, ubeti wa mwisho unaeleza vizuri kiburi na majivuno ya Wamvita, nataja mistari miwili tu ya kwanza:

*Mvita mji wa ndweo, ivumayo kwa k'elele*
*Ilit'ulile t'utio, p'anga za masimba wale...*

Mvita, city of pride, that roars with shoutings
Has brandished aloft brandishings, the swords of lofty lions.

Yalikuwa mazingira hayo, ule utamaduni wa kipekee uliojaa busara na mapokeo ya karne nyingi ambapo wewe ulizaliwa na kulelewa, ambapo wewe umekuwa ukianza kusikiliza mashairi ya Muyaka na ya wengineo, ile *Inkishafi*, zile tendi maarufu, nyimbo na misemo. Ulijifunza kwenda kama mwenda-pole, pia wewe hukunyamaza, ulikuwa kijana aliyejitosa katika bahari ya siasa iliyopigania haki na usawa wa watu wote nchini Kenya. Ulikuwa na uchungu na hamu ya kubadilisha mambo: Bado kijana ulikuwa huna budi ila kuona jinsi mji wa Mombasa ulivyokuwa unaanza kuporomoka na kupoteza cheo chake maalumu ulichokuwa nacho kabla ya Uhuru. Tabia yako, kama mzaliwa wa Mvita, na haja yako ya kupigania haki za Jimbo la Pwani la Kenya – hatua kwa hatua (tukumbuke tu karatasi yako, *Kenya: Twendapi?*) – umekuwa unachukuliwa kama adui wa serikali mpaka ulifungwa gerezani.

Lakini, turejee Dar es Salaam mwaka wa 1976. Wakati huo huo vijana wengi wa Chuo Kikuu walikuwa wafuasi wa siasa ya Ujamaa (kama wewe pia). Lakini, kwa wengi wenzio msimamo huu uliwafanya kukataa kabisa athari zote za kigeni, hata katika sehemu ya (ki)utamaduni. Kwa hivyo vijana wengi walilalamika kuhusu maingilio ya Kiarabu katika mashairi ya kizamani, (ya akina Muyaka bin Haji , Zahidi Mngumi, Alii Koti au Mwalimu Sikujua), pia ile *Inkishafi* au zile tendi mashuhuri (kama *Utendi wa Tambuka* au *Utendi wa Mwana Kupona*), mpaka walikataa kabisa kuziangalia tungo hizo kama tungo za kiafrika.

Hawa wenzio walitaka kubadilisha muundo na yaliyomo katika tungo za Kiswahili na kuunda mashairi mapya ya Kiswahili kwa mpango wa „free verse' - tukumbuke tu mashairi ya akina Ebrahim Hussein, Crispin Hauli na Euphrase Kezilahabi (taz. Kahigi 1975:35).

Lakini wewe umeendelea kusimama kama mwamba baharini kulinda na kuhifadhi urithi wa ushairi wa kizamani. Ulitunga *Utenzi wa Maisha ya Adamu na Hawaa* kwa mtindo wa zamani; tena, wakati wa kufungwa gerezani wewe ulitunga mashairi na nyimbo zilizotolewa nawe baadaye kama diwani yako ya kwanza iitwayo *Sauti ya Dhiki*. Hata hivyo, kama Shihabuddin Chiraghdin, mmoja wa wataalamu mashuhuri wa lugha ya Kiswahli, alivyoandika katika utangulizi wa *Sauti ya Dhiki* "... mashairi yake[ko] hayana maingilio ya miundo ya kigeni hata chembe, na mawazo yake[ko] yote yameambatana na Uswahili na Uafrika kwa jumla." Diwani hii ilikuza sifa yako iliyoendelea kuenea duniani, mpaka nchi ya Ujerumani.

Katika karatasi zangu nilizozipitia upya wakati wa kutayarisha hotuba hii, niliyaona tena makaratasi machache uliyonipa wakati ule huko Dar es Salaam, kwa mfano: 'Tanzu za Ushairi wa Kiswahili na Maendeleo Yake', 'Wajibu wa Mshairi wa Kiswahili Katika Jamii Yake' au 'Ushairi wa Kiswahili na Matumizi ya Lugha'. Mada za makala hayo zinaonyesha vizuri jinsi wewe ulivyojishughulisha na dhamira hizi muhimu, bado, katika miaka sabini ya karne iliyopita. Hizi dhamira zimekuwa kiini cha hoja zako mpaka leo: ushairi wa kizamani wa Kiswahili, lugha ya Kiswahili na matumizi yake, na wajibu wa mshairi.

Vilevile, bado, huko Dar es Salaam, ulianza kazi yako kama mhariri. Ule *Utenzi wa Fumo Liongo* ulikuwa kitabu cha kwanza ulichokihariri; vingi vingine vilifuata: tenzi na diwani za mashairi. Hata mpaka leo unaendelea na kazi yako ya uhariri. Juu ya hayo, tunangojea kwa hamu *Kale ya Washairi wa Pemba: Kamange na Sarahani* (kimeshachapishwa sasa na Mkuki na Nyota, Dar es Salaam; taz. Abdalla 2011) na diwani ya Omar Babu!

Wakati wa kazi yako katika Idhaa ya Kiswahili ya BBC, wewe umezuru Ujerumani mara mbili - kwanza ili kuhudhuria Kongamano la Jan-Heinz Jahn huko Mainz, na baadaye mwaka wa 1986 ulikuja kwa ajili ya kongamano liitwalo, Language Standardization in Africa' lililoandaliwa tena na Chuo Kikuu cha Mainz. Kila mara ulitoa makala kuhusu ushairi wa kizamani au umuhimu wa lugha ya Kiswahli. Lakini, jambo ninalokumbuka hasa tangu wakati huo ni sauti yako - Nani angeweza kusahau sauti yako? Sauti yako ina mshindo mkuu, sauti iliyobaki ndani ya kichwa changu, bado inayonikumbusha mazungumzo yetu kuhusu mambo ya ushairi wa kizamani.

Baada ya kuhamia kwako huku mji wa Leipzig, tulikutana mara nyingi, angalau mara moja kila mwaka, kwa ajili ya Kongamano la Kiswahili huko Bayreuth.

Mwishoni, nataka kutaja jambo moja tu, nalo ni warsha yetu huko Bayreuth miaka michache iliyopita tulipokutana kuhariri nyimbo za Fumo Liyongo. Pamoja na wataalamu wengine kutoka Kenya, London na Ujerumani, tulifanya ,kazi ya ki-Gudruni' – kama wazee walivyosema. Tulisoma pamoja miswada ya zamani ya Kiswahili kwa khati za Kiarabu, tuliyoipata kutoka kwa maktaba mbalimbali, na tulijadili maneno magumu (mara chache, hata waalimu wazee, marafiki zetu kutoka Mombasa, ambao ni waungwana watulivu, wenda-pole, walipandwa na hasira na wakagombana mpaka wakachoka, na sisi tukaendelea na kazi yetu).

Tukalinganisha nakala mbalimbali ili kupata mtindo mzuri wa kila utumbuizo; na mwishowe tulikuwa tumechagua nyimbo kumi na nane kuwa kiini cha mkusanyiko wetu wa mashairi yaliyotungwa na Liyongo peke yake - kwa mujibu wa ujuzi wetu, utafiti wetu na majadiliano ya wazee. Na wewe umetufurahisha na nakala ya,"Sauti ya Mvita" iliyotuwezesha kusikiliza rekodi kutoka mwaka wa 1952 wa ule utumbuizo mashuhuri kabisa uliotungwa na Liyongo na unaoanza kwa maneno yafuatayo:

> *Kiyakazi Sada / nakutuma / huyatumika*
> *Kamwambile mama / ni muyinga / siyalimka*
> *Afanye mkate / pale kati / tupa kaweka*
> *Nikereze p'ingu / mandakozi / yakaniuka ...*

Tusisahau kutaja ya kuwa wakati huohuo wa warsha yetu ya Liyongo, mtoto wako alizaliwa huko Hamburg - lakini, kumbe, jina lake si Liyongo wala Mringwari, bali Muyaka!

Mpendwa Abdilatif, nakushukuru sana kwa urafiki wako wa dhati uliodumu miaka thelathini na tano na tunatumai sana, inshallah, utadumu miaka mingi zaidi. Mungu akupe umri mrefu!

Lakini, tusikilize kwa makini sauti ya Muyaka bin Haji, aliyetunga ubeti ufuatao:

> *Aliyekimbia ole, mwendo wa myaka sitini*
> *Akenda umngojele, ukele mitilizini*
> *Ukamba:"Ndoo tukale, mwandani wangu mwandani"*
> *Akiuuza:"N'nani?", ukamba: "Si'mi weleo!"*

Asanteni.

# Othman Miraji Othman

Ndugu wote,

Mei tano hadi sita 2011 katika Chuo Kikuu cha Leipzig, Ujerumani, kulifanywa kongamano, na kauli mbiu ilikuwa: "Lugha ya Ndani Katika Kuivuka Mipaka: Ugunduzi wa Matumizi ya Utamaduni Kama Rasilimali ya Harakati za Kisiasa na za Upinzani Ndani ya Bara la Afrika na Kwengineko." Kongamano hilo, wakishiriki wasomi kutoka Ujerumani na nje, lilikuwa na madhumuni ya kumheshimu Abdilatif Abdalla na lilisadifu wakati alipostaafu kutoka chuo hicho kama mhadhiri wa miaka mingi katika masomo ya Kiafrika na lugha ya Kiswahili.

Kilichonivutia hasa katika kongamano hilo ni kuona vipi maprofesa katika chuo hicho cha Leipzig na kutoka kwengineko duniani walivyommwagia sifa na pongezi Abdilatif kama msomi wa Kiswahili, mshairi, mwalimu, mwanaharakati wa kupigania haki na uhuru katika nchi yake ya Kenya na hasa kama binadamu, tena muungwana. Nilisisimka pale nilipouona mlolongo mrefu wa wanafunzi wasiopungua 100, kila mmoja akiongoza kwenye jukwaa la mkutano kumkabidhi mwalimu wao huyo waridi au uwa dogo kama ahsante yao kwa kuwafundisha lugha ya Kiswahili, ambayo wanaicharaza vizuri. Wanafunzi wengine walisoma mashairi yao waliyomtungia kwa lugha ya Kiswahili. Mwalimu yeyote hupata faraja kubwa anapoona kazi yake imezaa matunda na inathaminiwa na wale waliofaidika nayo. Kwa miaka 15 Abdilatif amefundisha Leipzig.

Machi mwaka 1969, akiwa na umri wa miaka 22, Abdilatif Abdalla, mzaliwa wa Mombasa, alikuwa mfungwa wa mwanzo wa kisiasa katika Kenya huru. Alipewa kifungo cha miaka mitatu gerezani, akizuiliwa peke yake katika gereza la Kamiti, Nairobi, kutokana na mashtaka ya kuandika na kusambaza kijigazeti *Kenya: Twendapi?*, ambacho kilipinga kuandamwa vyama vya kisiasa vya upinzani, yeye mwenyewe akiwa mwanachama wa kimojawapo ya vyama hivyo, Kenya Peoples Union (KPU), kikiongozwa na Jaramogi Oginga Odinga. Mwaka 1973, mashairi yake aliyoyaandika gerezani, mengine akiyaandika katika karatasi za chooni, yalikusanywa katika kitabu *Sauti ya Dhiki*. Kitabu hicho kilipata zawadi ya Kenyatta ya Fasihi. Cha kushangaza ni kwamba zawadi hiyo aliyotunukiwa Abdilatif Abdalla ni yenye jina la marehemu Rais Kenyatta ambaye ndani ya mashairi hayo amebezwa vya kutosha!

Alipomaliza kifungo chake huko Kenya, Abdilatif alihamia Dar es Salaam, Tanzania, na kufanya kazi katika Taasisi ya Uchunguzi wa Kiswahili, akiwa na akina marehemu Mohammed Burhan Mkelle, Hamisi Akida na George Mhina, na pia akachangia kutungwa *Kamusi ya Kiswahili Sanifu*. Alibakia kama mwamba baharini kuulinda na kuuhifadhi urithi wa ushairi wa zamani, mfano ni kazi yake, akiandika kwa kutumia lahaja yake ya Kimvita: *Utenzi wa Maisha ya Adamu na Hawa*. Katika utangulizi wa *Sauti ya Dhiki*, Shihabuddin

Chiraghdin aliandika kwamba mashairi ya Abdilatif hayajaingiliwa na mitindo ya kigeni hata chembe na mawazo yake yameambatana na Uswahili na Uafrika, kwa jumla.

Makala yake, kwa mfano, "Tanzu za Ushairi wa Kiswahili na Maendeleo Yake", "Wajibu wa Mshairi wa Kiswahili Katika Jamii Yake", au "Ushairi wa Kiswahili na Matumizi ya Lugha", yanadhihirisha vipi alivyojishughulisha na dhamira hizo muhimu. Aliuhariri *Utenzi wa Fumo Liyongo*, akiwa Dar es Salaam.

Baada ya Dar es Salaam, kituo kilichofuata cha Abdilatif kilikuwa London, katika Idhaa ya Kiswahili ya BBC, kama mtangazaji. Hapo aliacha alama zake zinazokumbukwa hadi leo - ucheshi wake na kuingiza usanifu wa lugha kuwa ni sehemu ya shughuli za redio inayotangaza kwa lugha ya Kiswahili. Kwake yeye, habari inapowasilishwa kwa msikilizaji au msomaji inahitaji, licha ya kuwa na ukweli wa kuaminika, pia ichapukie na utamu wa lugha, acha pia kuwa na uzito wa kimsamiati.

Alipokuwa London ulikuwa wakati mgumu kwa Wakenya. Utawala wa Kenyatta na Moi uliyasahu kabisa malengo ya wananchi waliokwenda mwituni kuupigania Uhuru kutoka utawala wa kikoloni. Wakati huo Wakenya walio ndani na nje wakawa mbioni kuutangazia ulimwengu juu ya ukandamizaji uliokuwa ukifanywa na utawala wa Moi. Abdilatif pamoja na Wakenya wengine mjini London, akina Ngũgĩ wa Thiong'o na Yusuf Hassan, nikiwataja wachache tu, waliendesha harakati za kutaka kuleta mabadiliko.

Harakati hizo angalau zimezaa matunda kidogo hivi sasa, lakini sio kamili. Hata hivyo, hali ni afadhali kidogo sasa. Wakenya wana katiba mpya itakayowalinda yasikaririwe yale maovu yaliyofanywa zamani. Mwenyewe Abdilatif anasema kujitolea yeye na wenzake, huku wakifuatwa na makachero wa serikali ya Moi na kutishiwa hata kutaka kuuliwa, kulikuwa ni wajibu kwao; na yaliyobakia yataendelezwa na Wakenya vijana waliobakia. Aliwaambia watu waliomsikiliza katika kongamano hilo kwamba mapambano ni kama kujaribu kufungua kizibo cha chupa ya soda: Unajaribu kukitoa, unaposhindwa unampa mwenzako, yeye akishindwa anampa mwengine, hadi kizibo kinaanza kuregea; na kuna mtu mwishoni anakifungua kabisa na watu kuinywa ile soda. Yule mtu wa mwisho aliyekifungua kabisa kizibo haitwi kuwa ndiye shujaa pekee. La hasha! Ni wote waliojaribu kukifungua, wakikiregeza kidogokidogo, ndio mashujaa! Kwa hivyo hajioni yeye pekee kuwa ni shujaa, lakini kuna wengi wengine waliochangia.

Watayarishaji wa Kongamano hilo walilipamba na pia kumuenzi Abdilatif kwa kumualika kutoka Mombasa kaka yake Abdilatif, Sheikh Abdilahi Nassir, aliyekuwa mlezi wake na aliyemuongoza katika maisha yake. Abdilatif alitokwa na machozi kwikwi pale Sheikh alipoalikwa jukwaani kwani mwenyewe alikiri kwamba bila ya msaada wa Sheikh na uongozi wake asingefikia hapo alipofikia. Naye Sheikh hajatafuna maneno. Alikiri kwamba mafanikio aliyoyapata Abdilatif kiusomi, na kupendwa na watu, hayajamshangaza. Tangu alipokuwa mtoto Abdilatif alionyesha ishara zote kwamba katika maisha yake ataacha alama za kuvutia, na atakuwa tayari kwenda umbali wowote ili haki iwe juu, na hakuna kitu kingine kiwe juu ya haki.

Cha kushangaza! Abdilatif amefika darasa la saba katika shule ya msingi. Hajapata masomo yoyote ya juu shuleni wala ya Chuo Kikuu. Acha kuandika uzuri sana Kiswahili sanifu, lakini anakicharaza na kuandika vizuri sana Kiingereza. Amejisomesha mwenyewe na kwa kujichanganyisha na wasomi, hata kuwafanya wasomi nao wamtambue kuwa yeye ni gwiji wa ushairi na mtu mwenye busara ya hali ya juu. Na licha ya maarifa aliyoyapata kwa kukaa na miwaridi na miasumini, yaani wasomi, na kwa hivyo kunukia harufu nzuri za kuvutia - kiusomi na kitabia - Abdilatif, nimegundua, ana kipaji cha kuzaliwa. Mwenyezi Mungu amzidishie.

Na nilipomuuliza anatiwa ghera gani anapoandika shairi, alinijibu: Aya za Quran Tukufu. Unapofuatana naye barabarani mnapokuwa mnazungumza pamoja, pale ghafla unapoingia ukimya katika mazungumzo yenu, mara utamsikia akisoma Quran Tukufu kwa sauti nyororo ya mtindo wa Tajweed. Nami, hata kama mazungumzo yetu ya kabla yalikuwa yananivutia, husita nikiisikiliza sauti hiyo mpaka pale mwenyewe anaposita. Hufaidika ninapokuwa karibu na muungwana huyu wa Kimvita.

# Wanafunzi wa Chuo Kikuu cha Leipzig

## Kumkumbuka Bwana Abdilatif Abdalla –Mwalimu Wetu

Mwanzo wa mwaka mpya, jua likiamka, theluji inayeyuka
Ardhi inakosa blanketi yake nyeupe, laini.

Kila hadithi inakaribia mwisho wake
Baada ya kugeuza ukurasa wa mwisho, utupu na ukimya unatanda chumbani.

Oktoba ikifika, majani ya mti yanaanguka
Mti unasikitika katika uchi wake.

Ilikuwa karamu kubwa, tulikula, tukanywa, tukacheka, tukacheza
Sasa marafiki wote wameondoka, nyumba yangu tupu.

Kama mti, umelazimishwa kuyaacha matunda yake yakiiva
Waache watoto wakati wameshapevuka.

Mzee anahesabu makunyanzi na kutazama taswira shabihi yake
Anazurura na kuzurura katika kumbukumbu.

Wasafiri wanakutana barabarani
Wanajisindikiza na kuzungumza, halafu kila mmoja anafuata njia yake.

*  *  *

Theluji inapoyeyuka, maji yanatiririka ardhi kavu yenye kiu
Uhai mpya unazaliwa.

Ni sikukuu kusimama mbele ya rafu ya vitabu na kuvitazama
Tele dunia inangoja kutupokea kwao.

Baada ya usingizi fofofo, majira ya kuchipua yanayoamsha matunda yatoke na kuota
Mti unaona fahari na kuyaonyesha  mapambo yake mapya.

Natembea katika vyumba vitupu, na vicheko vya marafiki navisikia bado
Nikiendelea kufurahia kumbukumbu nzuri na kufurahia karamu ijayo.

Usisikitike watoto wako watakapoondoka
Watarudi na wajukuu.

Baada ya kuwaza na kuwazua, yule mzee mbele ya kioo anatabasamu
Amefahamu kwamba wingi wa maisha ya wazee ni utajiri
Na kila kipindi cha maisha kina wakati wake.

Dunia imejawa na kukutana. Kila mara watu wanakutana na kuaga. Kukutana kuchache
Utakumbukwa milele na milele.

# List of Contributors

*Rose Marie Beck*
Professor of African Languages and Literatures, University of Leipzig

*Ngũgĩ wa Thiong'o*
Novelist, essayist, political activist and Distinguished Professor of Comparative Literature and English, University of California, Irvine.

*Kai Kresse*
Associate Professor of African and Swahili Studies, Columbia University, New York

*Said Ahmed Khamis*
Poet, novelist, and Professor emeritus of African Literatures, University of Bayreuth

*Mohamed Bakari*
Professor of English Language and Literature, Fatih University, Istanbul

*Ken Walibora*
Novelist, writer, former Professor of African Languages and Literatures; Kiswahili Quality Manager, Nation Media Group, Nairobi

*Ahmed Rajab*
Journalist, writer for *Raia Mwema*; based in London

*Abdilahi Nassir*
Islamic scholar, former Managing Director (Oxford University Press, East Africa), former publisher (Shungwaya Publishers), former leader of Coastal Independence Movement; based in Mombasa

*Alena Rettova*
Senior Lecturer in Swahili and African Literatures, SOAS, University of London

*Ekkehard Wolff*
Professor Emeritus, African Languages and Literatures, University of Leipzig

*Irmtraud Herms*
Swahili Lecturer Emerita, African Languages and Literatures, University of Leipzig

*Jasmin Mahazi*
Doctoral student in Anthropology, Berlin Graduate School for the Study of Muslim Cultures and Societies, Freie Universitaet Berlin

*Gudrun Miehe*
Professor Emerita, African Languages, University of Bayreuth

*Othman Miraj Othman*
Former radio moderator and journalist, Deutsche Welle, Swahili Service, Cologne

Printed in the United States
By Bookmasters